International English

Teacher Resource Book

3

Eithne Gallagher
Else Hamayan

OXFORD
UNIVERSITY PRESS

W0006607

OXFORD
UNIVERSITY PRESS

Great Clarendon Street, Oxford, OX2 6DP, United Kingdom

Oxford University Press is a department of the University of Oxford. It furthers the University's objective of excellence in research, scholarship, and education by publishing worldwide. Oxford is a registered trade mark of Oxford University Press in the UK and in certain other countries

British Library Cataloguing in Publication Data
Data available

ISBN 9780198390336

10 9 8 7 6 5 4 3 2 1

Paper used in the production of this book is a natural, recyclable product made from wood grown in sustainable forests. The manufacturing process conforms to the environmental regulations of the country of origin.

Printed in Great Britain

Acknowledgements

Cover illustration by Fernando Juarez

The author and publisher are grateful for permission to include the following copyright material in print, audio and digital formats in this package.

Jill Atkins: *Yasmin's Parcels* (Readzone, 2013), copyright © Jill Atkins 2008, by permission of Readzone Books Ltd and the author.

Lauren Child: extracts from *Utterly Me, Clarice Bean* (Orchard Books, 2003), copyright © Lauren Child 2003, by permission of David Higham Associates.

Roald Dahl: letter to his mother, original kept at the Roald Dahl Museum and Story Centre, by permission of Dahl and Dahl Ltd.

John Foster: 'The Young Fox' from *Senses Poems* chosen by John Foster (OUP, 1996, 2005), copyright © John Foster 1996, by permission of the author.

Janine M Fraser: *Abdullah's Butterfly* illustrated by Kim Gamble (Collins, 1998), text copyright © Janine M Fraser 1997, by permission of HarperCollins Publishers, Australia.

Janet Grierson: extract from *Maui Catches the Sun* (Edgy Productions, 2006), by permission of Edgy Productions Ltd.

Timothy Knapman: 'The Upside-down Lion' from *Fables from Africa* (*Treetops*, OUP, 2010), copyright © Timothy Knapman 2010, by permission of Oxford University Press.

Roger McGough: 'The Sound Collector' from *Pillow Talk* (Viking, 1990), copyright © Roger McGough 1990, by permission of United Agents on behalf of the author.

John Malam: 'Desert Meerkats' from *Going Underground* (Project X, OUP, 2009), copyright © Oxford University Press 2009, by permission of Oxford University Press.

Alexander McCall Smith: extracts from *Precious and the Monkeys* (Polygon, 2011), published in the USA as *The Great Cake Mystery* (Random House, 2011), copyright © Alexander McCall Smith 2011, by permission of David Higham Associates.

UNICEF: 'Michael', and 'A Serious Business', from *A Life Like Mine: How children live around the world* (DK in association with UNICEF, 2002, 2006), copyright © Dorling Kindersley Ltd 2002, by permission of Dorling Kindersley Ltd.

Gini Wade: extracts from *Kesuna and the Cave Demons, Folk Tales of the World: A Balinese Folk Tale* (Dutton Children's Books, 1995), copyright © Gini Wade 1995, by permission of Penguin Books Ltd.

Kit Wright: 'Dad and the Cat and the Tree' from *The Magic Box* (Macmillan Children's Books, 2009), copyright © Kit Wright 1999, by permission of the author.

Although we have made every effort to trace and contact all copyright holders before publication this has not been possible in all cases. If notified, the publisher will rectify any errors or omissions at the earliest opportunity.

Any third party use of this material outside of this publication is prohibited. Interested parties should apply to the copyright holders indicated in each case.

Links to third party websites are provided by Oxford in good faith and for information only. Oxford disclaims any responsibility for the materials contained in any third party website referenced in this work.

MIX
Paper from
responsible sources
FSC® C007785
www.fsc.org

Contents

Contents of CD-ROM

- Interactive e-books

- Audio tracks
- Progress assessment charts
- Student Workbook answers
- Test questions, answers and mark schemes
- Additional printable classroom resources
- Child-friendly learning objective pages for class display

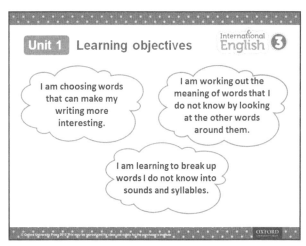

Introduction

How to use *Oxford International English* Level 3

This language and literacy course has been developed for and tested by teachers and students around the world in international schools and English medium schools. *Oxford International English* gives you the rich flavour of cultural diversity with all the quality ingredients of systematic literacy learning. It has been written and designed to complement both international curricula and national curricula.

Adding value

As a busy teacher, there are numerous demands on your time. *Oxford International English* supports your teaching goals by:

- ❱ Motivating and engaging your learners with dynamic themes and classroom activities.

- ❱ Delivering differentiated activities, allowing you to address the range of abilities in your class so each student works at his or her own level.

- ❱ Providing assessment: unit tests and termly check-up tests, clear mark schemes, as well as reading, writing and speaking and listening progress assessment criteria charts that help you level your students.

Student Book 3

The lesson notes in Teacher Resource Book 3 show you the **learning objectives** that are covered on each page of the Student Book along with the **success criteria** for the learning objective to help check that each student has achieved it. The CD-ROM has digital pages of all the learning objectives for you to display on the whiteboard.

Each **unit** of the Student Book is set out to allow a natural learning sequence of interest, inquiry, engagement, investigation and challenge. Using a rich range of literature – in various genres – and language, students interact with **cross-curricular topics** and themes whilst developing their English and literacy in a systematic and measurable way. The extra resources provided in Teacher Resource Book 3 and Workbook 3 give students the chance to **consolidate and apply** what they have learnt in class time.

All units follow a clear logical pattern of **skills development**. Look out for the skills focus at the top of each Student Book page.

Speaking and listening	Vocabulary and spelling
Reading fiction	Grammar and punctuation
Reading non-fiction	Reading poetry
Reading play scripts	Writing workshop

Four *Oxford International English* characters will guide the students through Student Book 3:

Johan

May

Kofi

Leyla

Workbook 3

This Workbook provides a unit-by-unit match to the Student Book topic with **further practice** and extension activities for independent work in class or as homework.

Students can do a **self-evaluation** of their learning at the end of each Workbook unit. This gives you and parents guidance on how to help them progress.

A **mini-dictionary** of vocabulary used in each unit is included at the end of the Workbook to help students work independently and develop their dictionary skills. There is also space for them to write their own new vocabulary with definitions in English and in home languages.

💿 Digital classroom resources

E-books of all the fiction, non-fiction, poetry, play scripts and corresponding Word Cloud lists are included on the CD-ROM. These can be used as interactive texts which can be manipulated on both a normal whiteboard and an interactive whiteboard. You can use these for whole class word and sentence focus. Each e-book also has audio recordings which allow students to practise listening and pronunciation. Please refer to the e-book user guide which can be found on the CD-ROM or the guided reading notes on page 182.

How is *Oxford International English* 'international'?

Culturally diverse classrooms

Oxford International English recognizes that your students are a diverse mixture of different nationalities using various different languages with different mother tongues. Even within a monolingual classroom, students are preparing to be global citizens aware of and engaged in cultural diversity in their communities. *Oxford International English* celebrates these aspects of your classes and facilitates both teacher and students to use this diversity as a learning tool so that students learn from each other as well with each other.

Maps

As a visual, colourful reference point, maps help students understand their place in the wider world and learn about other countries, languages and cultures. Maps are an integral part of the Student Book and can be used to locate where a person or story originates.

Stories, facts and poems from around the world

The reading extracts in each themed unit have been selected because they are either about a country or culture or have been written by a person from that country.

Global themes

From *Home and school* to *Why do we laugh?* each unit theme allows students to bring their own knowledge and experiences to the subject based upon their cultural heritage. The issues raised within the themes have a broad, universal appeal suitable for this age group.

How does it help students learning English as a second language?

Research has shown that learning a language and learning through that language is most successful when real contexts are used. *Oxford International English* uses authentic language and the type of real syntax that students would encounter in books, on the Internet, on television and in magazines. With the right scaffolding, correct pace and structure that *Oxford International English* offers, students learning English as a second language can access, enjoy and engage with English as both an academic subject and the means by which they will succeed across the curriculum.

Reading vocabulary in the Word Clouds and glossary definitions beforehand enables you to focus on low-frequency or difficult key words to aid understanding of the text extracts.

 Audio recordings of Word Cloud vocabulary provide listening, phonics and spelling practice. Audio text extracts provide examples of different intonation, speech rhythms and pronunciation patterns.

What about differentiation?

Your students, ranging from English as an additional or second language learners to English mother tongue learners, will have different cognitive abilities as well as different English language abilities. Some of your students will be brand new to your class *and* to learning English! To support you in this challenge *Oxford International English* uses differentiation in student activities.

Is for all ability students. In comprehension sections, these exercises are comprised of location and retrieval type questions for literal understanding.

B

Is slightly more challenging and for average ability students. In comprehension sections, these exercises consist of deduction and inference type questions.

C

Is the most challenging level and requires students to evaluate, interpret and create using what they have understood, their prior knowledge and their imagination. It is also the least structured type of activity.

···**Challenge**···

Is for high ability students to move onto after completing the other exercises or extension work.

How does *Oxford International English* help critical thinking skills?

Special features within Student Book 3 and Workbook 3 focus on developing students to be inquirers, questioning what they are discovering, prompting them to research further and encouraging them to consider how they learn.

Let's Talk! Allows students to practise guided speaking and listening skills. The theme of the unit and the visual stimuli also prompt students to consider what they want to know about the topic and how they will find out.

Discussion time
Do you think it is important to learn about stories from other cultures? Explain your answer to a partner.

Structure and guidance for the teacher is given in the lesson notes of this Teacher Resource Book. Students are required to think critically, form an opinion, give reasons and evidence for their opinions and debate a topic with their classmates or present a viewpoint.

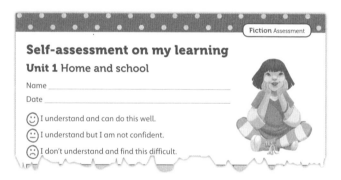

Within Workbook 3, students have the chance to reflect on their own learning, decide what they can do well and where they need more help. This builds ownership of and responsibility for their learning and provokes them to plan how they learn.

Does it work alongside a reading scheme?

Oxford International English can be used as stand-alone classroom material delivering a core but comprehensive language and literacy programme for the whole year. However, it is strongly recommended that *Oxford International English* Level 3 is used alongside a broad reading scheme which allows students access to a wide range of fiction and non-fiction in the form of printed material and e-books. This is the best way for children to develop an enjoyment of and interest in reading. It helps them to be successful not only in their English literacy but produces excellent reading strategies and comprehension skills across all areas of the curriculum. This is especially true for second language students whose overall academic success is dependent on their ability in English.

Oxford International English has been developed to link into and complement the **Oxford Reading Tree**, **TreeTops** and **Project X** reading schemes. There are extracts from books in these schemes in Student Book 3 for your students to enjoy.

As part of the **Oxford Reading Tree**, the **Treetops** series offers levelled reading books for children aged 7–11 years. This series offers the right book for every reader at each stage of their reading journey.

Project X is an innovative new whole-school reading programme with books for 21st-century children of all abilities.

Look at the Oxford University Press International Schools website for reading books and e-books that connect with the unit themes of *Oxford International English* Level 3. Use *Oxford International English* together with a reading scheme for a robust and complete literacy strategy for your students. www.oup.com/oxed/international

How can I check students' progress and measure their English level?

End of unit tests appear after the teaching notes in Teacher Resource Book 3 as short review tests to check learning objectives have been achieved. There are also three **Revise and Check** tests which are longer and require some simple revision and preparation. Mark schemes, answers and model answers for all tests are provided on the CD-ROM.

On the CD-ROM there are separate **progress assessment charts** for speaking and listening, reading and writing. Mid-way through the year and at the end of the year, use the descriptions in the charts to measure an individual student's ability and allocate the numerical 'level' if needed.

What extra teacher's resources are there?

A literacy glossary appears at the end of this Teacher Resource Book giving explanations of teaching and literacy terms.

Photocopiable classroom activity sheets for writing and planning stories, are provided on the CD-ROM in the 'printable resources' tab.

Model answers for the Student Book 3 exercises are provided in the teaching notes in this Teacher Resource Book and the Workbook 3 answers are provided on the CD-ROM.

Guided reading notes on **page 182** of this Teacher Resource Book are to be used with the complete story after Unit 9 of the Student Book.

How do I use the CD-ROM and the e-books?

1 Choose which resource you want and click on the tabs at the top of the screen.

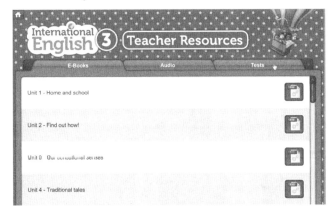

2 Click on the file icon to select the e-book and unit you want to see.

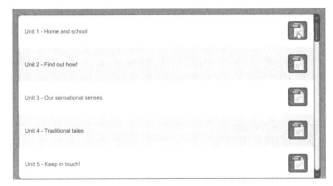

3 Press the 'Play' button to hear the audio of the e-book you have chosen. The audio will stop at the end of the page and start again after you turn the page and press 'Play'.

CD-ROM minimum system requirements

PC
- Pentium® 4 1.5 GHz/ Intel® Core™2 Duo 1.2GHz processor or equivalent
- 16 x DVD-ROM drive speed
- 512 MB RAM
- 1024 x 768 screen resolution with 16-bit colour depth
- 16-bit sound card with speakers or headphones
- Mouse or equivalent pointing device
- Keyboard or equivalent input device
- Adobe® Reader® 7
- Microsoft® Office 2003
- Internet Explorer® 7

Supported operating systems:
- Windows® XP Service Pack 3
- Windows Vista®
- Windows® 7

Mac (some e-book tools may not be available)
- Intel® Core™ Duo 1.33 GHz processor or equivalent
- 16 x DVD-ROM drive speed
- 512 MB RAM
- 1024 x 768 screen resolution with 16-bit colour depth
- Sound card with speakers or headphones
- Mouse or equivalent pointing device
- Keyboard or equivalent input device
- Adobe® Reader® 7
- Microsoft® Office 2003
- Adobe® Flash® Player 9
- Safari 5

Supported operating systems:
- Mac OS 10.6.8 Snow Leopard
- Mac OS 10.7.2 Lion
- Mac OS 10.8.1 Mountain Lion

Home and school

Warm-up objectives

Speak clearly and confidently in a range of contexts.

Take turns in discussion, building on what others have said.

Listen and respond appropriately to others' views and opinions.

Students talk about their homes and journeys to school in whole-group discussions and in pairs. They take it in turns in the discussions, listening to their classmates' opinions and responding appropriately.

Remember to display the child-friendly learning objectives to the class along with the child-friendly checklist that students can use to assess how well they achieve them.

We know that we have achieved these because:

▶ We can talk clearly about our homes and journeys to school.

▶ We know how to take turns in a conversation.

▶ We are able to listen and respond to the opinions of others.

② Unit warm up

Write the unit title on the board. In this unit students will be focusing on home and school. They will be particularly looking at their journeys to and from school.

Briefly describe your own journey to school and say 'so that is my journey to school' as you write the word 'journey' on the board. **Ask:** *How do you say 'journey', 'home' and 'school' in your home language?* (Be sure to include all the home languages.)

Read the quote with the class. **Ask:** *What is a proverb?* (A short well-known saying that states the truth.) *What does fool mean?* (A stupid person.) *Is it a good thing to ask questions?* (Yes.) Brainstorm on a chart why it is a good thing to ask questions in class. (We learn by asking, it's good to ask when we are not sure, etc.) Record answers on a chart and keep for further use.

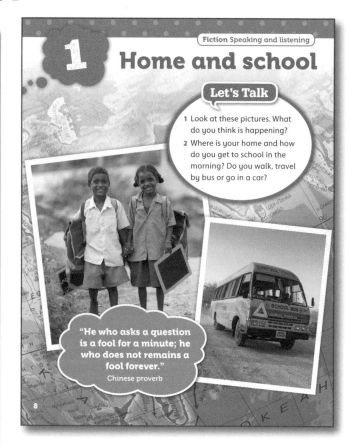

Fiction Speaking and listening

1 Home and school

Let's Talk

1 Look at these pictures. What do you think is happening?
2 Where is your home and how do you get to school in the morning? Do you walk, travel by bus or go in a car?

"He who asks a question is a fool for a minute; he who does not remains a fool forever."
Chinese proverb

8

③ Let's Talk

1 Focus attention on the illustrations and ask students what they think is happening in each picture. (Two children walking to school, a school bus taking children to school or home from school.) Students discuss their answer with a partner.

2 Ask students to describe where they live, how far from school their home is and how they get to school. Ask and answer as a whole group. Encourage students to listen and respond appropriately to others.

Tell students to ask how their peers get to school. They should ask as many people as they can in 5 minutes and record answers in their notebooks. Write prompts on the board: I walk to school, I come by car/bus, I cycle to school.

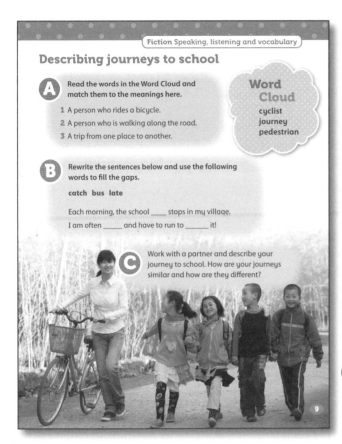

Fiction Speaking, listening and vocabulary

Describing journeys to school

A Read the words in the Word Cloud and match them to the meanings here.

1 A person who rides a bicycle.
2 A person who is walking along the road.
3 A trip from one place to another.

Word Cloud
cyclist
journey
pedestrian

B Rewrite the sentences below and use the following words to fill the gaps.

catch bus late

Each morning, the school _____ stops in my village,
I am often _____ and have to run to _____ it!

C Work with a partner and describe your journey to school. How are your journeys similar and how are they different?

9

Learning objectives

④ Infer the meaning of unknown words from the context.

Develop sensitivity to ways that others express meaning in their talk.

Students practise guessing the meaning of unknown words from the context. They work collaboratively to complete tasks. They work in pairs discussing journeys to school, listening and responding sensitively to their partner.

Remember to display the child-friendly learning objectives to the class along with the child-friendly checklist that students can use to assess how well they achieve them.

We know that we have achieved these because:

▶ We are able to use the new vocabulary.

▶ We can discuss how our journeys to school are the same and different.

▶ We listen to and respond sensitively to the way others express meaning.

⑤ Word Cloud definitions

Focus students' attention on the Word Cloud. Ask them to work in pairs and match the meanings from the context. Ask students which words helped them guess. *Example:* bicycle/cyclist. Share some word facts. *Examples:* the word 'journey' comes from the French word 'jour'; the word 'pedestrian' comes from the Latin word 'pedes', which means 'on foot'. Elicit how you say 'on foot' in classroom languages. Record answers on a chart.

Ask children to write the cloud words in their home languages. If they are unsure, they can use bilingual dictionaries, check on online translators or ask a parent, family member or other speaker of their home language. Note that students should write all new vocabulary in their New Word List (*see* Workbook).

cyclist a person who rides a bicycle.
journey a trip from one place to another.
pedestrian a person who is walking.

⑥ Student Book teaching notes and exercise answers

Students match the definitions to the meanings.

Answers:

1 cyclist
2 pedestrian
3 journey

Students rewrite the sentences filling in the missing words. Ask students to work individually. Then ask them to draw a picture under their sentence to illustrate their own journey to school. Ask them to compare their answers and share their drawing with a partner.

Answer:

Each morning, the school **bus** stops in my village. I am often **late** and have to run to **catch** it!

Students work in pairs to discuss how their journeys to school are similar and how they are different. Encourage them to talk about the things they see on their way to school.

⑦ Extension

Ask students to make a graph showing the number of children in the class who travel to school on foot, by car, by bus, etc. They can use the information they recorded in their notebooks during the Let's Talk exercise.

① Learning objectives

Read a range of story books.

Infer the meaning of unknown words from the context.

Students read the story of Abdullah and identify it as fiction. Students guess the meaning of words by paying attention to 1) illustrations, 2) the context of the story, 3) what they know about the structure of English and 4) what they know about their own mother tongue.

Remember to display the child-friendly learning objectives to the class along with the child-friendly checklist that students can use to assess how well they achieve them.

We know that we have achieved these because:

▶ We are able to read the story and identify it as fiction.

▶ We can guess the meaning of unfamiliar words by using the clues available to us.

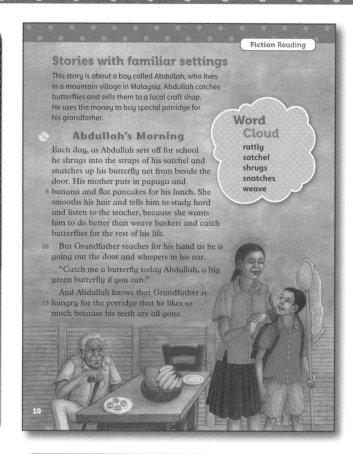

Stories with familiar settings

This story is about a boy called Abdullah, who lives in a mountain village in Malaysia. Abdullah catches butterflies and sells them to a local craft shop. He uses the money to buy special porridge for his grandfather.

Word Cloud
rattly
satchel
shrugs
snatches
weave

Abdullah's Morning

Each day, as Abdullah sets off for school he shrugs into the straps of his satchel and snatches up his butterfly net from beside the door. His mother puts in papaya and
5 banana and flat pancakes for his lunch. She smooths his hair and tells him to study hard and listen to the teacher, because she wants him to do better than weave baskets and catch butterflies for the rest of his life.
10   But Grandfather reaches for his hand as he is going out the door and whispers in his ear.
  "Catch me a butterfly today Abdullah, a big green butterfly if you can."
  And Abdullah knows that Grandfather is
15 hungry for the porridge that he likes so much because his teeth are all gone.

10

② Fiction reading notes

Use the CD-ROM or read the story yourself while students follow in their books. Read the introductory text with the students. **Ask:** *What kind of text is this?* (Fiction.) Explain that the setting for this story is a mountain village in Malaysia.

When you come to a word that is difficult, ask students to pay attention to pictures in the story, what is happening in the story, or things they know that will help them understand unfamiliar words. *Example:* for 'satchel', ask students to look at the illustration on page 11 that shows Abdullah with his satchel. Direct students' attention to the four factors that will help them to infer the meaning of that word: 1) illustrations, 2) context, 3) the structure of English and 4) the structure of the students' mother tongue. Put these four factors on a chart.

Begin to develop a 'side-by-side' chart of cognates (words that are similar in two or more languages, such as 'school' in English, 'escuela' in Spanish and 'sekolah' in Malay) that students can identify within the story from their own mother tongue.

For beginner-level students, model the actions. *Example:* for the word 'shrug', ask students to put on their satchels or backpacks, putting one on yourself, shrugging your shoulders as you do it. Point out students who are shrugging their shoulders. Ask students to shrug their shoulders. (Note that the meaning of the word 'shrug' in the text is different from the usual definition, which indicates an indifference or uncertainty.)

③ Word Cloud definitions

Read aloud the words in the Word Cloud or refer to the CD-ROM. Can students work out their meanings from the context? Ask students how they worked out the meaning, regardless of whether their guess was right or wrong.

rattly making a series of short, sharp sounds.

satchel a bag you wear over your shoulder or on your back, especially for carrying books to and from school.

shrugs raises and lowers the shoulders.

snatches takes quickly.

weave make a basket or cloth by lacing reeds or threads together.

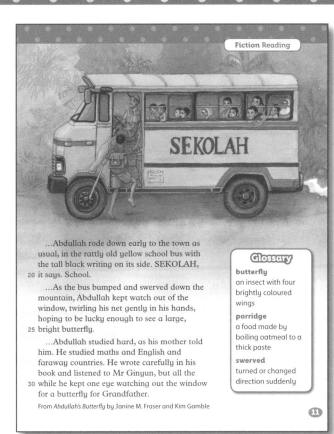

Fiction Reading

...Abdullah rode down early to the town as usual, in the rattly old yellow school bus with the tall black writing on its side. SEKOLAH,
20 it says. School.

...As the bus bumped and swerved down the mountain, Abdullah kept watch out of the window, twirling his net gently in his hands, hoping to be lucky enough to see a large,
25 bright butterfly.

...Abdullah studied hard, as his mother told him. He studied maths and English and faraway countries. He wrote carefully in his book and listened to Mr Ginyun, but all the
30 while he kept one eye watching out the window for a butterfly for Grandfather.

From Abdullah's Butterfly by Janine M. Fraser and Kim Gamble

Glossary

butterfly
an insect with four brightly coloured wings

porridge
a food made by boiling oatmeal to a thick paste

swerved
turned or changed direction suddenly

⑪

---

④ Learning objective

Identify different types of stories and typical story themes.

Students are introduced to the features of the narrative genre: stories with familiar settings. They read an extract in this genre and identify features such as character and setting. They discuss the similarities and differences between Abdullah's home and journey to school and their own.

Remember to display the child-friendly learning objective to the class along with the child-friendly checklist that students can use to assess how well they achieve it.

We know that we have achieved this because:

▶ We are able to identify the themes of Abdullah's story.

▶ We can identify similarities and differences between Abdullah's home and journey to school and our own home and journey to school.

⑤ Fiction reading notes

Refer students to the title of page 10 of the Student Book. Ask students what the word 'familiar' means. Does it make them think of another word they know (family)? Tell them it means 'well-known' or 'knowing something well'. Explain the meaning of the word 'setting' (the place in which a story takes place). Elicit from students words to describe a mountain village in Malaysia. Write the adjectives down without necessarily identifying them as such. This will come later in the unit. Make comparisons between students' own settings at home and Abdullah's setting in the story.

Ask students to name the characters in the story up to this point (Abdullah, his mother, his grandfather, Mr Ginyun). Ask them what they know about Abdullah's character. In this part of the story, Abdullah is torn between his desire to do something nice for his grandfather and his responsibilities at school. The author describes how Abdullah kept one eye watching out the classroom window. Ask students to think about one time when they kept one eye watching out the window. Elicit responses, share stories and, if time allows, write the themes of their stories on the board.

Ask: *Who wrote Abdullah's story?* (Janine M. Fraser and Kim Gamble.) *What is the story about?* (A Malaysian boy who catches butterflies to sell.) *Why is this part of the story called Abdullah's morning?* (Because it describes a typical morning, with Abdullah leaving for school.)

On a Venn diagram (a diagram of two overlapping circles showing relations between sets of things, *see* Guidelines), list the similarities and differences between the students' journeys from home to school and Abdullah's journey.

⑥ Extension

Students ask a parent, family member or other speaker of their home language for expressions such as 'keeping one eye watching out the window'. To integrate with art, ask students to illustrate these idiomatic expressions. Display the illustrations, with the sayings written in the students' home languages.

Learning objectives

① Answer questions with some reference to single points in the text.

Take turns in discussion, building on what others have said.

Listen and respond appropriately to others' views and opinions.

Students are guided to answer the comprehension questions in their own words rather than simply copying from the text. When they give their responses and answer any questions that the teacher or their peers ask, they are encouraged to do so in an appropriate way.

 Remember to display the child-friendly learning objectives to the class along with the child-friendly checklist that students can use to assess how well they achieve them.

We know that we have achieved these because:

▶ **We can answer the comprehension questions correctly.**

▶ **We take turns when we are talking to each other or the teacher.**

▶ **We listen when another person is talking and respond appropriately.**

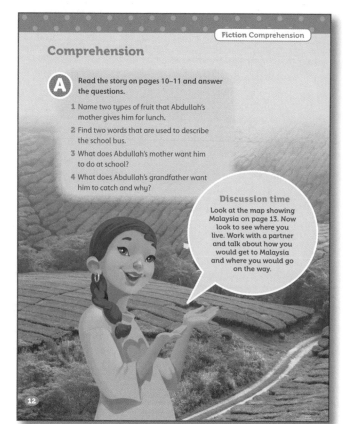

Fiction Comprehension

Comprehension

Ⓐ Read the story on pages 10–11 and answer the questions.

1 Name two types of fruit that Abdullah's mother gives him for lunch.

2 Find two words that are used to describe the school bus.

3 What does Abdullah's mother want him to do at school?

4 What does Abdullah's grandfather want him to catch and why?

Discussion time
Look at the map showing Malaysia on page 13. Now look to see where you live. Work with a partner and talk about how you would get to Malaysia and where you would go on the way.

12

To extend the exercise and ensure comprehension, ask students to compare the responses from the text with their own experiences. **Ask:** *What type of fruit do you bring to school? Who gives it to you? Find two words that describe the vehicle that brings you to school. What do your parents want you to do at school? Do you have a grandparent at home? Does he or she ask you to bring something home on your way back from school?*

② Student Book teaching notes and comprehension answers

Ⓐ

Students read the story again and answer the questions. Encourage students to give answers in their own words, rather than copying from the text. When students give you an exact copy of words from the text, ask them to expand the idea. ***Example:*** If a student says 'His mother puts in papaya and banana and flat pancakes for his lunch,' ask the student, 'Which of those three objects are fruit?'

Answers:

1 banana and papaya

2 any two of rattly, old or yellow

3 study hard and listen to his teacher

4 a butterfly, so that he can sell it and buy porridge for his grandfather

➡

③ Discussion time

Ask students to look at the map on page 13 and the map at the front of the Student Book or a wall map of the world. Show the students where you come from on the map and describe how you would get to Malaysia. Ask students to do the same. Ask students to bring from home the name of their home country or town, written in their home languages. Identify the location of the countries on the Student Book world map, a wall map or a globe.

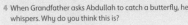

Fiction Comprehension

What do you think?

Use phrases from the story to help with your answers.

1   How would you describe the road that leads down to the town from Abdullah's village?

2   Do you think Abdullah is well behaved? Why?

3   Why do you think Abdullah's mother tells him to study hard?

4   When Grandfather asks Abdullah to catch a butterfly, he whispers. Why do you think this is?

What about you?

Do you think it is important to work hard at school? Will it help you in the future? Work with a partner and talk about your answer.

13

Learning objectives

④

Begin to infer meanings beyond the literal, for example about motives and character.

Consider how choice of words can heighten meaning.

Students imagine what the characters in the story are like. They focus on specific words and phrases that are powerful and add meaning and interest to the text.

Remember to display the child-friendly learning objectives to the class along with the child-friendly checklist that students can use to assess how well they achieve them.

We know that we have achieved these because:

▶ We can describe what characters in the story are like.

▶ We can identify words and phrases that add meaning to the story and make it more interesting.

⑤ **Student Book teaching notes and comprehension answers**

 B

Students refer to phrases in the story to help with their answers. When the correct or appropriate answers have been listed, ask students how they reached those conclusions. What clues did they use to form their answers? Give students time to prepare their statements and to present them to the rest of the class.

Answers:

1   Accept answers that use the phrase 'the bus bumped and swerved' and the notion of a mountain road to describe the road. As you discuss this question, ask the students to reflect on the use of the words 'bumped' and 'swerved'. **Ask:** *How would the meaning of this sentence be different if the author had used the word 'went' instead?*

2   Ask students to give a reason for their answer. Accept answers that bring up the fact that Abdullah studied hard, as his mother had told him to. He studied maths, English and faraway countries and wrote in his book carefully. He listened to Mr Ginyun. Some students may decide that he was not well behaved because he kept an eye out the window and he wanted to catch butterflies despite his mother's wishes against that.

3   Accept answers that refer to Abdullah's mother wanting him to do better than weave baskets and catch butterflies for the rest of his life.

4   Accept answers that refer to Abdullah's grandfather not wanting Abduallah's mother to hear what he was saying because he knew she did not want Abdullah to spend his time catching butterflies.

 C

Ask students to work in pairs to discuss whether they think it is important to work hard at school. Ask them to talk about what they want to achieve in the future and whether working hard at school will help them. Ask them to write two sentences about their future goals.

1 Learning objectives

Identify different types of stories and typical story themes.

Infer the meaning of unknown words from the context.

Students consider the themes and features of the story. Students infer the meaning of unfamiliar words using the four factors on the chart created earlier (*see* page 10).

 Remember to display the child-friendly learning objectives to the class along with the child-friendly checklist that students can use to assess how well they achieve them.

We know that we have achieved these because:

▶ We are able to identify the themes in Abdullah's story.

▶ We can guess the meaning of unfamiliar words.

Fiction Reading

Stories with familiar settings (continued)

On his way home from school, Abdullah is looking out of the window of the bus. He sees a beautiful butterfly and decides to get off the bus!

The Butterfly

Abdullah leapt out of his seat. He grabbed up his bag and butterfly net, and stumbled down the aisle.

"Wait," he said urgently. "Let me off."…

5 "You sure?" asked the driver. "It's still a mighty long walk home up the mountain."

But Abdullah nodded adamantly. He wanted to get off, now.

He waved to his friends hanging out the windows
10 and…ran back down the road to where he had seen the butterfly.

…Like a miracle, it was still there, rocking gently on a fern frond. He held his breath in wonder and excitement, because this was the
15 largest, most perfect butterfly of its kind he had ever seen.

…Abdullah stared, almost in a trance, as, with an upward sweep of its brilliant wings, the butterfly
20 launched itself off the plant and into flight.

From *Abdullah's Butterfly* by Janine M. Fraser and Kim Gamble

Word Cloud
adamantly
frond
rocking
trance

14

2 Fiction reading notes

Ask students what they think Abdullah is going to do by making predictions based on the title of the piece. Begin to read the story or refer to the CD-ROM. Stop at unfamiliar words and ask students to try to guess the meaning with the help of the four factors listed on the chart created earlier (*see* page 10).

Ask students to identify what kind of text this is (fiction) and what the theme of the story is. **Ask:** *Is it about butterflies?* (No.) Establish the themes of the story, talking about the titles of the two excerpts that you have read.

Ask students what this part of the story is about. Elicit words and phrases that describe how Abdullah felt when he saw the butterfly out of the school bus window. **Ask:** *What words tell us that he wanted to get off the bus quickly?* **Examples:** 'leapt out of his seat', 'urgently', 'adamantly', 'he wanted to get off, now.'

Ask students whether the text makes them form a picture in their mind of the butterfly Abdullah saw. How is the picture in their own mind different from the pictures of the butterfly on pages 14 and 15 of the Student Book. How is it similar?

3 Word Cloud definitions

Read aloud the words in the Word Cloud or refer to the CD-ROM. Ask students to guess the meanings using the four factors listed on the chart created earlier (*see* page 10).

adamantly in a very determined way.

frond a large leaf with many divisions.

rocking moving gently backwards and forwards or from side to side.

trance a dreamy state, like sleep.

4 Extension

Produce an acrostic (a composition where you make a word or phrase out of each of the letters of a word) by writing a word or phrase for each of the letters of the word 'butterfly'. *Example:*

Beautiful

Useful

Trembling

Tree

Exciting

Rainbow

Flower

Lovely

Yellow

Comprehension

A **Which three sentences below are true?**

1 Abdullah had to stay on the bus.
2 The butterfly landed on a fern.
3 Abdullah was amazed and excited.
4 Abdullah wanted to catch the butterfly.

B **What do you think?**

Use phrases from the story to help with your answers.

1 Why do you think Abdullah wanted to get off the bus?
2 Find words that describe the butterfly. Can you think of any others?
3 How do you think Abdullah felt when the butterfly flew into the air?

C **What about you?**

What do you think Abdullah did next? What would you have done if you were Abdullah?

Challenge
Think of something exciting that happened to you at or after school. Describe it to your friend.

15

Learning objectives

5

Answer questions with some reference to single points in the text.

Begin to infer meanings beyond the literal, for example about motives and character.

Consider words that make an impact, for example adjectives and powerful verbs.

Students answer questions about specific events or actions in the text. They answer questions by imagining things beyond the information given directly in the extract. They examine words that make the story more powerful.

Remember to display the child-friendly learning objectives to the class along with the child-friendly checklist that students can use to assess how well they achieve them.

We know that we have achieved these because:

▶ **We can answer specific questions about the story.**

▶ **We can imagine what the characters are like.**

▶ **We can identify special words that make the story more interesting and the meaning more powerful.**

---

6 **Student Book teaching notes and comprehension answers**

Students read the story again to find the three true statements.

Answers:

2, 3 and 4

B

1 Remind students to think beyond the information given directly in the extract. Give beginner second language students options to choose from.
Ask: *Was it because he wanted to walk home? Was it because he had forgotten something at school?*

Answer:

Because he saw a beautiful butterfly flying by and he had been waiting all day to catch one so he could sell it and buy porridge for his grandfather.

2 The adjectives 'beautiful', 'large', 'perfect', 'brilliant' are from the text. Encourage students to come up with other adjectives as well. Direct their attention to the illustrations of the butterfly and elicit adjectives that describe it: any colour, delicate, light, spotted or dotted, etc. Ask students to pick one or two words that the authors have used to make the butterfly really special. *Example:* 'brilliant'. **Ask:** *Are there words for actions in the extract that also make the action sound special?* *Example:* launched.

3 Accept answers such as 'surprised', 'sad', 'angry', 'upset', 'disappointed', etc. Ask students to explain why they think Abdullah would have felt these feelings. Ask them what they know about what Abdullah wanted and what his character was like.

Ask students to work in pairs to decide what they think Abdullah did next. Ask for responses to be shared with the rest of the class. Next, ask students to decide whether they would have done the same thing. If not, what would they have done? As students give their responses to both questions, put their answers in one or two words on the board, with sad endings on the left and happy endings on the right. Point out the differences.

7 **Challenge**

Share with students something exciting that has happened to you. Then ask students to do the same with a partner. Ask for volunteers to share their experiences.

Learning objective

1

Collect examples of nouns and adjectives, and use the terms appropriately.

Students decide what category various words are and place them in the appropriate column on a chart. They use the words 'noun' and 'adjective' in their oral language.

Remember to display the child-friendly learning objective to the class along with the child-friendly checklist that students can use to assess how well they achieve it.

We know that we have achieved this because:

▶ We can determine which words are nouns and which are adjectives.

▶ We can use the terms 'nouns' and 'adjectives' appropriately.

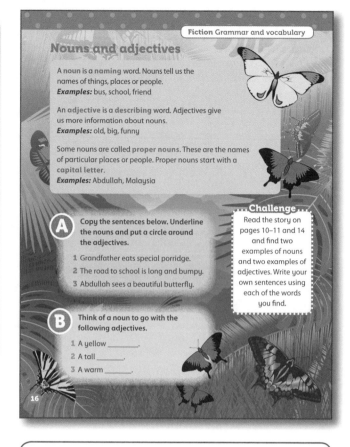

Fiction Grammar and vocabulary

Nouns and adjectives

A **noun** is a **naming** word. Nouns tell us the names of things, places or people.
Examples: bus, school, friend

An **adjective** is a **describing** word. Adjectives give us more information about nouns.
Examples: old, big, funny

Some nouns are called **proper nouns**. These are the names of particular places or people. Proper nouns start with a **capital letter**.
Examples: Abdullah, Malaysia

...Challenge...
Read the story on pages 10–11 and 14 and find two examples of nouns and two examples of adjectives. Write your own sentences using each of the words you find.

A Copy the sentences below. Underline the nouns and put a circle around the adjectives.

1 Grandfather eats special porridge.
2 The road to school is long and bumpy.
3 Abdullah sees a beautiful butterfly.

B Think of a noun to go with the following adjectives.

1 A yellow _____.
2 A tall _____.
3 A warm _____.

16

Student Book teaching notes and grammar and vocabulary exercise answers

2

Read the information about nouns and adjectives in the box with the class. Use two objects such as two balls or two apples of different colours and have two charts ready, one with the heading 'NOUNS' and one with the heading 'ADJECTIVES'. These will be filled with the appropriate words during the lesson.

Show students the object. **Ask:** *What is this called?* (Apple/ball, etc.) Explain that the word used to name the object is a noun and, as you say that, write the word 'apple' or 'ball' (or the name of the object you have brought in) on the NOUNS chart, on the left-hand side, all lower case. Point out other nouns, such as desk, book, window, etc., as well as pointing out individual students and writing their names on the right-hand side, beginning with a capital letter. Ask what the difference is between the two columns. When it is clear that the right-hand side contains names of particular places or people, label the column as 'Proper nouns'.

Next, take out the other object, of a different colour from the first. Elicit adjectives describing the colour of the object and write the words down on the ADJECTIVES chart. Do the same with big and small books, far and near, etc. Then, elicit the words describing various objects around the classroom, adding them to the chart.

A

Students copy the sentences and underline the nouns and circle the adjectives.

Answers:

1 Grandfather (noun), porridge (noun), special (adjective)
2 road (noun), school (noun), long (adjective), bumpy (adjective)
3 Abdullah (noun), butterfly (noun), beautiful (adjective)

B

Students think of nouns to go with the adjectives yellow, tall and warm.

Answers:

Accept whatever noun makes sense with each adjective.

Challenge

3

Model the activity by picking one noun and one adjective from the words selected by the students. *Example:* I wish I had long wings so I could fly. Accept all sentences that students produce as long as they use nouns and adjectives accurately.

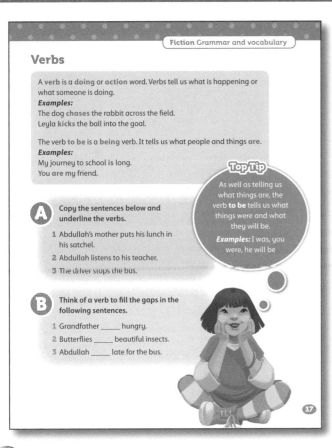

Fiction Grammar and vocabulary

Verbs

A **verb** is a **doing** or **action** word. Verbs tell us what is happening or what someone is doing.
Examples:
The dog **chases** the rabbit across the field.
Leyla **kicks** the ball into the goal.

The verb **to be** is a **being** verb. It tells us what people and things **are**.
Examples:
My journey to school **is** long.
You **are** my friend.

Top Tip

As well as telling us what things are, the verb **to be** tells us what things were and what they will be.
Examples: I was, you were, he will be

A Copy the sentences below and underline the verbs.

1 Abdullah's mother puts his lunch in his satchel.
2 Abdullah listens to his teacher.
3 The driver stops the bus.

B Think of a verb to fill the gaps in the following sentences.

1 Grandfather _____ hungry.
2 Butterflies _____ beautiful insects.
3 Abdullah _____ late for the bus.

17

---

(4) ## Learning objective

Collect examples of verbs, and use the term appropriately.

Students identify verbs as action words in sentences, and add verbs to a chart. They investigate the verb 'to be' and use the word 'verb' in their oral language.

Remember to display the child-friendly learning objective to the class along with the child-friendly checklist that students can use to assess how well they achieve it.

We know that we have achieved this because:

▶ **We can determine which words are verbs.**
▶ **We can use the term verbs appropriately.**

(5) ## Student Book teaching notes and grammar and vocabulary exercise answers

Prepare a chart with the heading 'VERBS'. Take a bite of one of the apples that you used for the noun and adjective activity, or throw one of the balls in the air. Elicit the word 'eat' or 'throw'. Write 'eat' or 'throw' on the VERBS chart. Continue acting out various actions – 'shrug', 'catch', 'stumble', etc. Give orders for various actions to students, and write down the verbs on the chart.

Explain that whereas verbs such as 'eat' and 'throw' indicate an action, there is another verb that indicates 'being'. Write the verb 'to be' and 'am', 'is' and 'are' on the chart, giving examples of each. Show students that 'am' goes with 'I', 'are' with 'you', 'we', 'they', and 'is' with 'he', 'she' and 'it'.

Write the eight pronouns (I, you, he, she, it, we, you and they) on the board. Give students sticky papers with the three forms of the verb 'to be' in the present tense (am, is, are) and ask individual students to come up and stick one of the papers under the appropriate pronoun. Show how 'to be' can also be used for things that happened (was, were) or things that will happen (will be).

Give students time to investigate how the verb 'to be' works in their home languages. Refer students to the exercises on page 17. Students work individually to complete the exercises.

A

Students copy the sentences and underline the verbs.

Answers:

1 puts
2 listens
3 stops

B

Students fill the gaps in the sentences.

Answers:

1 is/was
2 are/were
3 is/was

(6) ## Extension

1 Students make an adjective/noun/verb collage using drawings they do themselves or pictures they cut from magazines. They make a 'Can you see?' poster to go with it, where they list the nouns, adjectives and verbs seen in the pictures.
2 Ask students to find out how you say 'adjective', 'noun', 'proper noun' and 'verb' in their home languages. Display collages and words for these parts of speech in all the home languages.

1 Learning objectives

Consider how choice of words can heighten meaning.

Collect examples of verbs and adjectives, and use the terms appropriately.

Students focus on verbs and adjectives that carry special meaning and they add words to the charts of adjectives and verbs.

Remember to display the child-friendly learning objectives to the class along with the child-friendly checklist that students can use to assess how well they achieve them.

We know that we have achieved these because:

▶ **We can determine which words are verbs and which are adjectives.**

▶ **We can identify powerful verbs and adjectives.**

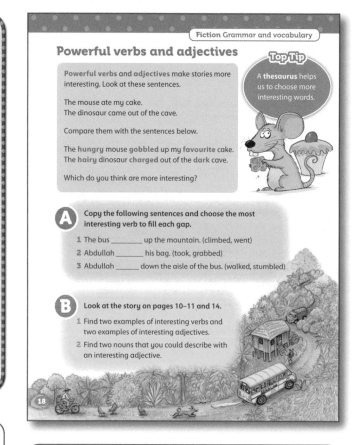

Fiction Grammar and vocabulary

Powerful verbs and adjectives

Top Tip

A **thesaurus** helps us to choose more interesting words.

Powerful **verbs** and **adjectives** make stories more interesting. Look at these sentences.

The mouse ate my cake.
The dinosaur came out of the cave.

Compare them with the sentences below.

The **hungry** mouse **gobbled** up my **favourite** cake.
The **hairy** dinosaur **charged** out of the **dark** cave.

Which do you think are more interesting?

A Copy the following sentences and choose the most interesting verb to fill each gap.

1 The bus _____ up the mountain. (climbed, went)
2 Abdullah _____ his bag. (took, grabbed)
3 Abdullah _____ down the aisle of the bus. (walked, stumbled)

B Look at the story on pages 10–11 and 14.

1 Find two examples of interesting verbs and two examples of interesting adjectives.
2 Find two nouns that you could describe with an interesting adjective.

18

2 Student Book teaching notes and grammar and vocabulary exercise answers

Ask students to look at some of the full-colour illustrations in the Student Book. Now show them an illustration in black and white, such as a copy of one of the Student Book pages as shown in the Teacher Resource Book. Ask them which they like better. It is extremely unlikely that any of them will choose the black-and-white one. Ask them why they chose the picture in colour. Tell them that words can have the same effect. They can make a sentence more colourful, brighter and more interesting.

Read the introductory text about powerful verbs and adjectives. Make sure the students understand the meanings of 'hungry', 'gobbled', 'favourite', 'hairy', 'charged' and 'dark'. If not clear, mime or show what each word means. Ask students why they think the sentences with powerful adjectives are more interesting (they bring to life, they tell me exactly what was happening, they give me interesting information about what's happening, etc.).

 A

Students choose the most interesting word to fill the gaps. Act out the two choices for each statement so that students see the difference.

Answers:

1 climbed
2 grabbed
3 stumbled

 B

Students refer to the story on pages 10–11 and 14 of the Student Book and answer the questions.

Answers:

1 Accept answers such as 'reaches' and 'leapt', 'brilliant' and 'tall'.
2 Accept answers such as 'mountain', 'road', 'wings'.

3 Top Tip

Show students a thesaurus. Write down on the board: 'The angry man walked away.' Look up (or have a student look up) 'angry' in the thesaurus and pick 'furious' as a replacement. Act out 'angry' and 'furious', making 'furious' look much more dramatic and expressing stronger emotion than 'angry' and ask students which one is more interesting. Do the same with 'walk' and 'march', making 'march' more exaggerated than 'walk'.

New spellings

When learning new spellings, it helps to break the word into **syllables** or chunks.
Example: but-ter-fly

When words are spelt with **two vowels together**, the vowels usually make one sound rather than two.
Examples: read, snail, sound

Top Tip

Words in English are made up of vowels and consonants.

Vowels: a, e, i, o, u

Consonants: The rest of the alphabet

 A Here are some of the new words you have learnt in this unit.

**journey satchel floating
porridge weave**

1 Read, say and listen to the words.
2 Write the words down, breaking them into syllables. Which word has only one syllable?
3 Write a sentence using each of the new words.

 B Look at the new words in A above.

1 Find the vowels in each word.
2 Do any of the words have two vowels together? What sound do the vowels make?

Challenge

Read the story on pages 10–11 and 14. Find two examples of words that are spelt with two vowels together. Write a sentence using each of the words.

19

Learning objectives

④ **Use effective strategies to tackle blending unfamiliar words to read, including sounding out, separating into syllables, using context.**

Use effective strategies to tackle segmenting unfamiliar words to spell, including segmenting into individual sounds, separating into syllables, applying known spelling.

Students analyse words in their reading and in their writing and look for their components, including the number of syllables. Students sound out words that have two vowels together.

Remember to display the child-friendly learning objectives to the class along with the child-friendly checklist that students can use to assess how well they achieve them.

We know that we have achieved these because:

▶ **We can separate words into syllables and count the number of syllables in words.**

▶ **We can identify, sound out and spell words that have two vowels together.**

⑤ **Student Book teaching notes and phonics and spelling exercise answers**

Use strips of paper with single syllables written on them making up the following words: but-ter-fly, jour-ney, satch-el and por-ridge. Make enough copies so that students can work in pairs. Give each pair of students a set of syllable strips. Ask them to put them together to make words. When students are done, write the words on the board. Read the words, tapping each syllable with a ruler as you read it. Ask students to read with you, and then to read with their partners as they tap each syllable. Write 'syllable' under each syllable on the board.

Point to the vowels in the words, and remind students of the five vowels (a, e, i, o, u). Point to the words that have two vowels together. Next, read the word and ask students to listen to the sound of those two letters. Tell them 'See how these two vowels make one sound?' Ask students to complete the exercises on page19.

 A

Students look at some of the new words they have learnt in the unit and answer the questions.

Answers:

1 Students read, say and listen to the words.
2 jour-ney, satch-el, rock-ing, weave
3 Accept any sentence that is meaningful and makes sense.

 B

Students look at the words in A and answer the questions.

Answers:

1 (journey) ou/e, (satchel) a/e, (rocking) o/i, (porridge) o/i/e, (weave) ea/e
2 journey (ou), floating (oa), weave (ea)

⑥ **Challenge**

Read the box with the students. Ask them to find two examples in the extracts of words that have two vowels together. Ask them to say the words out loud and listen to the sound the vowels make. Students then write a sentence using each of the words.

Learning objective

① Identify different types of story and typical story themes.

Students are introduced to the features of the narrative genre: writing a story with a familiar setting. They will read an extract in this genre and identify features such as character and setting.

Remember to display the child-friendly learning objective to the class along with the child-friendly checklist that students can use to assess how well they achieve it.

We know that we have achieved this because:

▶ We understand what fiction means and that familiar setting stories take place in everyday situations.

▶ We know what setting and character mean.

② Writing workshop teaching notes

Model writing

Fiction with a familiar setting falls into the category of narrative genre. Explain to students that types within this genre include adventure, fairy-tale, horror story, epic, science fiction and romance. The structure of the text goes through the stages in this order:

1 The setting, situation and characters are introduced.
2 One or more problems emerge as events unfold.
3 A solution emerges (although a major problem can remain unresolved until the end of the story).
4 A message may come from the story (a moral or word of wisdom).

Elicit ideas for familiar settings; make a list of them (home, school, park, etc.). Tell students they are going to write a story in a familiar setting.

Direct children to the title of the text. Read it out loud. Ask students for another word for house (home). Ask if they can explain the difference between these two words (a house is a building where people live; a home is the place where you live, but it can also mean the place where you were born or the place where you are looked after). Draw a chart on the board and ask children how they say house and home in the home languages.

⇨

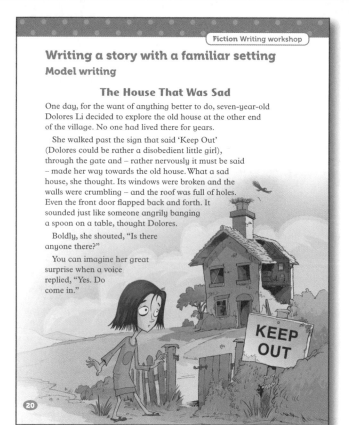

Fiction Writing workshop

Writing a story with a familiar setting
Model writing

The House That Was Sad

One day, for the want of anything better to do, seven-year-old Dolores Li decided to explore the old house at the other end of the village. No one had lived there for years.

She walked past the sign that said 'Keep Out' (Dolores could be rather a disobedient little girl), through the gate and – rather nervously it must be said – made her way towards the old house. What a sad house, she thought. Its windows were broken and the walls were crumbling – and the roof was full of holes. Even the front door flapped back and forth. It sounded just like someone angrily banging a spoon on a table, thought Dolores.

Boldly, she shouted, "Is there anyone there?"

You can imagine her great surprise when a voice replied, "Yes. Do come in."

KEEP OUT

20

Refer students to the picture. **Ask:** *Does the little girl live in the house?* Ask students to turn to a partner and say (predict) what they think the story is going to be about. Point to the chart for learning unknown words from context and read though the four factors (*see* page 10). Read the text with the students. Ask students if they can guess the meanings of the words: 'explore', 'disobedient', 'crumbling', 'flapped', 'banging' and 'boldly'. Students read the text silently again. Check for understanding with beginner students. Give them the gist of the story and have them write key vocabulary in their New Word List (*see* Workbook).

Refer students to the picture again. **Ask:** *What does the sign mean?* Elicit how you say 'Keep Out' in their home languages. **Ask:** *Should you go into a place with a sign that says 'Keep Out'?* Ask the students to think in pairs about reasons for 'Keep Out' signs. Students share their ideas with the whole group.

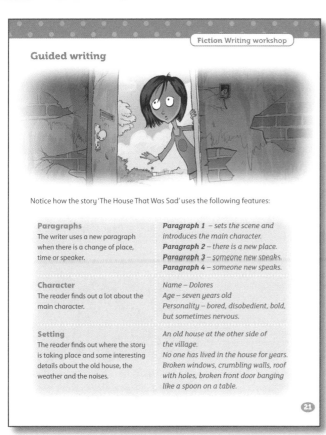

Guided writing

Fiction Writing workshop

Notice how the story 'The House That Was Sad' uses the following features:

Paragraphs	Paragraph 1 – sets the scene and introduces the main character.
The writer uses a new paragraph when there is a change of place, time or speaker.	Paragraph 2 – there is a new place. Paragraph 3 – someone new speaks. Paragraph 4 – someone new speaks.
Character	Name – Dolores
The reader finds out a lot about the main character.	Age – seven years old Personality – bored, disobedient, bold, but sometimes nervous.
Setting	An old house at the other side of the village.
The reader finds out where the story is taking place and some interesting details about the old house, the weather and the noises.	No one has lived in the house for years. Broken windows, crumbling walls, roof with holes, broken front door banging like a spoon on a table.

21

③ Learning objectives

Begin to organize writing in sections or paragraphs in extended stories.

Develop descriptions of settings in stories.

Write portraits of characters.

Students develop their knowledge of settings and characters and the importance of writing in paragraphs. Using the table, they identify the features in the extract and relate their learning to other familiar stories.

Remember to display the child-friendly learning objectives to the class along with the child-friendly checklist that students can use to assess how well they achieve them.

We know that we have achieved these because:

▶ **We understand that by writing in paragraphs we make our stories easier to read.**

▶ **We can identify setting and character in familiar stories.**

▶ **We understand that using adjectives makes the setting and character more interesting for the reader.**

④ Writing workshop teaching notes

Guided writing

Read through the table on page 21 of the Student Book with the students. Ask them to write the words 'paragraphs', characters' and 'setting' in their notebooks. Elicit how they say these words in their home languages.

In pairs, students find the beginning of each new paragraph in the text on page 20.

Elicit names of characters from other books the students have read. Ask them to give one sentence describing the personality of the character. In pairs, students find the information about Dolores in the text.

Mention a story that is familiar to the students and ask them to describe the setting to their partner. Individually, students find the description of the setting in the extract and underline it. Point out that the description of the setting does not end in the first paragraph.

With books closed, elicit adjectives that describe Dolores and the house. Write them on a chart. Encourage students to write new words in their New Word List (*see* Workbook).

Lead a group discussion on why paragraphs, character and setting are important in a good story. *Example:* A setting that is described well makes the reader feel that they are there. The more the reader feels they know the character, the more the story will flow and the readers will want to know more. Writing in paragraphs makes a story easier to read. Show students a chunk of text without paragraphs and one with to emphasize their importance.

NB whenever possible, encourage students from the same language background to talk through their learning in their home languages.

① Learning objectives

Plan main points as a structure for story writing.

Begin to organize writing in sections or paragraphs in extended stories.

Choose and compare words to strengthen the impact of writing.

🔘 Remember to display the child-friendly learning objectives to the class along with the child-friendly checklist that students can use to assess how well they achieve them.

We know that we have achieved these because:

▶ We can write a paragraph plan with the main points to be covered in each paragraph.

▶ We can use interesting adjectives to describe the setting and character.

② Writing workshop teaching notes

Draw the outline of two large houses on the board and write 'House' on the roof of one and 'Home' on the other. Ask students to copy this into their notebooks. Briefly in pairs, students brainstorm words they associate with house and home. (House: walls, windows, roof, door, rooms, housework, etc. Home: family, parents, brothers, sisters, pets, warm, cosy, safe, homework, etc.) Ask students to share their words with the whole class and list them inside the drawings on the board. Students copy any words they didn't come up with into their notebooks.

Ask students to look back at the 'House That Was Sad' story. **Ask:** *Do you think the story has a good title? Why?* (Because it is not a home, etc.)

Your writing

Explain to the students that they are now going to finish the story with a happy ending. Refer them to the picture of Dolores smiling and the picture with the house all done up. **Ask:** *What can you see? How do you think the characters feel? What do you think the*

Writing a story with a familiar setting

Your writing

Finish the story 'The House That Was Sad' with a happy ending. Write a paragraph plan to help you plan your story. In the plan, write a sentence that sums up what is going to happen in each paragraph.

Remember to use a new paragraph when you change any of the following:

Time	Ten minutes later...
Place	They walked into the kitchen.
Character	The old lady tiptoed into the room.
Action	Suddenly, a door burst open.
Speaker	The old man declared, "I want laughter back in this house!"

Remember to include some details about what the house looks like inside, as well as any noises and smells. You could even bring in what something feels like. It will make your description of the house much more interesting for the reader!

If the house becomes a happy house, you might want to describe the outside so it does not look sad anymore!

22

---

smells would be like?, etc. Ask students to close their eyes and think about what could have happened. Ask them to write down their ideas (quick write, 5 minutes only). Second language students can do this in their home languages.

Students now turn their ideas into a paragraph plan. They write one sentence only to sum up their ideas for the paragraph. Direct their attention to the rules for starting a new paragraph and read through these. Remind them also to indent each new paragraph and show them where this happens in the 'sad house' extract.

The students are now very familiar with the topic and ready to write for an extended period of time. Monitor students' progress. Beginner English learners can be encouraged to write their story in their home languages. The teacher can scribe for children whose oral skills are more developed than their writing skills.

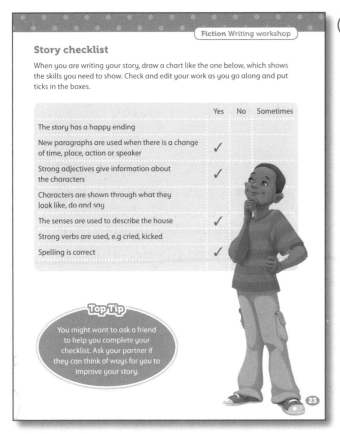

Story checklist

When you are writing your story, draw a chart like the one below, which shows the skills you need to show. Check and edit your work as you go along and put ticks in the boxes.

	Yes	No	Sometimes
The story has a happy ending			
New paragraphs are used when there is a change of time, place, action or speaker	✓		
Strong adjectives give information about the characters	✓		
Characters are shown through what they look like, do and say			
The senses are used to describe the house	✓		
Strong verbs are used, e.g cried, kicked			
Spelling is correct	✓		

Top Tip

You might want to ask a friend to help you complete your checklist. Ask your partner if they can think of ways for you to improve your story.

(23)

Learning objectives

(3)

Identify misspelt words in own writing and keep individual spelling logs.

Take turns in discussion, building on what others have said.

Listen and respond appropriately to others' views and opinions.

Students use a checklist to check their story has the necessary features. They work with a partner, discussing ways in which their story can be improved.

Remember to display the child-friendly learning objectives to the class along with the child-friendly checklist that students can use to assess how well they achieve them.

We know that we have achieved these because:

▶ We can identify misspelt words and edit our work.

▶ We can work with a partner and talk about ways to improve our stories.

(4) Writing workshop teaching notes

Story checklist

Refer students to the story checklist. Decide together which points are relevant to their writing. Make a checklist chart together, similar to the chart on page 23 of the Student Book. ***Example:***

1 The setting is interesting and there are details describing it.
2 There is a new paragraph when there is a change of time, place or speaker.
3 The characters are described well. We know what they look like and we know about their personalities.
4 The story has a happy ending.

Review the following words with second language students: 'setting', 'paragraphs', 'time', 'place', 'describe', 'personality' and 'happy ending'. Encourage them to put new vocabulary in their New Word List in English and their home languages (*see* Workbook). Ask students to copy the checklist on to loose-leaf paper. Tell them to read through their stories and put ticks in the boxes to show they have used the skill.

Read the Top Tip together and ask students to share their writing with a friend. Remind them to be good listeners and to suggest ways for improvement in an appropriate manner.

Teachers should conference individually with students, focusing at this stage on meaning over form. As the students' confidence develops, teachers can ask them to identify spelling errors in their writing and give them strategies to help them learn words they find difficult.

NB Second language learners may use their home languages when they cannot find the English words. Spelling and syntax may reflect patterns used in their home languages, too. When this occurs the teacher should not consider it as an error but rather a teaching point.

(5) Extension

1 Students can write more stories in familiar settings. Second language students can write these in their home languages and translate them into English to share with their teacher and peers (*see* Guidelines).
2 Beginner students can use the words generated in the home/house activity to write a few sentences about their home. They can do this as a dual language text, writing first in their home languages and then in English.

End of Unit Test

Question Paper

Reading: fiction

Read the extract and answer the questions.

Abdullah Plays a Trick

When he got off the bus at the stop near the school, Abdullah saw a dainty, darting dragonfly. He nimbly whisked it into his net, but five sen was not enough to buy Grandfather the porridge he likes so much.

5 Then, in the schoolyard, hunched down in a puddle by the drinking tap he saw a small green forest frog. Abdullah grinned with glee. He carefully scooped it into his net and sneaked into the classroom.

He hung his bag on its hook, and when he was sure no-one was looking he slipped the frog into Siew Lian's desk and slunk out to kick the soccer ball with his friends.

10 During class, Siew Lian reached into her desk to get out her writing book. Four cold sticky frog feet stepped onto her hand. She screamed and jumped out of her seat and shook the creature off, making such a fuss that everyone began to laugh. Mr Ginyun was cross.

"It's just a little frog that made its bed in your desk last night, Siew
15 Lian," he said. "Sit down and do your work, and don't be such a silly."

Abdullah smirked. Siew Lian looked around and saw and pulled a face at him.

From *Abdullah's Butterfly* by Janine M. Fraser and Kim Gamble

Glossary

dragonfly an insect with a long, thin body and two pairs of wings.

pulled a face made an expression on your face that showed you didn't like something.

sen the money used in Malaysia.

slunk moved slowly and quietly in a way so as not to attract attention.

smirked smiled in a way that shows you are pleased with yourself or have gained an advantage over someone else.

sneaked moved quietly and secretly.

whisked put quickly into.

Comprehension

(A) **Give evidence from the text to support your answers.**

1 What did Abdullah see close to the drinking tap?

_____ [1]

2 Why did Siew Lian reach into her desk?

_____ [1]

3 Why did everyone in class start to laugh?

_____ [1]

(B) **Give evidence from the text to support your answers.**

1 Do you think Abdullah was good at catching butterflies? Explain your answer.

_____ [2]

2 Why do you think Mr Ginyun was cross?

_____ [1]

3 Why did Siew Lian pull a face at Abdullah?

_____ [1]

(C) **Give evidence from the text to support your answers.**

1 Why do you think Abdullah 'grinned with glee' when he saw the frog?

_____ [1]

2 Why didn't Abdullah want anyone to see him go into the classroom with the frog?

_____

_____ [2]

3 How do you think Siew Lian felt when she put her hand into her desk? Explain your answer.

_____

_____ [2]

Writing: fiction

Read the extract below.

After School

"Did you study hard at school today?" asked Abdullah's mother when she came home from the weaving workshop. Because she wants him to do more than weave baskets and catch butterflies for the rest of his life.

"Did you catch me a butterfly today, Abdullah?" asked Grandfather.
5 Because he was hoping to have some of his favourite porridge for tea that night.

Abdullah shook his head.

"It doesn't matter," said Grandfather.

But it did to Abdullah. He thought he would never see another
10 butterfly, so large and beautiful again.

"There is always tomorrow," said Grandfather. "You can always catch me a butterfly tomorrow.

...If he could catch another dragonfly tomorrow, and perhaps a scorpion, and a beetle or two...there would be enough to buy
15 Grandfather the porridge he likes so much.

But not today. There was not time enough left today.

Tomorrow.

From *Abdullah's Butterfly* by Janine M. Fraser and Kim Gamble

Glossary
beetle an insect with hard, shiny covers over its wings.
dragonfly an insect with a long body and two pairs of wings.
porridge oatmeal boiled in water to make a thick paste you can eat.
scorpion an animal that has claws and a poisonous sting in its tail.
weave to make things by passing threads or strips over and under each other.

The extract on page 26 ends with the word 'Tomorrow'. What do you think Abdullah did the next day? Write the next three paragraphs of Abdullah's story.

Please use a separate sheet of paper.

Organize your story in paragraphs. Use a new paragraph when there is a change of place, time, action or speaker. Remember to include the following features:

Setting

Where was Abdullah? Describe the place. Include details of what the place looked like as well as any noises or smells. What time of day was it?

Characters

Include details that tell the reader about Abdullah's character and his appearance. Who was Abdullah with? What were they doing?

Events

What happened? How did Abdullah, his mother and his grandfather feel about it? Did Abdullah catch a butterfly for his grandfather? What did his mother say?

[20]

2 Find out how!

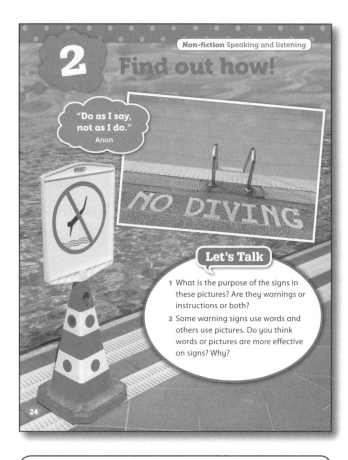

Non-fiction Speaking and listening

2 Find out how!

"Do as I say, not as I do."
Anon

NO DIVING

Let's Talk

1 What is the purpose of the signs in these pictures? Are they warnings or instructions or both?
2 Some warning signs use words and others use pictures. Do you think words or pictures are more effective on signs? Why?

24

① Warm-up objectives

Speak clearly and confidently in a range of contexts.

Take turns in discussion, building on what others have said.

Listen and respond appropriately to others' views and opinions.

Students explore the purpose of signs and the language associated with them. They discuss pictures of 'No diving' signs, and learn that signs can be warnings and instructions. They compare signs that use words with signs that use pictures or symbols, and discuss which they think works better and why.

Remember to display the child-friendly learning objectives to the class along with the child-friendly checklist that students can use to assess how well they achieve them.

We know that we have achieved these because:

▶ We can listen to our classmates and answer their questions appropriately.

② Unit warm up

Draw grass on the board and stick figures of an angry adult and a child. Add speech bubbles saying: 'Why are you walking on the grass, when I told you not to?' and 'But YOU are walking on the grass!' Model the dialogue with feeling. Divide the class in half, and ask one half to play the child, the other the adult.

Write the quote under your picture, reading it aloud: *"Do as I say, not as I do." Anon.* **Ask:** *What does this mean?* Help students by asking which word is the verb. (Do.) **Ask:** *What does 'do' mean?* (To perform an action; to carry out something.) Elicit how students say 'do' in their home languages. Point to 'Anon'. Ask if anyone can guess its meaning. (Short for anonymous, which means someone whose name is unknown.)

③ Let's Talk

Direct attention to the pictures and read Let's Talk. Explain 'sign' (a notice that gives instruction or warning in words or as a symbol), 'warning' (words that tell you to be careful of something) and 'instruction' (something that tells you what to do). Point to the 'No diving' symbol. **Say:** *A sign is a board or notice that tells or shows people something. It can be a warning saying* ⇨

'Don't do it.' Act it out. Now point at something with an instruction on it. (Fire extinguisher, etc.)

1 Direct attention to the two signs and ask what the message is. (No diving.) Ask students to decide in pairs if they are warnings, instructions or both.

2 Read question 2 aloud. Ask students to discuss in pairs whether they think words or pictures work better as signs, and why. Ask individuals for their response. Point out that pictures and symbols can be understood in any language. Ask students to vote on which they think is better.

Ask students to write the words 'sign', 'warning', 'instructions' and 'effective' in English and their home languages in their New Word List (*see* Guidelines, page 192, and Workbook).

Refer to the scene on the board. **Ask:** *What sign could be displayed?* (Keep off the grass.) Ask students to describe signs seen on their way to school, or walk around school looking for signs.

④ Extension

Ask students to collect images of common signs and make a collage of the most effective, explaining their choices orally. Students could also research signs from their home countries on the Internet to produce home-language collages. Display the work.

Learning objectives

Listen and remember a sequence of instructions.

Develop sensitivity to ways that others express meaning in their talk and non-verbal communication.

Students continue to look at instruction words, and practise using them with reference to safety rules. They work individually and with partners to complete the tasks, listening and responding appropriately and respecting others' opinions.

Remember to display the child-friendly learning objectives to the class along with the child-friendly checklist that students can use to assess how well they achieve them.

We know that we have achieved these because:

▶ We can listen and follow instructions.

▶ We can work well with a partner to complete tasks.

(6) Word Cloud definitions

Remind students to add new words to their New Word List in English and their home languages (*see* Guidelines, page 192, and Workbook).

instruction something that tells you what to do.

safety being safe and protected.

warning a sign of danger; words that tell you to be careful of something.

(7) Student Book teaching notes and exercise answers

Point to the illustration and ask what the girl is doing. Accept listening to music, travelling in a car, etc. Point to the seatbelt and ask what it is. (A seatbelt.) **Ask:** *Why is it important to wear a seatbelt?* (To stop you being injured in a car accident; to stop you being thrown out of the seat, etc.) *Where else do we wear seatbelts?* (On a bus, on a plane, etc.)

Instruct students to look at the Word Cloud on page 25 of the Student Book, and match words to the meanings. Write on the board: '1 ... means being safe and protected.' and so on. Ask students for the words to fill in the gaps, and read the full sentence together.

Answers:

1 safety 2 instruction 3 warning

Ask students if they have ever travelled by plane. **Ask:** *Who gives instructions on a plane?* (Pilot, flight attendant, etc.) *What do they give instructions for?* (Putting on seatbelts, oxygen masks, etc.) Explain what these are. Teach and mime the words 'fasten' (to join something firmly to another thing) and 'unfasten' (to undo something joined together). Ask what the un– in 'unfasten' means. (Not.) Model 'take-off' and 'landing'.

Answer:

2, 3, 1

Ask students to work in pairs to find three reasons for following safety signs and rules. **Ask:** *Can you think of other warning signs and safety instructions?*

(8) Extension

Students work in pairs to share how they get to school, and write safety rules for their journeys. Bilingual students could write the rules as a dual-language text (*see* Guidelines, page 192).

Learning objectives

1

Read and follow instructions to carry out an activity.

Infer the meaning of unknown words from the context.

Students explore a set of instructions for making a paper mask. They follow the steps in theory (no mask is produced), and identify the layout and features of instruction text, such as numbering, illustration and labelling.

Remember to display the child-friendly learning objectives to the class along with the child-friendly checklist that students can use to assess how well they achieve them.

We know that we have achieved these because:

▶ We understand that it is important to read instructions carefully.

▶ We understand that we have to follow instructions in the correct order.

▶ We use all the clues available to us to understand unfamiliar words.

2 Non-fiction reading notes

Refer students to the images on page 29 of the Student Book. **Ask:** *What does the word 'mask' mean?* (A decorative covering for the face.) *What do you think these masks are used for?* (Carnival, a play.) *How do you say 'mask' in your home languages?* Tell students they are going to find out how to make paper masks.

Direct attention to the instructions for making a paper mask on page 26 of the Student Book. You can also use the e-book on the CD-ROM, along with its spotlight and highlighting tools, to focus on specific areas of the page. **Ask:** *Do you think these instructions look clear? Can you say why?* (Laid out well, numbered instructions, illustrations, etc.)

Read through the list of materials, ensuring understanding of the words. Show students the objects if available, and ask for their home-language names. **Ask:** *Why do you think it is important to put the list of materials at the beginning?* (Getting the materials is the first thing you have to do, etc.) *Why is it a good idea to lay the list out in a column?* (To see what you need clearly.)

➡

Instructions

The instructions below explain how to make a mask using a balloon and tissue paper.

From Balloon to Mask

Word Cloud
cardboard
glue
scissors
shiny
stable

Materials
Small cardboard box · Pin
Balloon pump · Modelling clay
Coloured tissue paper · Sticky tape
Balloon · Scissors
Glue mixture · Paintbrush

Make sure the balloon is roughly the size of your own head.

1 Blow up a balloon and place it in a shoebox to keep it stable. The balloon will form the basic shape of your mask.

2 Use modelling clay to make the eyebrows, nose, mouth and chin. Attach these shapes to the balloon with sticky tape.

3 Cut long strips of differently coloured tissue paper and stick them over the whole face area using the glue mixture.

4 Build up the balloon with lots of layers of tissue paper. Leave to dry overnight and the tissue paper will turn hard and shiny.

26

Now read the numbered instructions in order, stopping at unfamiliar words and encouraging students to guess the meaning. You can also refer to the e-book and the audio on the CD-ROM.

Ask: *Why is it important to read the instructions all the way through at least once before you begin?* (To get the gist of the task; to make sure you have everything you need and understand what you have to do before you begin.) **Ask:** *Why do you think instructions are numbered?* (So that the task can be completed in the right order.)

3 Word Cloud definitions

Ask students to place the words correctly on the NOUNS, ADJECTIVES and VERBS charts (*see* Unit 1, page 16).

Remind students to add new words to their New Word List (*see* Workbook) in English and their home languages. You can also refer to the audio on the CD-ROM.

cardboard a material like paper but much thicker.
glue a substance used to stick things tightly together.
scissors a cutting instrument with two blades.
shiny having a smooth, glossy surface.
stable fixed, not moving.

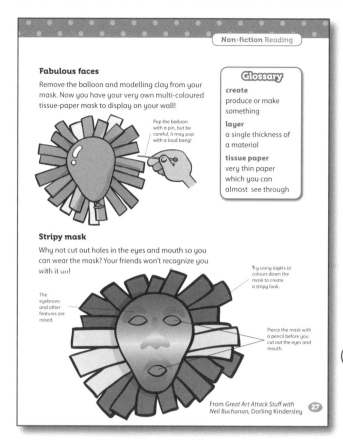

Non-fiction Reading

Fabulous faces

Remove the balloon and modelling clay from your mask. Now you have your very own multi-coloured tissue-paper mask to display on your wall!

Pop the balloon with a pin, but be careful, it may pop with a loud bang!

Stripy mask

Why not cut out holes in the eyes and mouth so you can wear the mask? Your friends won't recognize you with it on!

Try using layers of colours down the mask to create a stripy look.

The eyebrows and other features are raised.

Pierce the mask with a pencil before you cut out the eyes and mouth.

From *Great Art Attack Stuff with Neil Buchanan*, Dorling Kindersley   27

Glossary

create
produce or make something

layer
a single thickness of a material

tissue paper
very thin paper which you can almost see through

4 Non-fiction reading notes

Direct students' attention to the illustrations on pages 26 and 27 of the Student Book, and ask why these are helpful. (They show what the mask should look like at each stage.) Tell students to cover the written instructions 1–4 with a finger or pencil. **Ask:** *Would you be able to make the mask by just looking at the pictures?* (No. Although students may think they could.) *Why?* (The illustrations don't give detail about the materials used, how to apply them, length of drying time, etc.) Direct students to the relevant instruction to help them understand this point.

Ask students to cover illustration 3 and read the instruction. Ask why the picture is important here. (The picture shows how the paper strips should hang over the edge of the box.) Point out that without the picture, they would not know to do this from the text.

Tell students that it's important to have written and illustrated instructions, as they work together to make the task clearer.

⇨

Read the final instructions for making the mask with the class, stopping and explaining any words. **Ask:** *Do you know what the instructions on the illustrations are called?* (Labels.) Point out that labels help explain the details of the illustration. ('The eyebrows and other features are raised.') They also give extra instruction on how to do something. ('Pop the balloon with a pin.')

Refer students to the Stripy mask section, and read it through, including the labels. Ask students why these extra ideas are put at the end, and not with the other instructions. (To keep the basic instructions clear and to the point.) Point out that illustrated instructions should always end with a picture of the final object. Finally, refer to the CD-ROM and listen to the audio with the class.

5 Glossary

Read the words in the Glossary aloud together. Challenge students to be the first to find each word in turn in the instructions. Ask them to read the sentence containing the word.

'Try using layers of colours down the mask to **create** a stripy look.' (Stripy mask label, top right)
'Build up the balloon with lots of **layers** of **tissue paper**.' (Instruction 4)
'Cut long strips of differently coloured **tissue paper**…' (Instruction 3)
'Now you have your very own multi-coloured **tissue-paper** mask…' (Fabulous faces, first paragraph)

6 Extension

Students could make masks modelled over balloons, either following these instructions, or using their own ideas. Prepare an invitation to the exhibition of masks in the classroom. Point out that instructions and invitations are types of non-fiction text. Make copies to distribute to teachers and other classrooms.

Learning objectives

1

Scan a passage to find specific information and answer questions.

Read and follow instructions to carry out an activity.

Answer questions with some reference to single points in the text.

Consider ways that information is set out on a page.

Understand the term non-fiction.

Take turns in discussion, building on what others have said.

Students search the instructions for specific information. They identify the features of instruction text, and consider layout and the value of illustrations and diagrams. They debate whether or not it's best to follow instructions. They also focus on the fact that instruction text is non-fiction, as it represents something that's real.

Remember to display the child-friendly learning objectives to the class along with the child-friendly checklist that students can use to assess how well they achieve them.

We know that we have achieved these because:

▶ **We can correctly answer the questions posed by looking over the instructions.**

▶ **We can hold a debate, defending our point of view and listening carefully to others' opinions.**

▶ **We can talk about the ways that information is set out on a page.**

▶ **We understand that instruction text is non-fiction.**

2 Student Book teaching notes and comprehension answers

A

Ask students to work in pairs, and mark their answers orally as a group.

Answers:

1 A cardboard box. Also accept 'a solid box', 'a hard box', 'a strong box', but lead students who give this answer to producing the word 'cardboard'.

2 It's used to make the shapes of the eyebrows, nose and mouth. Ask students what would happen if they did not make the shapes with the modelling clay. (The mask would have a flat surface and it would not look like a face.)

Non-fiction Comprehension

Comprehension

A Read the instructions on pages 26–27 and answer the questions.

1 What kind of box will help to keep the balloon stable?

2 What is the modelling clay used for?

3 In which step is the sticky tape used?

4 How can the tissue paper be used to give a stripy effect?

Discussion time

In groups discuss whether you read instructions or try to do things for yourself. If you buy a new game do you read the instructions? Give reasons for your answers.

28

3 Instruction number 2. It's used to attach the clay features to the balloon.

4 By using layers of colours down the mask. The answer is in the top right-hand label of the Stripy mask illustration on page 27 of the Student Book.

3 Discussion time

Read the Discussion time box aloud. Refer students to the illustration. **Ask:** *Which boy do you think will be first to make the plane?* (The boy reading the instructions.) *Why do you think the other boy has left his instructions in the box?* (He enjoys working things out for himself; he isn't good at following instructions, etc.)

Divide the students into two groups and assign one group to defend the idea that when you're about to do something new, you just try to do it by yourself. Assign the other group to defend the opposite: that when you are about to do something new, you first read about it and try to get instructions on how to do it.

When each group has had enough time to develop their argument, create groups of four or six students, with equal numbers from each group. Give students time to discuss and argue their point of view. Ask for comments and a show of hands as to which side they preferred. Then ask them if their choice would depend on the situation.

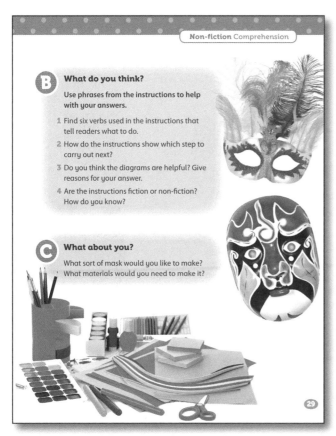

(4) Student Book teaching notes and comprehension answers

Answers:

1   blow up, place, use, attach, cut, stick, build up, leave, remove

    Make sure that students haven't included other verbs in the instructions that do not tell readers what to do.

2   The instructions are numbered, so you follow the order. They are placed in such a way that they are close to one another. They go from left to right and from top to bottom, which is the way English is read.

    Ask students if all languages are read in the same direction as English. (No: Arabic, Urdu and Hebrew read from right to left; Asian languages from top to bottom.) Show students examples, if available.

3   Yes, they show us visually rather than with just words, so it makes it easier to know what to do and what something should look like at each stage.

4   Non-fiction, because they have to do with something real.

Encourage students to go beyond repeating the mask-making instructions on pages 26–27 of the Student Book. *Example:* talk about using different materials; how they would like to decorate their masks, etc.

(5) Extension

Ask students to work in pairs or groups to write instructions for decorating the finished mask shown on page 27 of the Student Book. Ask them to imagine that coloured tissue was unavailable, so they had to use plain white paper to make the mask. Tell them to use the instructions on pages 26–27 of the Student Book as a guide, and to include illustrations and labelling.

Learning objectives

(1)

Read and follow instructions to carry out an activity.

Read information texts and begin to make links between them.

Make a record of information drawn from a text, for example by completing a chart.

Students examine the instructions for making a grass head, and identify the main features of instruction text. They compare these instructions with those for the mask on pages 26–27 of the Student Book, and complete a Venn diagram recording their similarities and differences. They also learn the names of a range of materials.

Remember to display the child-friendly learning objectives to the class along with the child-friendly checklist that students can use to assess how well they achieve them.

We know that we have achieved these because:

▶ We know how to make a grass head by following written instructions.

▶ We can correctly identify texts as fiction and non-fiction.

▶ We can identify an instruction text and its common features.

▶ We can record similarities and differences between two texts using a Venn diagram.

Instructions (continued)

Read the following instructions for how to make a grass head, using a pair of tights, some garden compost and grass seed.

Make a Grass Head

Word Cloud
compost
decorate
elastic band
pipe cleaners
tights

You will need:
Pair of clean, thin tights
Compost
2–3 teaspoons of grass seed
Elastic band
Items for decorating the head, such as stick-on eyes and pipe cleaners
Small pot

1 First, cut a piece from the foot end of the tights, about 20 cm (8 inches) long.
2 Next, put a little compost into the toe end and sprinkle in the grass seed.
3 Then, fill the foot with compost to make a ball about the size of a tennis ball.
4 Tie a knot at the open end to stop the compost coming out.
5 Draw a little compost out at the 'front' of the head and tie an elastic band round to make a nose.
6 Finally, decorate your grass head, for example with stick-on eyes and glasses made from pipe cleaners.

To make the grass grow, pour some water into a small pot. Rest the head on the pot with the tied end hanging in the water. The water will gradually soak through to the grass seed. The grass will start growing after about a week. Add more water to the pot at least every two days.

30

differences and similarities. Elicit their ideas, and record them in the correct section. (Mask has more illustrations, labels, extra ideas, tools needed, instructions reading left to right and down, etc. Grass head has less illustration, instructions read down, etc.) Now ask for similarities and put these in the central, shared section. (Materials list, numbered stages, illustration of final result, command verbs, words showing a new stage such as 'next', summing up, etc.)

Ask students which set of instructions they think is best, and hold a vote on it by show of hands. Ask students why they voted a particular way.

(2) Non-fiction reading notes

Tell students they are going to look at the instructions for making a grass head. Refer them to the illustration.

Write the words 'INSTRUCTION TEXT' on the board. Read through the instructions on page 30 of the Student Book, stopping at unfamiliar words and encouraging students to work out their meaning by looking at the clues available. You can also refer to the e-book and the audio on the CD-ROM.

Ask students to read through the instructions again in pairs, and make a note of the main features. Elicit their ideas, writing them on the board. (List of materials, numbering stages, illustrations, etc.) Discuss why each is useful.

Draw a Venn diagram on the board (see Guidelines, page 193). On one side write 'Mask', on the other 'Grass head'. Working in pairs, ask students to compare the instructions for the grass head with those for the mask on pages 26–27 of the Student Book, noting

(3) Word Cloud definitions

Ask students to work in pairs to guess what the words mean. Remind them to add them to their New Word List (see Workbook) in English and their home languages. You can also refer to the audio on the CD-ROM.

compost a mixture of decayed plants that makes the soil better.

decorate to make an object more beautiful.

elastic band a strip that can stretch and return to its original size.

pipe cleaners flexible wires with a twisted, fuzzy-fabric coating.

tights thin clothing that covers the legs closely from the waist to the toes.

Student Book teaching notes and comprehension answers

⑤

Answers:

 A

2, 3, 4

B

1 Any three of: 'First', 'Next', 'Then', 'Finally'.
2 To close the bottom of the head tightly so that the compost does not fall out. Also accept: if you don't use the elastic band, the compost will fall out when you turn the head right-side up.
3 We must add water, and continue to do so at least every other day, because if we don't add water, the grass seeds cannot grow. Plants need water in order to grow. If we don't add water, the seeds will dry up and we won't have grass growing.

C

Allow students to work in pairs if they would like to, but each student should produce their own set of instructions.

Within the Student Book page:

Comprehension

A Which three sentences are true?
1 You do not need to add water.
2 A grass head is made from tights, compost and grass seeds.
3 The grass will grow after about a week.
4 You can add eyes and glasses to the grass head.

Challenge
Work in pairs and take it in turns to give your partner instructions for how to draw a decorated grass head. At the end, look at your pictures. Were the instructions good? How could they be improved?

B What do you think?
1 Find three words that the writer uses to show the start of a new stage.
2 What is the elastic band used for?
3 Why is it important to water the grass head?

C What about you?
How would you decorate your grass head? Write some step-by-step instructions for how to add the decorations.

31

Learning objectives

④

Scan a passage to find specific information and answer questions.

Answer questions with some reference to single points in the text.

Students answer questions about the instructions for a grass head on page 30 of the Student Book. They also write step-by-step instructions for decorating a grass head, and give and take verbal instructions for producing a drawing of it.

Remember to display the child-friendly learning objectives to the class along with the child-friendly checklist that students can use to assess how well they achieve them.

We know that we have achieved these because:

▸ We can answer the questions posed to us correctly.
▸ We can write instructions.
▸ We can give and receive instructions orally.

Challenge

⑥

Read the instructions in the Challenge out loud. Pairs of students give each other instructions for making a drawing of a decorated grass head, without seeing what is being drawn. Point out the illustrations on pages 30–31 of the Student Book as a starting point. When they have finished, tell students to swap their pictures. Were their instructions successful? Ask them to decide how they could be improved, and try again if there's time.

Extension

⑦

Ask students to bring in pictures of head sculptures that can be found either in historical or art museums in their home countries. If possible, parents or other home members should identify where the picture was taken and, if known, whose head it is, and write it out in English and in their home languages.

When the pictures have all come in, display them on the wall. You can also mark the place they came from on a wall map. Explain that head sculptures exist in practically all cultures, and are based on the identities of the people who are represented. Elicit what type of people are honoured with a sculpture of their head. (Religious leader, politician, artist, etc.)

① Learning objectives

Understand that verbs are necessary for meaning in a sentence.

Maintain accurate use of capital letters and full stops in showing sentences.

Students focus on verbs and sentences and learn what characterizes them. They practise using capital letters and full stops, and finding verbs. They identify sentences and turn jumbled words into sentences.

Remember to display the child-friendly learning objectives to the class along with the child-friendly checklist that students can use to assess how well they achieve them.

We know that we have achieved these because:

▶ We can correctly identify sentences and verbs.

▶ We can write sentences with capital letters and full stops.

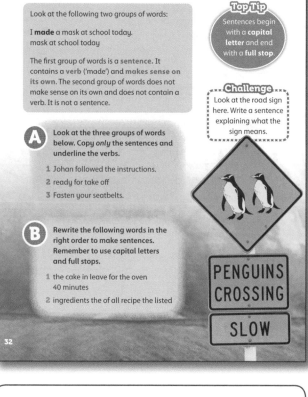

Non-fiction Grammar and punctuation

Sentences

Look at the following two groups of words:

I **made** a mask at school today.
mask at school today

The first group of words is a **sentence**. It contains a **verb** ('made') and **makes sense on its own**. The second group of words does not make sense on its own and does not contain a verb. It is not a sentence.

Top Tip

Sentences begin with a **capital letter** and end with a **full stop**.

Challenge

Look at the road sign here. Write a sentence explaining what the sign means.

 A Look at the three groups of words below. Copy *only* the sentences and underline the verbs.

1 Johan followed the instructions.
2 ready for take off
3 Fasten your seatbelts.

 B Rewrite the following words in the right order to make sentences. Remember to use capital letters and full stops.

1 the cake in leave for the oven 40 minutes
2 ingredients the of all recipe the listed

32

② Student Book teaching notes and grammar and punctuation exercise answers

Read the description of a sentence. Follow up by giving more examples, preferably from the students' own writing. Write them on the board and change some to non-sentences by leaving out the verbs.

Make sure students understand that it's not just the presence of a verb that makes a full sentence. Write the words 'mask at school today' on the board, and add the word 'made' to the beginning. **Ask:** *Is this a complete sentence?* Point out that it isn't, because we don't know who made a mask. So, even if there is a verb in the group of words, it may not be a full sentence.

Refer students to the Top Tip about capital letters at the beginning and full stops at the end of sentences. Tell students that not all languages have capital letters; for example, Arabic doesn't. Ask students to find out from their parents or other home members if sentences in their home languages have a capital letter at the beginning and a full stop at the end.

Answers:

A

1 and 3 are sentences. Verbs are 'followed', 'fasten'.

B

1 Leave the cake in the oven for 40 minutes.
2 The recipe listed all of the ingredients.

Tell students that a good clue for putting a jumble of words into a sentence is the verb. Look for the verb first, and then it can be easier to work out the sentence.

③ Challenge

Refer to the 'PENGUINS CROSSING' sign. Read out the Challenge. Ask students to work in pairs, but write their own sentences. Ask a few students to read them out, writing them on the board. Accept anything resembling: 'Go slowly. There may be penguins crossing the road.'

Explain that in this part of the world, there are penguins crossing roads, so this sign warns cars to slow down. **Ask:** *Are there penguins where you live, other than in a zoo? How about in your home countries? Where do penguins exist in the wild?* (Antarctica, South America, South Africa, Australia, New Zealand, etc.)

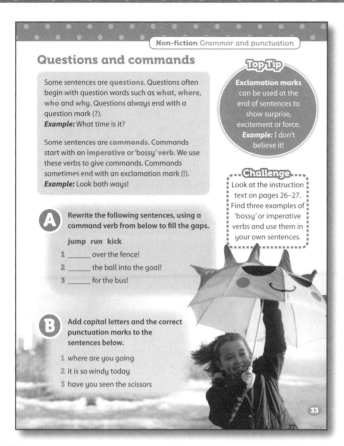

Non-fiction Grammar and punctuation

Questions and commands

Some sentences are **questions**. Questions often begin with question words such as **what**, **where**, **who** and **why**. Questions always end with a question mark (?).
Example: What time is it?

Some sentences are **commands**. Commands start with an **imperative** or 'bossy' verb. We use these verbs to give commands. Commands sometimes end with an exclamation mark (!).
Example: Look both ways!

Top Tip

Exclamation marks can be used at the end of sentences to show surprise, excitement or force.
Example: I don't believe it!

Challenge

Look at the instruction text on pages 26–27. Find three examples of 'bossy' or imperative verbs and use them in your own sentences.

A Rewrite the following sentences, using a command verb from below to fill the gaps.

jump run kick

1 _____ over the fence!
2 _____ the ball into the goal!
3 _____ for the bus!

B Add capital letters and the correct punctuation marks to the sentences below.

1 where are you going
2 it is so windy today
3 have you seen the scissors

33

(4)

Learning objective

Use question marks and exclamation marks.

Students examine sentences that are questions and commands. They continue to observe how important verbs are in sentences and learn to produce sentences with question marks and exclamation marks.

 Remember to display the child-friendly learning objective to the class along with the child-friendly checklist that students can use to assess how well they achieve it.

We know that we have achieved this because:

▶ We can correctly use punctuation in questions and commands, as well as in statements.

(5) Student Book teaching notes and grammar and punctuation exercise answers

Tell students that all sentences need some kind of mark at the end. **Ask:** *What is the most common mark you see at the end of a sentence?* (Full stop.) *Can you describe it?* (A dot on the line.) Show them sentences with full stops from the fiction they read in Unit 1 (*Abdullah's Butterfly* and *The House That Was Sad*), and the non-fiction instructions for the mask in this unit.

Tell them there are also sentences that end with other kinds of marks. Draw a question mark on the board. **Ask:** *What is this?* (Question mark.) Show them sentences from the fiction texts in Unit 1 that end with question marks (*see* pages 14 and 20 of the Student Book). Many questions begin with *Wh–* words. Ask students to find the two questions on page 29 of the Student Book that begin with *Wh–* (the questions in C). Ask students to find other sentences with question marks in their books. (Many of the questions in the exercises have question marks.)

Tell students that another kind of mark makes you pay attention, and is used at the end of sentences that tell you to do things. Draw an exclamation mark on the board. These sentences have command verbs called 'imperatives'. They mean 'you <u>must</u> do this'.

Answers:

A

1 Jump over the fence!
2 Kick the ball into the goal!
3 Run for the bus!

Point out how the exclamation mark helps you pay attention. Read the sentences with an emphasis that gives them urgency. Make sure that students have used capitals to begin their sentences.

B

1 Where are you going?
2 The wind blew her away!
3 Have you seen the scissors?

(6) Top Tip

Show students the sentence, 'Your friends won't recognize you with it on!' on page 27 of the Student Book.

Ask students to look back at any of their other writing, and see if they would like to add exclamation marks to any of the sentences.

(7) Challenge

Read the Challenge with the students. Tell them to work in pairs to find three examples of imperative (bossy) verbs in the mask-making instructions, pages 26–27 of the Student Book. ('Blow', 'place', 'Use', 'Attach', 'Cut', 'Stick', 'Leave', 'Remove', 'Pop', etc.) Ask them to write their sentences individually.
Example: 'Remove your boots before coming indoors'; 'Leave the book on the table'; 'Cut the pizza in half'. Invite volunteers to read their sentences.

Learning objectives

1

Continue to improve consistency in the use of tenses.

Understand that verbs are necessary for meaning in a sentence.

Students practise using words associated with tense and begin to develop an understanding of the concept of tense. They investigate the verb endings *–ing*, *–s* and *–ed*.

Remember to display the child-friendly learning objectives to the class along with the child-friendly checklist that students can use to assess how well they achieve them.

We know that we have achieved these because:

▶ We know that adding the word endings *–ing*, *–s* and *–ed* to a verb tells us when something happens.

▶ We know the grammatical word for these verb endings is 'tense'.

Non-fiction Grammar

Tenses

We use different **tenses** to say **when** something happens.

We use a verb in the **present tense** to tell us about things that are happening **now**.
Examples:
The horse **jumps** over the fence.
The horse **is jumping** over the fence.

We use a verb in the **past tense** to tell us about things that happened **in the past**. Verbs in the past tense often end with **ed**.
Example: The horse **jumped** over the fence.

Top Tip

When we use a present tense with 'he', 'she', 'it' or the name of a person or thing, we must remember to add an 's' to the verb.

Examples:
She plays basketball every Saturday.

Harshil eats the apple.

A Find the verbs in the following sentences. Write down whether the verbs are in the present or past tense.

1 The penguins dived into the sea.
2 Ahmed is cleaning his teeth.
3 Rahini and Anna listened to the music.

B Rewrite the sentences changing the verbs to the past tense.

1 The parrot lands on the branch of the tree.
2 The referee picks up the ball.
3 Aisha waits for the bus to arrive.

34

---

2 Student Book teaching notes and grammar exercise answers

Write the word 'VERBS' in a cloud in the centre of a large sheet of paper.

Ask: *What do you know about verbs?* (A verb tells you what someone or something is doing. Every sentence needs to have a verb.) *How do you say the word 'verb' in your home languages?* Those who can should write 'verb' in their home languages on the sheet. Ask the others to find out from a parent, other home member or other speaker of their home languages, and add it next time.

Write some examples of regular verbs on the board. ('play', 'jump', 'walk', 'like', etc.) Working in pairs, ask students to write two sentences with these verbs using the endings *–ing*, *–s* and *–ed*. Do not use the word 'tense' yet. Take a sample sentence from each pair and write it on another sheet of paper. Write the sentence exactly as the students say it (mistakes and all).

At the top of the sheet write '*–ing*', '*–s*' and '*–ed*'. **Say:** *These word endings tell us <u>when</u> something happens, and the grammatical word for this is 'tense'.* Write 'tense' next to the endings. Read one of the sentences with verb + ing. **Say:** *This shows us that the action is happening <u>now</u>.* Write on the board: 'verb + ing = now'.

⇨

Next, choose a sentence with verb + s, and say that this is also a way of saying something is happening now. Write 'verb + s = now' on the board. Finally choose a sentence with verb + ed. **Ask:** *When do you think what happened in the sentence took place?* (In the past.) Write 'verb + ed = past' on the board.

Read the Tenses introduction on page 34 of the Student Book. Ask them to find out how they say 'tense' in their home languages. Ask students to complete exercises A and B in pairs.

Answers:

1 past **2** present **3** past

1 landed **2** picked **3** waited

3 Top Tip

Read aloud the Top Tip and examples. Write 'he/she + verb + s' on the board. Elicit more examples from the students, prompting them with a regular verb to use if necessary. Avoid any that end in *–ch* at the moment, as these take *–es*.

Non-fiction Grammar, spelling and phonics

Adding –ed and –ing to verbs

We can often add –ed or –ing to verbs without changing the rest of the spelling.
Examples: shout, shouted, shouting

When a verb ends in e, we drop the e before adding –ed or –ing.
Examples: dance, danced, dancing

When a verb ends in a short vowel followed by a consonant, we **double** the consonant before adding –ed or –ing.
Examples: slip, slipped, slipping

Top Tip

Short vowels have a short, snappy sound. Saying the words out loud will help you to know whether the vowel is short. *Examples:* drop, skip, grab

A Add –ing or –ed to the verbs below and use them to fill the gaps.

rest wash eat

1 My uncle _____ his car last Sunday.
2 Amy is _____ a piece of fruit.
3 The lion is _____ in the sun.

B Find the misspelled words in the sentences below and rewrite the words with the correct spellings.

1 Amy is bakeing a cake.
2 The car stoped so the children could cross the road.
3 The fish are swiming in the sea.

35

---

(4) Learning objectives

Learn rules for adding – ing, –ed to verbs.

Identify misspelt words in own writing and keep individual spelling logs.

Students continue to practise adding –ing and –ed to verbs, and learn spelling rules associated with them. They learn to drop the 'e' from verbs ending in –e before adding –ing and –ed. They also learn to double the consonant before –ing and –ed in verbs ending in a short vowel followed by a consonant, and discover how to spot these. They practise these rules by identifying misspelt verbs in sentences.

 Remember to display the child-friendly learning objectives to the class along with the child-friendly checklist that students can use to assess how well they achieve them.

We know that we have achieved these because:

▶ We know to drop the 'e' from verbs ending in –e before adding –ing and –ed.

▶ We know to double the consonant before –ing and –ed in verbs ending in a short vowel followed by a consonant.

▶ We can identify short vowels by their short, snappy sound when we say the words aloud.

---

(5) Student Book teaching notes and grammar, spelling and phonics exercise answers

Prepare cue cards with familiar verbs in their base form (without –ing or –ed), such as 'dance', 'shout', 'laugh', etc. Include verbs that illustrate the spelling rules for verbs ending in –e, such as 'smile', and with a short vowel followed by a consonant, such as 'tap', and verbs where the spelling remains unchanged, such as 'jump'.

Elicit the meaning of the words 'verb' and 'tense'. (Accept 'verb' is a doing word, and the 'tense' of the verb tells us the time of the action.) Elicit the endings that show the action is happening now (–ing and –s) and the action happened in the past (–ed).

Place cue cards on the table and call one student at a time to read the verb to themselves and act it out.
Ask: *What is* X *doing?* (Dancing, reading, etc.) Encourage them to say the whole sentence: *X is dancing.* Write their responses on a chart.

Point to sentences with regular verbs and ask students how they would change to show past. Together read the 'Adding –ed and –ing to verbs' box.

On the board make three columns with the headings: 'No Change', 'Drop the E', and 'Double the Consonant'. Refer students to their sentences on the chart. Together identify the verbs and which column they belong to. Write them in the appropriate column.

Students work in pairs to complete exercises A and B.

Answers:

A

1 washed **2** eating **3** resting

B

1 baking **2** stopped **3** swimming

(6) Top Tip

Together, read the Top Tip on how to identify short vowels. Elicit more examples of verbs with a short vowel followed by a consonant. (Stop, hop, hum, etc.)

Learning objectives

Read and follow instructions to carry out an activity.

Read a range of information texts and begin to make links between them.

Students learn to tell how a task is to be accomplished through a sequence of steps or actions. They look at model instructions for cleaning teeth, and consider the tools and materials needed and what has to be done at each stage. Action verbs and imperative (command) forms of verbs are identified in the text.

Remember to display the child-friendly learning objectives to the class along with the child-friendly checklist that students can use to assess how well they achieve them.

We know that we have achieved these because:

▶ We can follow step-by-step instructions.

▶ We can recognize the action verbs that tell us what is to be done.

▶ We know that the command (bossy) form of the verb is used in instructions.

② Writing workshop teaching notes

Model writing

Hold a class discussion about the importance of keeping teeth clean. Use whatever props are available. (Photo of a child with a cavity, diagrams of teeth, advertisements for tooth care, dentist's chair, etc.) If you have no props, just point to your own teeth. **Ask:** *What causes teeth to go bad?* (Too many sweets; too much sugar; not brushing your teeth, etc.) Ask students to work in pairs and take turns to show their partner how they brush their teeth, telling them when they do it, what they use and how they do it. Invite individuals to share how they brush their teeth with the class.

Once the context is established, tell students they are going to learn how to write good, clear instructions. Refer them to the instructions for cleaning teeth on page 36 of the Student Book. Point out that instructions:

▶ Usually list the materials (the things needed) in the order they are required.

▶ Are listed in steps.

▶ Are often accompanied by illustrations or diagrams.

Non-fiction Writing workshop

Writing instructions
Model writing

How to Clean Your Teeth

What you will need:
Toothbrush
Tube of toothpaste
Glass
Water
Towel

1 Get ready...
First, pick up your toothbrush and hold it firmly in one hand. Take the tube of toothpaste in your other hand. Remove the top and squeeze a small amount of toothpaste onto the brush. Put the top back on the toothpaste tube.

2 Get brushing...
Next, brush all your teeth for two minutes.

3 Get sorted...
Then, fill a glass half full with water, and use this to rinse your mouth. Spit the water from your mouth into the sink. Turn on the tap so that the 'toothpaste water' is rinsed away and wash your toothbrush under the tap.

4 Finally...
Dry your mouth with a towel. Your teeth should now be clean!

36

Ask students to read the whole extract quietly. (Act out verbs for beginner second language students.)

Next ask them to read each step and identify the verbs. Ask students to call out verbs, and write them on the board. ('pick', 'Take', 'Remove', etc.) **Ask:** *What form is this verb in? Is it present or past? Is it telling you what to do?* Elicit the 'bossy' or command form, the imperative.

In pairs, students then take turns reading each step and acting it out to each other. Invite a couple of volunteers to demonstrate to the class.

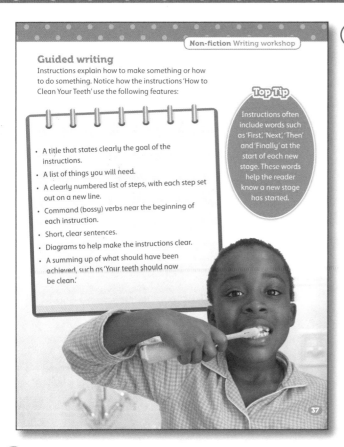

Non-fiction Writing workshop

Guided writing

Instructions explain how to make something or how to do something. Notice how the instructions 'How to Clean Your Teeth' use the following features:

- A title that states clearly the goal of the instructions.
- A list of things you will need.
- A clearly numbered list of steps, with each step set out on a new line.
- Command (bossy) verbs near the beginning of each instruction.
- Short, clear sentences.
- Diagrams to help make the instructions clear.
- A summing up of what should have been achieved, such as 'Your teeth should now be clean.'

Top Tip

Instructions often include words such as 'First', 'Next', 'Then' and 'Finally' at the start of each new stage. These words help the reader know a new stage has started.

37

(4) Writing workshop teaching notes

Ask students to work in pairs to think of things they might need instructions for. Elicit ideas, writing them on the board. (Recipes, rules for games, science experiments, etc.)

Guided writing

Point out that when we write instructions to make or do something, the writing follows the same pattern. Read through the Guided writing chart in the Student Book. With the help of students, turn each statement into a question, writing them on a chart.

- ▶ Does the title state clearly the goal of the instructions?
- ▶ Is there a list of things you will need?
- ▶ Is there a clearly numbered list of steps? Does each step have a new line?
- ▶ Are there command (bossy) verbs near the beginning of each instruction?
- ▶ Did the author use short, clear sentences?
- ▶ Did the author give some advice?
- ▶ Are there diagrams to help make the instructions clear?
- ▶ Is there a summing up of everything that has been done?

Refer students to the instructions for cleaning teeth. Ask them to take turns asking and answering the questions in pairs. Work with beginner second language students to explain 'list', 'step', 'advice', 'diagram' and 'sum up'. Encourage them to write new words in their New Word List in English and their home languages (*see* Guidelines, page 192, and Workbook). New arrival students can follow the instructions from the pictures, draw a picture and write what is happening in their home languages.

Read the Top Tip with students. Make a list of the conjunctive adverbials ('first', 'next', 'then' and 'finally') in the extract. Ask students to write how they say these words in their home languages. Point out that these words show a sequence and are used to link the text. Ask students to identify the punctuation mark that always follows these words. (Comma.)

(3) Learning objectives

Establish purpose for writing, using features and style based on model texts.

Develop range of adverbials to signal the relationship between events.

Consider ways that information is set out on a page.

Students consider ideas for their own set of instructions for making or doing something. They use a guided writing chart to study the features of teeth-cleaning instructions. They also learn that the words 'first', 'next', 'then' and 'finally' help the reader know that a new stage has started.

🔘 Remember to display the child-friendly learning objectives to the class along with the child-friendly checklist that students can use to assess how well they achieve them.

We know that we have achieved these because:

- ▶ We can identify different kinds of writing by looking at how they are presented on the page.
- ▶ We know that using words such as 'first', 'next', 'then' and 'finally' help to make our instructions clearer.

Learning objectives

Establish purpose for writing, using features and style based on model texts.

Consider ways that information is set out on a page.

Students write their own set of instructions for making or doing something. They follow the writing structure and features associated with creating instructions found on page 37 of the Student Book. They are reminded to include the goal (what is to be achieved by following the steps), the materials needed, the steps in the process and illustrations or diagrams to clarify the task/product/steps.

Remember to display the child-friendly learning objectives to the class along with the child-friendly checklist that students can use to assess how well they achieve them.

We know that we have achieved these because:

▶ We are able to recognize the structure for writing instructions.

▶ We can use words like 'first', 'next', 'then' and 'finally' to connect the steps in our instructions.

② Writing workshop teaching notes

Bring the instructions for four **simple** board games to class. (Snakes and Ladders, Ludo, etc.) Tell the students that they are going to write their own set of instructions.

Refer students to the list of ideas on page 38 of the Student Book. Read through it. **Say:** *Turn to your partner and think of four different things you could write instructions for.* Set a time limit to complete this task. Ask students to call out their ideas, without repeating suggestions already made. Write the ideas on the board.

Next, review the process quickly. (Title, materials, steps, command (bossy) verbs, short sentences, advice, diagrams and sum up.)

⇨

Writing instructions
Your writing

Write your own set of instructions. These could be on how to do one of the following:

- Sweep a floor
- Get from school to home
- Make a cup of tea
- Operate a computer game
- Play a game
- Make a model aeroplane
- Do a handstand or cartwheel
- Hold a successful birthday party
- Make some Mexican tortillas

Whatever you choose, remember to:

- Have a clear aim. What is it someone will be able to do at the end if they follow the instructions?
- Use some diagrams to help make the instructions clear.

38

Divide the class into four and hand out the instructions for board games. Ask students to look at them and decide if they are clearly written or not. Set a time limit, as they are not going to play the game. Tell them to look quickly at the instructions, and see if they follow the pattern and are explicit.

Your writing

Students are now ready to start writing their set of instructions. Tell them they should look at pages 36 and 37 of the Student Book to remind them of the structure. Give ample time for writing. Beginner second language students can write the instructions in their home languages. Scribe for students who can express their ideas, but who are not yet ready to write. Circulate, referring students to the guided writing chart if you notice something missing. Encourage the use of diagrams and illustrations to help make their instructions clearer.

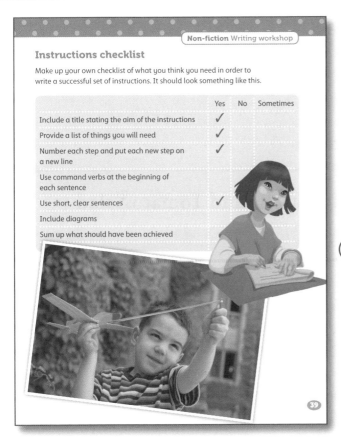

Instructions checklist

Make up your own checklist of what you think you need in order to write a successful set of instructions. It should look something like this.

	Yes	No	Sometimes
Include a title stating the aim of the instructions	✓		
Provide a list of things you will need	✓		
Number each step and put each new step on a new line	✓		
Use command verbs at the beginning of each sentence			
Use short, clear sentences	✓		
Include diagrams			
Sum up what should have been achieved			

Prepare a sign 'Do Not Disturb!' and place it on a table where you can work with students individually. Make sure that everyone has an opportunity to speak to you. Focus mostly on the structure of the text, but point out repeated errors in spelling and tell the student to write the word in their personal spelling list.

Encourage them to write new words in their New Word List (*see* Guidelines, page 192, and Workbook) in English and their home languages.

④ Extension

1 Students collect samples of instructions in their home languages. Look at these as a class, and talk about similarities and differences with English. Display the instructions in different scripts alongside English examples in the classroom.

2 Make a class recipe book. Involve parents or other home members by asking them to help their child write a simple recipe in their home languages. Ask students to write dual-language texts in their home languages and English. Make sure they do their best writing and colour their diagrams and pictures carefully. Make a cover with a title, such as *A Multilingual Cook Book* By Class 3. Display the book in the school library.

③ Writing workshop teaching notes

Instructions checklist

Students work in small groups to make a checklist for writing instructions similar to that on page 39 of the Student Book. Each student in the group should write one.

As a whole class write the first two steps together. ***Example:***

1 Write a title that shows what you are going to do: 'How to…'
2 Write a list of the things you need.

Ask students to continue working on steps 3, 4, 5, 6 and 7. They should discuss the remaining points in their group and finish writing the checklist.

Tell students to open their books at page 39 of the Student Book, and ask them to compare the list they prepared with the checklist. Tell them to add any points they may have missed. Remind students that they need to use the checklist to check their own and each other's writing.

➪

End of Unit Test

Question Paper

Reading: non-fiction

Read the extract and answer the questions.

Insalata Caprese Recipe – Mozzarella and Tomato Salad

Preparation time: 10 minutes

Serves 3

Ingredients:

500g (1lb) ripe tomatoes
250g (8oz) fresh mozzarella
8–10 fresh basil leaves
1/4 cup of olive oil
Pepper and salt (if necessary)
Bread

Instructions:

1 First, use a knife to cut the tomatoes into thin slices.

2 Next, cut the mozzarella into thin slices.

3 Then, tear the basil into small pieces by hand.*

4 Place one slice of tomato, then one slice of mozzarella on a serving dish. Overlap the slices and continue until all the slices have been used.

5 Sprinkle with olive oil.

6 Season with a little salt and pepper, if necessary.

7 Finally, add the torn basil leaves.

8 Serve with bread.

Buon appetito!

* Do not cut basil with a knife, as the steel of a knife makes the edges of the leaves black.

Glossary

basil a herb with green leaves that is used in cooking.

ingredients the items included in a recipe.

mozzarella a white Italian cheese.

slices thin, flat pieces of something, cut from a larger piece.

Comprehension

A **Give evidence from the recipe to support your answers.**

1 How many people can this recipe feed?

_____ [1]

2 How many grams of tomatoes are needed?

_____ [1]

3 How long does the salad take to prepare?

_____ [1]

B **Give evidence from the recipe to support your answers.**

1 Does the writer think salt and pepper is always needed in this recipe? Explain your answer.

_____ [2]

2 Why do you think the writer has put numbers next to the steps in the instructions?

_____ [1]

3 Find four words that the writer uses to help the reader follow the order of the steps.

_____ [4]

C **Give evidence from the recipe to support your answers.**

1 List four examples of 'bossy' or command verbs in the instructions.

_____

_____ [4]

2 Do you think diagrams or photographs would help to make the recipe more clear? Explain your answer.

_____

_____ [2]

3 Write a sentence summing up what will have been achieved if the instructions have been followed.

_____ [2]

Writing: non-fiction

1 Imagine you are planning a party. Complete the instructions below telling your friend how to make some sandwiches. Use the words in the glossary to help you.

How to Make a Chicken Sandwich

What you need:

Bread
Cooked chicken, chopped into small pieces
Butter
Salt and pepper
Mustard

Instructions:

1 First, put all the ingredients on the table.

2 Then, _____

3 Next, _____

4 Finally, _____

_____

Glossary

mustard a yellow paste which is used to give food a hot taste.

sandwich two slices of bread spread with butter, with a filling such as jam, meat or cheese between them.

slice a thin, flat piece cut off something (noun); cut something into thin, flat pieces (verb).

spread cover the surface of something.

2 **Now write the instructions for one of the following:**

- Playing your favourite game.
- Making your favourite snack.
- Operating a computer game.
- Making a cup of tea.
- Getting from school to home.

Please use a separate sheet of paper.

Remember to include the following in your instructions:

- Give a title that says clearly the goal of your instructions.
- Write the list of things that will be needed.
- Put each step on a new line.
- Number each new step.
- Use words such as 'First', 'Next' and 'Finally' to help the reader follow the order, from one step to another.
- Use bossy verbs at the beginning of each instruction.
- Use short sentences.
- Give some advice.
- Use diagrams to make your instructions clear.
- Sum up at the end, saying what will have been achieved if the instructions have been followed.

[20]

3

Our sensational senses

"Children, like
animals, use all their
senses to discover
the world."
Eudora Welty

Let's Talk

1 What words would you use to
describe what the girl in this
picture can see, feel and smell?

2 We have five senses, sight,
hearing, taste, touch and smell.
Which is your favourite sense?

40

1 Warm-up objectives

Speak clearly and confidently in a range
of contexts.

Take turns in discussion, building on what
others have said.

Listen and respond appropriately to others'
views and opinions.

Students practise the language they need for
talking about their senses. They identify objects
using touch, smell, taste, hearing and sight, and
create a chart for them. They also relate the
words for the senses to those used in their
home languages.

Remember to display the child-friendly
learning objectives to the class along with the
child-friendly checklist that students can use to
assess how well they achieve them.

We know that we have achieved these because:

▶ We know what the sense words 'touch',
'taste', 'smell', 'hear' and 'see' mean.

▶ We know how to take turns listening and
speaking.

▶ We know how to use describing words for
describing the senses.

2 Unit warm up

1 Make a chart of five columns, headed 'SENSES'.
Find objects that can be heard, touched, smelled,
tasted and seen, and hide them in a bag (*see*
Guidelines re use of realia, page 188). *Example:*
cotton wool, bell, perfume, bag of sweets, detailed
picture.

Join the students in a semi-circle. Ask students
to close their eyes and use their senses to guess
what the objects are. *Example:* spray perfume,
rub cotton wool on hands, ring bell, rattle the bag
of sweets, pass the drawing around. Tell students
to open their eyes. Were they right? Identify the
objects. Ask which senses helped them guess the
objects, and write them as column headings on
the chart: 'See', 'Hear', 'Taste', 'Touch', 'Smell'. Give
each student a sweet to show taste.

2 Refer to the title of the unit and ask for the
meaning of 'sensational'. (Fantastic, exciting, etc.)
Say: *We used our senses in the game we played*

⇨

earlier. *Let's write a definition for senses.* (We are
able to see, hear, taste, touch and smell. These are
our senses.) Ask students to write the definition
in their home languages and put new words in
their New Word List (*see* Guidelines, page 192, and
Workbook) in English and their home languages.

3 Draw the students' attention to the quote and
read it together: *"Children, like animals, use all their
senses to discover the world." Eudora Welty.* **Ask:**
What words could be used instead of the commas?
('are' and 'they'.) Check understanding of the word
'discover'. (To find something out.) **Ask:** *How do
you say this in your home languages?* Ask students
to turn to a partner and say if they agree with the
quote. Invite several students to share their ideas
with the class.

3 Let's Talk

Point to the photo. **Ask:** *What season do you think it is?
How do you know?* (Summer or Spring; flowers are
growing.) *What's the name of the flower she's smelling?*
(Buttercup.) *How do you say buttercup in your home
languages?* If they don't know, suggest they ask
family members. Ask students to answer the Let's Talk
questions in pairs.

Senses words

Poetry Speaking, listening and vocabulary

A Look at the words in the Word Cloud and match them to the meanings here.

1 A smell that you sense with your nose.
2 A sound that you hear with your ears.
3 A taste that you sense in your mouth.

Word Cloud
flavour
noise
scent

B Copy out this table and put the words into the right column. Some of the words might fit in more than one column.

wet red delicious crunchy purple loud cold sweet tasty fruity

See	Hear	Taste	Touch	Smell
yellow	quiet	salty	soft	scented

C Work with a partner and take it in turns to talk about your favourite food. Think of words to describe how the food looks, tastes, smells, feels and sounds when you eat it.

41

④ Learning objectives

Infer the meaning of unknown words from the context.

Develop sensitivity to ways that others express meaning in their talk and non-verbal communication.

Working together, students extend their vocabulary by exploring sense words and the adjectives that describe them. They discuss favourite foods, animal noises and the scent of flowers. They sort adjectives into a SENSES chart and learn that some adjectives can apply to more than one sense.

Remember to display the child-friendly learning objectives to the class along with the child-friendly checklist that students can use to assess how well they achieve them.

We know that we have achieved these because:

▸ We can guess the meaning of words that describe senses in context.
▸ We can take it in turns to talk about our favourite food.
▸ We can work well with a partner.

⑤ Word Cloud definitions

Remind students to add new words to their New Word Lists (see Workbook) in English and their home languages. Write these unfinished sentences on the board. Ask students to complete them orally:

'I like … -flavoured ice-cream best.'

'My cat makes a … noise when it's hungry.'

'The scent of this flower makes me think of …'

Ask how students say these words in their home languages. Draw attention to 'scent', pointing out the silent 'c'.

flavour the taste and smell of something.
noise a sound that may be loud or unpleasant.
scent a perfume.

⑥ Student Book teaching notes and exercise answers

Ⓐ

Students complete the exercise in pairs. Check orally.

Answers:

1 scent **2** noise **3** flavour

Ⓑ

Read through the word list. Check for understanding. Ask students to act out 'wet', 'delicious', 'tasty', 'crunchy', 'loud', 'cold'. **Ask:** *What do we do to show something is delicious without using words?* (Rubbing tummy, etc.) *How do you show this in your home languages?* Ask what kind of words they are. (Adjectives.) Review the definition of adjective. (A describing word.)

Instruct students to copy the table into their notebook. Warn them that some words might fit in more than one column. Students complete exercise B individually and compare in pairs. Complete the SENSES chart together. Ask for more words, using flashcards of food as prompts if necessary. *Example:* lemon – sour, etc. Encourage students to put new words in their New Word List (see Workbook) in English and their home languages.

Answers:

See: purple, red. **Hear:** crunchy, loud. **Taste:** crunchy, delicious, fruity, sweet, tasty. **Touch:** cold, wet. **Smell:** delicious, fruity, sweet.

Ⓒ

Ask students to guess your favourite food. Mime eating it, and describe its taste, smell, etc. Now ask pairs to do the same.

Learning objectives

(1)

Read a poem.

Write and perform a poem.

Infer the meaning of unknown words from the context.

Students explore the illustrated poem 'The Sound Collector' to learn words associated with sound, and act out the poem. They then adapt the poem, replacing sound with taste or smell. They also learn how titles are clues to what they are about to read. The structure of English and their home languages is explored.

Remember to display the child-friendly learning objectives to the class along with the child-friendly checklist that students can use to assess how well they achieve them.

We know that we have achieved these because:

▶ We can read, write and act out a poem.

▶ We can use all the clues available to us to understand unfamiliar words that describe sounds and the objects that make them.

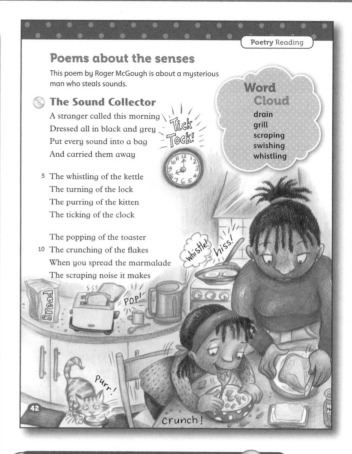

Poems about the senses

This poem by Roger McGough is about a mysterious man who steals sounds.

The Sound Collector

A stranger called this morning
Dressed all in black and grey
Put every sound into a bag
And carried them away

5 The whistling of the kettle
The turning of the lock
The purring of the kitten
The ticking of the clock

The popping of the toaster
10 The crunching of the flakes
When you spread the marmalade
The scraping noise it makes

42

Word Cloud

drain
grill
scraping
swishing
whistling

(2) Poetry reading notes

The poem can be illustrated with the help of the following items: large bag, key, bowlful of crunchy cereal, piece of toast, picture of a grill, picture of a bathtub, long piece of cloth, picture of stairs. Or you can explain the poem by pointing to items in the illustration, miming and making the noises, or inviting students to do so. You can add drama by dressing in black and grey like the stranger.

Tell students that, so far, they have read stories about home and school, and information text. Now they are going to read poems about their senses. Read the second verse of 'The Sound Collector'. After each line, make the sound described. **Ask:** *Which sense is the poem about?* (Hearing.) Mime by cupping an ear. **Ask:** *How did you guess that? Look at the poem in your book, what other clues are there that the poem is about sound?*

Ask: *What does the title say?* ('The Sound Collector'.) Explain that titles are very important because they let us know what we are going to read about. Tell students that the poem is about a man who steals sounds. **Say:** *Let's see what sounds this stranger is going to steal in this poem.*

(3) Word Cloud definitions

Make the sound that each word indicates and ask students to write the meaning in their New Word List (*see* Guidelines, page 192, and Workbook), either in English and their home languages, or by a simple drawing that shows the word. You can also refer to the audio on the CD-ROM.

drain a pipe carrying water or dirty liquid away.

grill part of a cooker that heats and cooks food from above.

scraping a harsh sound that you get when you pass something over a rough surface.

swishing a light, brushing sound.

whistling a sharp, clear sound we make by puckering our lips and blowing.

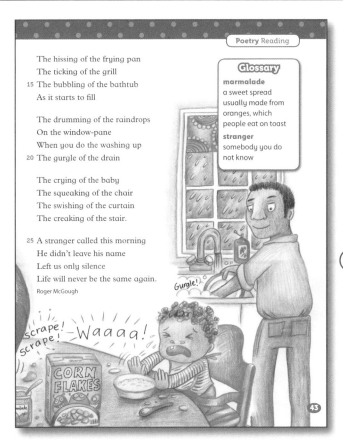

Poetry Reading

The hissing of the frying pan
The ticking of the grill
15 The bubbling of the bathtub
As it starts to fill

The drumming of the raindrops
On the window-pane
When you do the washing up
20 The gurgle of the drain

The crying of the baby
The squeaking of the chair
The swishing of the curtain
The creaking of the stair.

25 A stranger called this morning
He didn't leave his name
Left us only silence
Life will never be the same again.
Roger McGough

Glossary

marmalade
a sweet spread usually made from oranges, which people eat on toast

stranger
somebody you do not know

Ask pairs of students to choose either taste or smell from the chart of senses. Ask them to copy the first verse of the poem and change the word 'sound' to 'smell' or 'taste'. Direct them to the second verse of the poem. Ask them to change the sounds in that verse to smells or tastes to make a poem called 'The Smell Collector' or 'The Taste Collector'. If necessary help students with words for things that smell or taste, as well as with words that represent smells and tastes. Ask for volunteers to read their poem aloud to the class.

5 Glossary

Draw attention to the Glossary words 'marmalade' and 'stranger'. Ask students to read these aloud. Challenge students to be the first to find these words in the poem, and ask them to read the lines:

'A stranger called this morning...' (Lines 1 and 25)

'When you spread the marmalade...' (Line 11)

4 Poetry reading notes

Using the SENSES chart made in the unit warm up (*see* pages 48–49), begin making a list of the sounds in the 'Hearing' column. Make the noises or ask a student to do so. Use the objects if they are available and/or direct the students' attention to the illustration showing the object that makes the noise.

Assign each student (or pair of students) one of the sounds in the poem (there are 16). Tell them that you are the sound collector. Walk around the class while they make the sounds, then touch a student's desk and make a sweeping gesture as though taking something. They must immediately stop making their sound. Continue until all the sounds are collected. **Ask:** *How did it feel when I took your sound? How did it feel when it got quieter in the classroom, and then we had silence?*

After this brief activity, ask each student or pair in turn to make their noise, and direct the class to look at the poem. **Ask:** *What is that sound called? What makes that sound? Show me* (the object).

Next, read the poem, stopping to make sure that all the words are clear. You can also refer to the e-book and audio on the CD-ROM.

Learning objectives

(1)

Answer questions with some reference to single points in the text.

Read a range of story, poetry and information books and begin to make links between them.

Students examine text in order to find answers to questions about specific parts of the poem they have read. They also identify the use of rhyme in the poem, and learn that poetry is the only text type to use rhyme regularly, although not all poems rhyme.

Remember to display the child-friendly learning objectives to the class along with the child-friendly checklist that students can use to assess how well they achieve them.

We know that we have achieved these because:

▸ We can answer questions about specific parts of the poem we have read, such as a particular event or action.

▸ We can identify a type of text as poetry if it rhymes, and understand that not all poems rhyme, and that story and information texts do not rhyme.

(2) Student Book teaching notes and comprehension answers

Read the poem one more time, stopping at every word that represents a sound, and ask the student or students who made that sound to make it again.

Ask: *What do you notice about the second and fourth line of each verse of the poem?* (The last words rhyme.) Tell them that many poems have words that rhyme. **Ask:** *Did the stories and information text that you've read have words that rhyme like this?* (No.) If any students produced rhyming lines when replacing sounds with smells or tastes in the poem, point that out. Praise the work but assure students that some poems do not rhyme at all. Make a chart of the three text types. Write 'rhyme (sometimes)' under 'Poetry', and 'no rhyme' under 'Fiction' and 'Non-fiction'. You can refer students to the extracts in Unit 1 and the instruction texts in Unit 2 so that they can see the difference in layout clearly, too. Ask students to find out from parents or other home members if poems in their home languages rhyme.

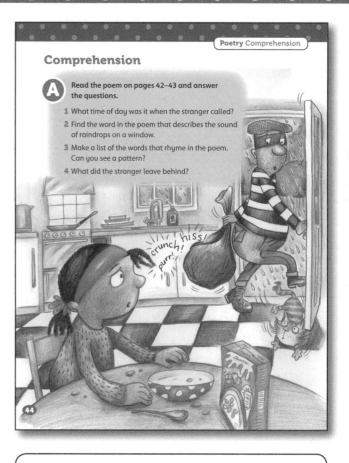

Comprehension

A Read the poem on pages 42–43 and answer the questions.

1 What time of day was it when the stranger called?

2 Find the word in the poem that describes the sound of raindrops on a window.

3 Make a list of the words that rhyme in the poem. Can you see a pattern?

4 What did the stranger leave behind?

44

Answers:

1 The morning.

Ask students to refer to the four-factor clues chart developed in Unit 1 (*see* page 10), and tell you what they used as clues to answer this question. **Ask:** *Does the illustration look like your own homes at breakfast time? How are they different? Are there any sounds that aren't in the poem that you hear in the morning at home?*

2 'drumming'.

Ask: *Are raindrops the only things that make that sound? How did we make that sound when I stole your sounds?* (Drums; tapping fingers on desk.)

3 'grey' – 'away', 'lock' – 'clock', 'flakes' – 'makes', 'grill' – 'fill', 'pane' – 'drain', 'chair' – 'stair', 'name' – 'again'. The second and fourth lines of every verse rhyme.

Read the rhyming words aloud, stressing the sound that makes the words rhyme, and invite students to join in.

4 'silence', no sound.

Poetry Comprehension

B

What do you think?

Use phrases from the poem to help with your answer.

1 Which sounds in the poem do you like the most? Are there any you dislike?

2 Which words in the poem are the most effective?

3 Can you think of any other sounds the sound collector could have taken?

4 At the end of the poem, why does the poet say life will never be the same?

C

What about you?

How would you feel if the world became silent? Which sounds would you miss the most? Are there any sounds you would not miss?

Discussion time

Imagine the sound collector had come to your school. Think of four words to describe the sounds he might have taken. In a group, compare your words.

45

Learning objectives

3

Consider words that make an impact, such as adjectives and powerful verbs.

Take turns in discussion, building on what others have said.

Listen and respond appropriately to others' views and opinions.

Students discuss sounds that make an impact on them, including their favourite and least favourite sounds. They continue to focus on words that sound like the noise they make, which have particularly strong images. Guidance is provided for following acceptable rules of conversation.

Remember to display the child-friendly learning objectives to the class along with the child-friendly checklist that students can use to assess how well they achieve them.

We know that we have achieved these because:

▶ We can identify words that sound like the noise they make and recognize how a simpler word would not have the same effect.

▶ We know how to take turns in listening and speaking.

▶ We can participate in discussions without hurting anyone's feelings and by listening to each other and taking turns.

4 # Student Book teaching notes and comprehension answers

B

1 Ask students to look at the poem and remember all the sounds that the class made. Tell them to pick their favourite and least favourite sounds. When students share their answers, make sure they listen and respond appropriately to others' choices.

2 Remind students how authors use words that are particularly powerful and describe things in a very clear way. Remind them of the powerful words they read in the extract from *Abdullah's Butterfly* in Unit 1. Ask students to pick words (adjectives or verbs) that make the poem come alive. Ask why they picked that particular word. Suggest that perhaps some verbs are powerful because they make the sound itself, such as 'hiss' or 'crunch'. **Ask:** *Can you find other verbs in the poem that make their sound?* ('purr', 'pop', 'bubble', 'swish', 'tick', 'gurgle', 'squeak', 'creak'.)

3 Ask students to look at the pictures on pages 42–45 of the Student Book. **Ask:** *Can you see any other sounds represented here?* Point out the sink as a clue. (Whooshing of the tap water, bursting of bubbles, clinking of plate, etc.)

4 Accept answers such as, life without sounds would be very boring, perhaps dangerous, etc.

C

Tell students to cover their ears as they think about being in a silent world. Ask individuals to discuss the sounds they would and wouldn't miss, giving reasons. Share your choices as well, indicating appropriate manner for agreement or disagreement. ***Example:*** *That's very good, Hanka. I'd miss the sound of birds singing, too. But you know what? I'd also miss the sound of a kettle whistling, as I like my cup of coffee. That must be something you don't like!*

5 # Discussion time

Ask students to stand outside the classroom in pairs and jot down the words for four sounds they can hear. Compare the words, writing them on the board. Monitor discussion among students, making sure they take turns and listen to each other.

Learning objectives

1

Read a range of poetry.

Practise learning and reciting poems.

Students listen to the poem 'The Young Fox' and try to spot words describing the senses. They look at the use of rhyme and see how this makes poetry different to fiction and non-fiction texts. They are challenged to remember the order of events.

Remember to display the child-friendly learning objectives to the class along with the child-friendly checklist that students can use to assess how well they achieve them.

We know that we have achieved these because:

▶ We can identify texts as poetry by the use of rhymes.

▶ We understand that story texts and information books don't use rhyme.

▶ We can remember the order of events in a short poem.

Poetry Reading

Poems about the senses (continued)

This poem by John Foster is about a young fox that uses its senses to find out if it is safe to leave its home.

Word Cloud
creeps
danger
peer
sniffs

The Young Fox

At night, the young fox pokes its head
Out of its den beneath the shed.

It listens with its pointed ears
To hear if there is danger near.

5   Its sharp nose sniffs the air and tells
If there are any dangerous smells.

Its sharp eyes peer from left to right
Watching for movements in the night.

If it senses it's safe, then up it leaps
10   And off across the fields it creeps.

John Foster

46

---

2   Poetry reading

Read the introduction to 'The Young Fox'. Tell students that this is another poem about the senses. Ask them to listen and see if they can tell which ones. Tell them to write down any sense words they hear.

Read the poem, stopping at words that students may not understand. Get them to look for clues as to meaning. Point out the Word Cloud words. You can also refer to the e-book and audio on the CD-ROM.

Read the poem again and ask students to close their books. Challenge them to remember what happens. Give prompts. *Example: What does the fox do first?* (Pokes its head out from its den.) *What does it do next?* (Listens for danger.) And so on. Write answers on the board and then open books. Did they remember the poem correctly?

Ask: *Since this is a poem, what do you expect to find at the end of lines?* (Rhyming.) Point out the rhyming words. ('head' – 'shed', 'ears' – 'near', 'tells – smells', 'right' – 'night', 'leaps' – 'creeps'.)

Ask: *Which senses does the author mention?* (Hearing, smell and sight.) *Which words show that it's those three senses?* ('listens', 'ears', 'hear', 'nose', 'sniffs', 'smells', 'eyes', 'peer', 'watching'.) Add them to the SENSES chart (*see* pages 48–49).

⇨

In pairs, ask students to compare the two poems in Unit 2, recording similarities and differences. Divide the board into columns headed 'Similarities' and 'Differences'. Record students' ideas under the correct heading. *Example:* **Similarities:** both about senses, have rhyme, contain something bad (stealing sounds, possible danger), etc. **Differences:** one sense/three senses, people/fox, morning/night, four-line verse/two-line verse, etc.

Ask: *Which poem do you like best? Why?*

3   Word Cloud definitions

Ask for volunteers to act out creeping, peering and sniffing, and to behave as though they are in danger.

Remind students to add new words to their New Word List (*see* Workbook) in English and their home languages. You can also refer to the audio on the CD-ROM.

creeps moves slowly with the body close to the ground.

danger something that may cause harm.

peer look with narrowed eyes for something that is difficult to see.

sniffs smells through the nose with a short, loud intake of air.

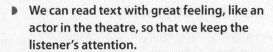

Comprehension

A Which three sentences below are true?

1 The fox lives in a shed.
2 The fox listens for sounds of danger.
3 The fox has a good sense of smell.
4 If it is safe, the fox creeps across the fields.

B What do you think?

Use phrases from the poem to help with your answer.

1 Which three senses does the fox use to check for danger?
2 Do you think the fox has good hearing? Why?
3 Why do you think the poet chose the word 'creeps' in the last verse?
4 Which words in the poem do you think are most effective? Give reasons for your answer.

C What about you?

Why do you think the young fox needs to check for danger before leaving its den?

Challenge
With a partner, practise reading the poem 'The Young Fox' aloud. Take it in turns to read the verses. Express yourself as you read! Have fun. You can pretend to do the fox's actions as you read the poem.

47

Learning objectives

(4) **Begin to infer meanings beyond the literal, for example about motives and character.**

Consider words that make an impact, such as adjectives and powerful verbs.

Read aloud with expression to engage the listener.

Practise to improve performance when reading aloud.

Begin to adapt movement to create a character in drama.

Students answer questions about the poem to test their ability to infer meaning beyond the literal. The impact of using powerful words is seen by replacing them with plainer words. Students also practise reading aloud with expression and acting like the fox.

Remember to display the child-friendly learning objectives to the class along with the child-friendly checklist that students can use to assess how well they achieve them.

We know that we have achieved these because:

▶ **We can identify words that create powerful images, and recognize how a simpler word would not have the same effect.**

▶ We can read text with great feeling, like an actor in the theatre, so that we keep the listener's attention.

▶ We understand from the words used in the poem how the fox feels and how it moves.

(5) Student Book teaching notes and comprehension answers

A

Answers:

2, 3 and 4 are true. Sentence 1 may trick students. The fox lives 'beneath', not 'in' the shed. Explain 'beneath'. (Under.) Act it out by putting objects beneath something, such as a desk or table.

B

1 Hearing, smell, sight.
2 Yes. Ask students how they knew the fox had good hearing. (What they know about foxes; the phrase 'pointed ears'.) **Ask:** *Is 'pointed' a powerful adjective? Would the line have been as effective if the author had left out that word?*
3 The word 'creeps' shows that the fox is being careful, because it is a slower movement that would be safer for the fox, etc. **Ask:** *Is 'creeps' a powerful word? Would the line have been as effective if the author had used 'goes'?*
4 Many words in the poem are powerful words. What is important is the explanation students give. Contrast the powerful words with plainer, less expressive and more generic words. ***Example:*** 'pokes' with 'puts', 'peer' with 'look', 'leaps' with 'jumps'. Read the powerful words with exaggerated expression and mime the actions.

C

Accept any answer having to do with the fact that foxes are hunted by people as well as larger animals.

(6) Challenge

Students practise reading 'The Young Fox' with a partner, taking turns to read the verses. Encourage students to read with expression, and act out the fox's actions as they do so. Ask for volunteers to perform their reading to the whole class.

You could also give pairs of students one line each from the poem, and ask one to read it and the other to act the part of the fox. Put the pairs together to perform the whole poem.

① Learning objective

Use effective strategies to tackle blending unfamiliar words, including identifying known suffixes and prefixes.

Students learn about prefixes and root words, and practise how to use the prefixes *un–* and *dis–*. The idea of root words is demonstrated using the image of a tree with roots. Students learn how this knowledge can help them with spelling.

Remember to display the child-friendly learning objective to the class along with the child-friendly checklist that students can use to assess how well they achieve it.

We know that we have achieved this because:

▶ We understand and can use the words 'prefix' and 'root word'.

▶ We know that a prefix comes at the beginning of the word, and can name words with the prefixes *un–* and *dis–*.

▶ We know that a prefix changes the meaning of a root word.

② Student Book teaching notes and vocabulary and spelling exercise answers

Prepare a 'PREFIX' chart with five columns on a large sheet of paper, and write the prefixes '*un–*', '*dis–*', '*re–*', '*pre–*' and '*de–*' across the top. Fold the chart concertina style, and then fold it to show only *un–* and *dis–*. Prepare a similar chart on smaller sheets for students.

Write the word 'prefix' in the centre of the board. Ask if anyone knows its meaning. (A word or syllable added to the front of a word to change or add to its meaning.) Write this definition on the board, reading it aloud. Point out that 'pre' means 'before' and that prefixes are always at the beginning of the word.

Explain that *un–* and *dis–* both mean 'not'. Ask students for words that begin with *un–* and *dis–*. A greater number of *un–* words are likely to be suggested, so add more *dis–* words as they occur during classwork.

Ⓐ

Read through the words with students, check for understanding and pair students to make the new words.

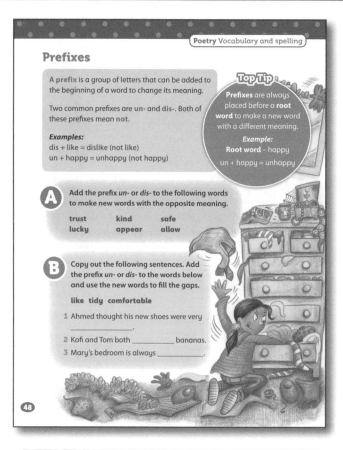

Poetry Vocabulary and spelling

Prefixes

A **prefix** is a group of letters that can be added to the beginning of a word to change its meaning.

Two common prefixes are **un-** and **dis-**. Both of these prefixes mean **not**.

Examples:
dis + like = dislike (not like)
un + happy = unhappy (not happy)

Top Tip

Prefixes are always placed before a **root word** to make a new word with a different meaning.
Example:
Root word – happy
un + happy = unhappy

Ⓐ Add the prefix *un-* or *dis-* to the following words to make new words with the opposite meaning.

| trust | kind | safe |
| lucky | appear | allow |

Ⓑ Copy out the following sentences. Add the prefix *un-* or *dis-* to the words below and use the new words to fill the gaps.

like tidy comfortable

1 Ahmed thought his new shoes were very _____.
2 Kofi and Tom both _____ bananas.
3 Mary's bedroom is always _____.

48

Answers:

trust – distrust, lucky – unlucky, kind – unkind, appear – disappear, safe – unsafe, allow – disallow

Ⓑ

Focus attention on the picture. Discuss the untidy room, and ask students to compare it with their own bedrooms. Ask students to complete B individually. Check orally.

Answers:

1 uncomfortable **2** dislike **3** untidy

③ Top Tip

Demonstrate the idea of root words. Write 'prefix' on the board, and draw a tree trunk coming away from it with many roots. Write 'like' and 'happy' on two roots, and '*dis–*' and '*un–*' above 'prefix'. Explain that root words are words that have a meaning of their own but can be added to, either with a prefix (before the root) or a suffix (after the root). Say that root words can often help us find out what a word means or where it comes from.

④ Extension

Ask: *Do your home languages use prefixes like these?* Ask students to talk about the concept of prefixes with their parents or other home members in their home languages. Invite students to share similarities and differences.

Poetry Vocabulary and spelling

More prefixes

A The prefix *re-* means 'again'. Rewrite the following sentences, adding the prefix *re-* to the verbs.

1 The family visited their favourite beach.
2 Kofi filled his glass with water.
3 The football team arranged the game.

Top Tip

Knowing about **prefixes** and **root words** is useful for spelling. Prefixes form separate syllables, so they help you break down words into smaller parts.

B The prefix *pre-* means 'before' and the prefix *de-* means 'remove' or 'make opposite'.

1 Add the prefix *pre-* or *de-* to the following words to make a new word.
   historic frost view value
2 Write a sentence using each of the new words you made in 1.
3 How have the prefixes changed the meaning of the words in 1?

C Use a dictionary to find two new words that begin with the prefixes *un-, dis-, de-, re-* and *pre-*. Working with a partner, take it in turns to test each other on the spelling and meaning of the words.

49

---

(5) Learning objectives

Extend earlier work on prefixes.

Use a dictionary or electronic means to find the spelling and meaning of words.

Students practise breaking down words into smaller parts. They investigate the prefixes *re–*, *pre–* and *de–*, and find appropriate root words. Dictionaries are used to find new words.

Remember to display the child-friendly learning objectives to the class along with the child-friendly checklist that students can use to assess how well they achieve them.

We know that we have achieved these because:

▶ We can name words with the prefixes *re–*, *pre–* and *de–*.

▶ We can use our understanding of prefixes and root words to help us with spelling .

▶ We can use a dictionary to find new words.

(6) Student Book teaching notes and vocabulary and spelling exercise answers

Open the PREFIX chart to reveal the other prefixes. Review the meaning of prefix.

⇨

Point to the heading *re–* on the chart and explain that it means 'again'. Gather ideas for *re–* words from students, writing them in the column. ***Example:*** rewrite, redo, retell, etc. Go to the drawing of the tree with roots. Add *'re–'* to the prefixes, and root words to the roots. **Ask:** *Does the word 'rely' belong here? Why not?* ('ly' carries no meaning without *re–*.)

Read through the words in A with students and check for understanding. Ask students to write the answers individually.

Answers:

1 revisited **2** refilled **3** rearranged

Introduce the prefixes *pre–* (before) and *de–* (remove or make opposite) in the same way, finding words for the chart and adding them to the tree along with root words. Give examples of words that don't belong, such as 'premium' and 'delicious', saying why. Ask students to work in pairs to make new words. Check for understanding of root words.

Answers:

1 prehistoric, defrost, review, devalue
2 Ask several students to share their sentences. Write them on the board and ask for feedback from the class on usage and word order.

In pairs, students use a dictionary to find two new words beginning with the prefixes introduced (*un–*, *dis–*, *re–*, *pre–* and *de–*). Instruct students to test their partner for spelling and meaning of the words. Check again for understanding of root words.

(7) Top Tip

Use the board to show how breaking words into syllables (segments) can help students remember spelling. Encourage them to keep their prefix charts in their writing folder, and put new words in their New Word List (*see* Workbook) in English and their home languages.

(8) Extension

Ask students to complete their individual prefix charts, adding any words they find from their current reading or in dictionaries. Elicit words they have found, and add correct words to the classroom's PREFIX chart.

Learning objectives

①

Identify different types of play scripts and typical themes.

Read a range of story, poetry and information books and begin to make links between them.

Read play scripts and dialogue, with awareness of different voices.

Students explore the main features of a play script and learn how writing a play script is different from writing a story. They read an extract containing conversation from the story *Lost Shoes* and discover how this can be turned into a play script.

Remember to display the child-friendly learning objectives to the class along with the child-friendly checklist that students can use to assess how well they achieve them.

We know that we have achieved these because:

▶ **We can understand the main differences between a play and a story.**

▶ **We can make links between stories, plays and poems.**

▶ **We understand the importance of tone of voice and facial expressions in reading dialogue.**

② Writing workshop teaching notes

Divide a large sheet of paper into two columns, one headed 'Story' and the other 'Play'. Tell students to copy this into their notebooks. Elicit the meaning of 'story'. (Words that tell of real or imaginary events.) Now elicit the meaning of 'play'. (A story acted on stage or on television.) Ask students how they say these in their home languages. Tell students to work in pairs and discuss the differences between stories and plays, recording them under the correct headings. (You can read a story yourself; stories have pictures; people act in plays, etc.)

Refer students to the picture of the messy room. Ask them to talk about the picture in pairs, and decide if the title is a good one.

Model writing

Read the conversation to the class, changing tone of voice with character. Point out the speech marks and ask why they are there. (To show that someone is talking.) Remind students that the beginning of the extract has been highlighted with blue for people's speech, orange for an action and green for the speaker's name or part.

Writing a play script
Model writing

Read the conversation below. In the first two paragraphs, the words that are spoken are in blue. Notice that there are speech marks (" ") around the words. The words in orange describe *how* the words are spoken and the actions of the characters. We show what we are thinking by how we talk, the expressions on our faces and how we move. The names of the characters are in green.

Lost Shoes

"I can't find my shoes!" wailed seven-year-old George Green, desperately searching under his bed. "I've looked everywhere!"

"They must be somewhere, George. You would have taken them off last night before you went to bed," said George's dad, scratching his head. "Let's search the room together. Are you ready? On top of the bed?"

"No," said George.

"Under your desk?"

"No," said George.

"Behind your computer?"

"No," said George.

"Then," Dad declared, "you are just going to have to go to the birthday party with no shoes on. Let's go. You don't want to be late. Mum's waiting downstairs to take you."

"Perhaps no one will notice," George muttered, as he glanced down at his bright green socks. He sighed, "What shall I do?"

50

Ask some comprehension questions to ensure that everyone has understood the context. **Ask:** *Why does George need his shoes?* (He is going to a birthday party.)

Read the extract again, focusing on vocabulary. Ask students to guess the meanings of 'wailed' (cried), 'desperately' (anxiously), 'scratching' (scraping with fingernails), 'nervously' (worriedly), 'muttered' (grumbled or mumbled), 'glanced' (to take a quick look). Ask students to find another two words that are used for 'said' ('declared', 'sighed'). Elicit their meanings: 'declared' (said something firmly) and 'sighed' (breathed out heavily). Mime sighing.

Divide students into threes, and ask them to re-read the extract as Dad, George and the Narrator (the storyteller). Students playing Dad and George read the speech of their characters (text between speech marks); the Narrator reads the rest of the story.

Student Book page

Play script Writing workshop

Guided writing

Change the conversation on page 50 into a play script. Use the following features in your play script.

Characters
In play scripts, the speaker (highlighted in green in the text on page 50) is written in bold on the left-hand side of the page.

Dialogue
The words inside the speech marks on page 50 (highlighted in blue) are the words the characters say. There is no need to use speech marks in a play script.

Stage directions
Words such as 'scratching his head' on page 50 (highlighted in orange) can be used as instructions for the actors. Stage directions tell the actors what to do on stage and how to say their words. Put the stage directions in brackets.

The opening is done for you.

George (*desperately searching under the bed*) I can't find my shoes! I've looked everywhere!

Dad (*scratching his head*) They must be somewhere, George.

Your writing

Add your own ending to the play script. Does George find his shoes or go to the party with no shoes? Or does he wear his slippers or someone else's shoes? You decide. You might have to introduce new characters, such as George's mum and sister.

51

Story	Play script
You can read a story yourself. Stories often have pictures. Lots of descriptions. Can write what people are thinking. Speech marks.	A story acted on stage or television. People acting and singing. People talking and doing things. Actors need directions. Facial expression and voice matter. No speech marks. Action. Performance.

Guided writing

Inform students that they are going to turn the extract from *Lost Shoes* into a play script.

Read through the features of play scripts. Review on the board that:

▶ Name goes on left in bold.

▶ No speech marks in play script.

▶ Stage directions go inside brackets.

Remind students that stage directions tell actors what they must do and how they should say their lines. Point to the example 'scratching his head', highlighted in orange in the extract on page 50 of the Student Book. Refer students to the Guided writing example (the opening). Ask them to copy this into their notebooks.

Working in groups of three, students decide who is responsible for finding names of speakers, what they say, and what they do in the extract. Together the group writes the characters, dialogue and stage directions.

Your writing

Ask students to work individually and write their own endings to the play script. Read aloud the introduction to Your writing, and refer them to the model on the board. Allow beginner students to write in their home languages. Scribe for those who can speak but are not yet able to write. Invite students to share their endings with their groups. Groups can take turns acting out the ending.

Ask for volunteers to perform to the whole class.

---

(3) ## Learning objectives

Write simple play scripts based on reading.

Use reading as a model for writing dialogue.

Students collaborate to write a short play script based on reading the story *Lost Shoes*.

Remember to display the child-friendly learning objectives to the class along with the child-friendly checklist that students can use to assess how well they achieve them.

We know that we have achieved these because:

▶ **We can turn a story into a play script.**

▶ **We can write stage directions.**

▶ **We can write dialogue.**

(4) ## Writing workshop teaching notes

Direct attention to the chart headed 'Story' and 'Play'. Add the word 'script' to 'Play' to make 'Play script'. Explain that this means the words in a play. Brainstorm with the students other differences between stories and play scripts.

End of Unit Test

Question Paper

Reading: play scripts

Read the following story and answer the questions.

Food Glorious Food

Juan was so **excited**. He was going to have tacos for lunch. His mother had gone to the Mexican store the day before and she made him a special lunch to take to school.

"I have tacos for lunch today! They are so yummy!" **he announced to**
5 **Carl happily as they entered the classroom**.

"Tar-cos? What are tar-cos?" **laughed** Carl.

"Here, look!" answered Juan, **as he pulled out his lunch bag and started to open it**.

"Pee-yu!" **squealed Carl, as he looked into Juan's lunch bag**. "That
10 stinks! There are onions in there!"

Juan was puzzled and hurt. He quickly closed his lunch bag and quietly put it away.

"Tar-cos, tar-cos," **shrieked Carl, jumping up and down**.

Ms Green, the teacher, had been **watching this,** and she was
15 **horrified!** This was no good! She wanted her students to appreciate foods from different cultures, and to enjoy the tastes and smells of different kinds of food. So she decided to do something the next day.

"Listen up, everyone," **she announced**. "Tomorrow we will have a special lunch. We're going to have an international food party! Each of
20 us will bring something special that we eat at home."

The next day, the classroom smelled delicious.

Glossary

appreciate enjoy something and recognize its value.

stinks has an unpleasant smell.

tacos Mexican sandwich-like food consisting of tortillas, folded and filled with various mixtures, such as meat, cheese, tomato and lettuce.

yummy delicious.

Comprehension

A Give evidence from the extract to support your answers.

1 If we turned this story into a play script, which characters in the play would come on to the stage first?

_____ [2]

2 If this story were a play script, how many characters would have a speaking part? Name the characters.

_____

_____ [3]

3 If this story were a play script, what would the actor playing Juan be carrying as he entered the classroom?

_____ [1]

B Give evidence from the extract to support your answers.

1 How do we know which words are spoken in the text? Give an example.

_____ [2]

2 Why would the words in bold be useful to an actor?

_____ [1]

3 If you were acting the part of Carl, what would you do as you said the words 'Pee-yu!' in line 9?

_____ [1]

C Give evidence from the extract to support your answers.

1 Find three verbs that could be used in stage directions to tell actors how to speak their lines.

_____ [3]

2 Write a stage direction to help an actor show how Juan felt when he was putting away his lunch bag.

_____

_____ [2]

Writing: play script

In the extract below Ms Green's class are getting ready to have their international food party. Read the extract.

Food Glorious Food

"What did you bring for the international food party?" asked John Smith, **proudly showing off the chocolate cookies his Mum had made**.

"Come on, let me see what is in your fancy box," he **insisted**.

Yuri **sighed heavily, trying to hide her decorated lunch box**. She
5   did not want him to see the sushi her Mum had made for her.

"I have some Japanese food," she **whispered quietly**.

Ms Green, the teacher, **clapped her hands to get everyone's attention**.

"Children, leave your food on the table and come and sit on the rug. I want each of you to tell us about the food you have brought."

10   **Yuri felt embarrassed and looked as if she was going to cry.** She didn't want to talk about sushi. She looked across at the table and wished she had brought pizza, cucumber sandwiches or a cake. Her food looked so different.

Aimee, Yuri's best friend, **sat next to her on the rug, took Yuri's**
15   **hand** and said "I can't wait to try Japanese food. I bet it's really yummy."

"Thank you," smiled Yuri.

"Yuri, what did you bring?" asked Ms Green.

"A Japanese dish made with rice called sushi." **Yuri said nervously**.

"I love sushi," **beamed Ms Green**. "It's one of my favourite Japanese dishes."

20   "John, what have you brought?" continued Ms Green.

Glossary

beamed smiled happily.

bet to be sure about something.

embarrassed feeling shy or awkward.

fancy decorated, not plain.

insisted said very firmly.

sushi a Japanese food made of cooked rice and other ingredients such as fish or meat.

Turn the 'Food Glorious Food' story into a play script. Then, add your own ending.

Please use a separate sheet of paper

Organize your play script with the following features:

Characters

Write the name of the speaker on the left-hand side of the page. Think about Yuri and how she might feel at the party. Do her classmates like sushi? You can introduce other characters and describe the food they brought.

Dialogue

Write the words that are spoken to the right of the speakers' names. Remember there is no need to use speech marks in a play script.

Stage directions

The words in bold in the story on page 62 can be used to write instructions that tell the actors what to do and how to say their lines. Remember to put the stage directions in brackets.

Begin like this:

John (proudly showing off the chocolate cookies) What did you bring for the international food party?

John (insisting) Come on, let me see what's in your fancy box?

Yuri …

[20]

4 Traditional tales

① Warm-up objectives

Speak clearly and confidently in a range of contexts.

Take turns in discussion, building on what others have said.

Listen and respond appropriately to others' views and opinions.

Students explore the cultures and traditions of Bali, Indonesia, by asking and answering questions. They learn that dancing is an important Balinese tradition. They share information about their own traditions, building an awareness of their growing identities and those of others.

Remember to display the child-friendly learning objectives to the class along with the child-friendly checklist that students can use to assess how well they achieve them.

We know that we have achieved these because:

▶ We show respect for other cultures and traditions.

▶ We listen with interest.

▶ We respond with respect.

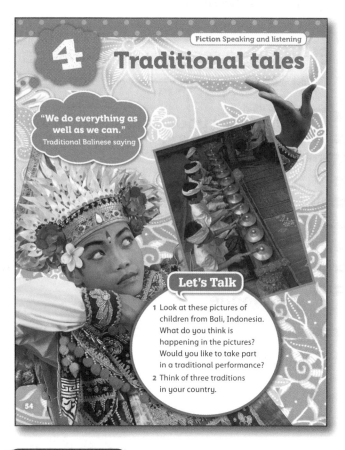

4 Traditional tales

"We do everything as well as we can."
Traditional Balinese saying

Let's Talk

1 Look at these pictures of children from Bali, Indonesia. What do you think is happening in the pictures? Would you like to take part in a traditional performance?

2 Think of three traditions in your country.

54

② Unit warm up

Ask students to suggest another word for 'tale'. (Story.) Say that tales begin and end in the same way in many languages. Give the example: 'Once upon a time…' and 'They all lived happily ever after'. Ask if they know how to say these phrases in their home languages. Make a multilingual poster named 'BEGINNINGS AND ENDINGS', displaying different scripts for story openings and endings.

Read the quote aloud together: *"We do everything as well as we can." Traditional Balinese saying.* Elicit if students know where Balinese is spoken. (The island of Bali.) If you have a Balinese speaker, ask them to translate the quote. Find Bali on a world map, and point out that it is an island. Ask how students say 'island' in their home languages.

Read the quote again. Ask students to turn to their partners and decide together what the quote means. Invite several pairs to share their ideas with the class. (Always do your best, etc.)

③ Let's Talk

Focus attention on the pictures on page 54 of the Student Book. **Ask:** *What do you think is happening?* (Dancing; playing musical instruments.) *Where do you think the dancer is from?* (Bali.) Explain that we say Bali for the country and Balinese for the people and the language.

Ask: *What's the dancer doing?* (Dancing.) *How do you say 'dance' in your home languages? What types of dancing have you heard of?* (Hip hop, funky, ballet, Irish dancing, etc.) Write the headings 'Modern' and 'Traditional' on the board, and add the dance forms that students suggest.

Underline 'Tradition' and ask students what it means. Write a definition together. (Customs and habits that are passed down from one generation to another.) **Ask:** *What sort of word is traditional?* (Adjective.) Ask students to find the noun 'tradition' and the adjective 'traditional' in Let's Talk. Quickly elicit these in their home languages and ask students to write them in their New Word List in English and their home languages (*see* Guidelines, page 192, and Workbook).

Students answer questions 1 and 2 in pairs.

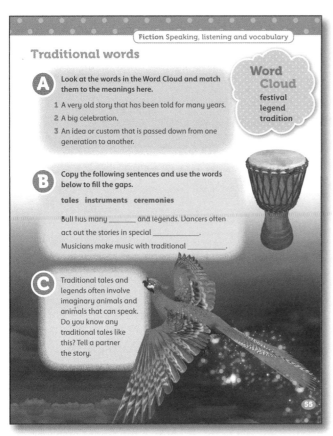

Fiction Speaking, listening and vocabulary

Traditional words

A Look at the words in the Word Cloud and match them to the meanings here.
1 A very old story that has been told for many years.
2 A big celebration.
3 An idea or custom that is passed down from one generation to another.

Word Cloud
festival
legend
tradition

B Copy the following sentences and use the words below to fill the gaps.

tales instruments ceremonies

Bali has many _____ and legends. Dancers often act out the stories in special _____.
Musicians make music with traditional _____.

C Traditional tales and legends often involve imaginary animals and animals that can speak. Do you know any traditional tales like this? Tell a partner the story.

⑤ Word Cloud definitions

Remind students to add new words to their New Word List in English and their home languages (*see* Guidelines, page 192, and Workbook).

festival a time when people arrange special celebrations, performances, etc.

legend an old story handed down from the past.

tradition customs and habits that are passed from one generation to another.

⑥ Student Book teaching notes and exercise answers

A

Read the words in the Word Cloud. Ask students to look at the three sentences and find any words that are new to them, then guess the meanings with a partner. Explain that a custom is a usual way of doing things. *Example:* using chopsticks, hands, knives and forks are customary ways of eating in different cultures.

Students complete A individually and check their answers in pairs. Do a quick matching check on the board.

Answers:

1 legend **2** festival **3** tradition

B

Students read the sentences and identify the missing words.

Answers:

tales, ceremonies, instruments

Ask students to draw a picture of a festival from their country. Students tell each other about their pictures. Ask them to write a dual-language text about their drawing in their home languages and English. Display these.

C

Ask students how tales usually begin and end. Point to the multilingual BEGINNINGS AND ENDINGS poster prepared in the Unit 4 warm up. Students tell each other a traditional tale involving animals, beginning by saying in their home languages, 'Once upon a time...' and ending in, 'They all lived happily ever after.'

⑦ Extension

Students work on the retelling of a traditional tale with parents, other home members or other speakers of their home languages. Invite them to come in and share tales with the students, retelling in English.

④ Learning objectives

Infer the meaning of unknown words from the context.

Speak clearly and confidently in a range of contexts.

Students learn the meanings of words associated with traditions. They exchange traditional tales that contain imaginary animals and animals that can speak.

Remember to display the child-friendly learning objectives to the class along with the child-friendly checklist that students can use to assess how well they achieve them.

We know that we have achieved these because:

▶ We can talk about our traditional stories.

▶ We can speak clearly and show respect for other cultures and traditions

▶ We can guess the meanings of new words about traditions from the context.

Learning objectives

1

Identify different types of stories and typical story themes.

Read a range of story books and begin to make links between them.

Infer the meaning of unknown words from the context.

Students read a traditional Balinese folk tale and investigate its similarities and differences to other texts they have read. They continue to guess the meaning of unfamiliar words by using the four-factor clues chart developed in Unit 1 (*see* page 10).

 Remember to display the child-friendly learning objectives to the class along with the child-friendly checklist that students can use to assess how well they achieve them.

We know that we have achieved these because:

▶ We can identify different types of stories and story themes.

▶ We use all the clues available to us to understand unfamiliar words.

2 Fiction reading notes

Introduce this traditional tale from Bali by reading aloud the introductory note.

Tell students that there are many characters who say things in this story. Direct the students' attention to the picture of Bawang. **Ask:** *Who do you think she is?* Write 'Bawang' on the board. **Ask:** *Who else do you think will say something?* Direct their attention to the picture of the fish. Write 'fish' on the board.

Begin reading the story, stopping at unfamiliar words and encouraging students to guess at the meaning by looking at the clues chart created in Unit 1 (*see* page 10). Make sure you stop at the words in the Word Cloud 'downstream' (line 10), 'gasped' (line 6), 'panting' (line 16), 'puffing' (line 15). Whenever the possibility arises, ask students whether something similar has happened to them, or whether they do things differently in their home. *Example:* read the first sentence. **Ask:** *Who washes the clothes in your home? Do you?* and *Do you go down to the river to wash clothes?* Read the second paragraph. **Ask:** *Have you ever lost something that belonged to your family that was important? How did you feel?*

You can also refer to the e-book and the audio on the CD-ROM.

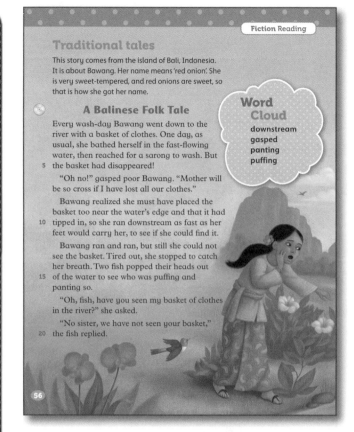

Fiction Reading

Traditional tales

This story comes from the island of Bali, Indonesia. It is about Bawang. Her name means 'red onion'. She is very sweet-tempered, and red onions are sweet, so that is how she got her name.

A Balinese Folk Tale

Every wash-day Bawang went down to the river with a basket of clothes. One day, as usual, she bathed herself in the fast-flowing water, then reached for a sarong to wash. But
5 the basket had disappeared!

"Oh no!" gasped poor Bawang. "Mother will be so cross if I have lost all our clothes."

Bawang realized she must have placed the basket too near the water's edge and that it had
10 tipped in, so she ran downstream as fast as her feet would carry her, to see if she could find it.

Bawang ran and ran, but still she could not see the basket. Tired out, she stopped to catch her breath. Two fish popped their heads out
15 of the water to see who was puffing and panting so.

"Oh, fish, have you seen my basket of clothes in the river?" she asked.

"No sister, we have not seen your basket,"
20 the fish replied.

Word Cloud

downstream
gasped
panting
puffing

56

3 Word Cloud definitions

When you get to these words in the story, you have an opportunity to reinforce the parts of speech you taught in Unit 1 (*see* page 16). Ask students to decide whether these words go in the NOUNS, ADJECTIVES or VERBS charts.

Remind students to add new words to their New Word List (*see* Workbook) in English and their home languages. You can also refer to the audio on the CD-ROM.

downstream the direction in which a river flows.
gasped breathed in suddenly because of a surprise.
panting breathing hard and quickly from being tired.
puffing breathing loudly from hard activity, such as running.

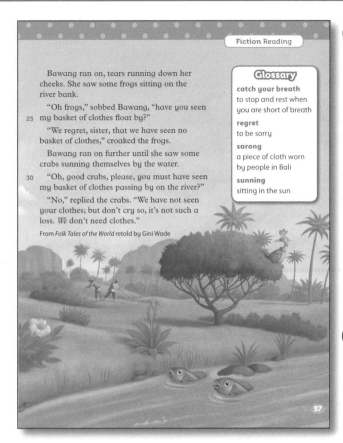

Bawang ran on, tears running down her cheeks. She saw some frogs sitting on the river bank.

"Oh frogs," sobbed Bawang, "have you seen
25 my basket of clothes float by?"

"We regret, sister, that we have seen no basket of clothes," croaked the frogs.

Bawang ran on further until she saw some crabs sunning themselves by the water.

30 "Oh, good crabs, please, you must have seen my basket of clothes passing by on the river?"

"No," replied the crabs. "We have not seen your clothes; but don't cry so, it's not such a loss. *We* don't need clothes."

From *Folk Tales of the World* retold by Gini Wade

Glossary

catch your breath
to stop and rest when you are short of breath

regret
to be sorry

sarong
a piece of cloth worn by people in Bali

sunning
sitting in the sun

⑤ Glossary

Draw attention to the Glossary words and phrases: 'catch your breath', 'regret', 'sarong' and 'sunning'. Ask students to read these aloud. Challenge students to be the first to find these words in the tale, and ask them to read the sentences.

'Tired out, she stopped to catch her breath.' (Line 13)

"We regret, sister, that we have seen no basket..." (Line 26)

'...she bathed herself... then reached for a sarong to wash.' (Line 3)

'...she saw some crabs sunning themselves by the water.' (Line 29)

⑥ Extension

Ask for volunteers or assign the following roles to students: Narrator, Bawang, two fish, three or four frogs, three or four crabs.

While the rest of the students are making space for these students to act out the story, go to each character (or set of characters) and point out the sections in the story that are their responsibility. Remind them to dramatize their parts and to say the words with feeling. Also, remind them that they need not say any of the narration, they only read the sentences <u>inside</u> the quotation marks. Remind the Narrator to speak only the words <u>outside</u> the quotation marks.

Give the readers a little time to practise, and then ask them to read the story as a play.

④ Fiction reading notes

If you are reading the story yourself, make sure to dramatize the dialogue as much as you can. Act upset when you speak the words that Bawang is saying. Gasp when the story says she gasped. Puff and pant when you get to that part of the story. Act like you are sobbing when the story says Bawang sobbed. Make your voice croak when you speak the words that the frogs say.

Whenever you get to a character saying something, point it out and write down their name on the board ('frogs', 'crabs').

Remind students of what they learned about script writing in Unit 3. These are the characters that would have lines to say if the story was written as a play.

When you finish reading the story, ask students if they can think of a better title for this part of the story. Accept anything that comes close to 'Bawang loses her family's clothes'. Write 'Theme:' on the board and the title that best represents the gist of the story. Then, write down the main points of the story as you elicit ideas from the students.

Learning objectives

(1)

Answer questions with some reference to single points in the text.

Begin to infer meanings beyond the literal, for example about motives and character.

Take turns in discussion, building on what others have said.

Listen and respond appropriately to others' views and opinions.

Develop sensitivity to ways that others express meaning in their talk.

Students answer questions about Bawang's story by focusing on specific events or points. They consider Bawang's character and work out the reasons for specific events in her story. They participate in discussions following the accepted rules of conversation, and describe the images the story brings to mind.

Remember to display the child-friendly learning objectives to the class along with the child-friendly checklist that students can use to assess how well they achieve them.

We know that we have achieved these because:

▶ We can correctly answer the questions posed.

▶ We can make guesses about events and characters in the story even though we don't see these described clearly in the text.

▶ We can participate in discussions, giving our opinion and listening to others' opinions.

(2) Student Book teaching notes and comprehension answers

Many of the answers to these questions can be summarized in one word, and others have key words in the sentences that form the answer. Take advantage of this to review the parts of speech. As students call out their answers, ask them which column in the NOUNS, ADJECTIVES and VERBS charts (*see* Unit 1, page 16) fits their words.

Answers:

(A)

1 fish, frogs, crabs
2 'to see who was puffing and panting so.'

   This answer is taken exactly as it is shown in the text. Encourage students to give answers in their

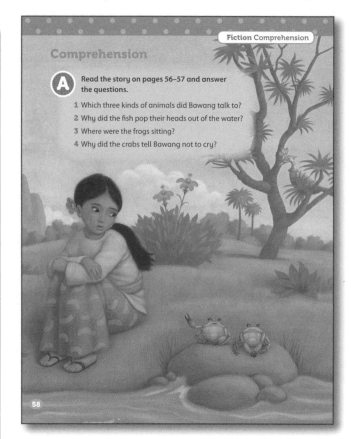

Fiction Comprehension

Comprehension

(A) Read the story on pages 56–57 and answer the questions.

1 Which three kinds of animals did Bawang talk to?
2 Why did the fish pop their heads out of the water?
3 Where were the frogs sitting?
4 Why did the crabs tell Bawang not to cry?

58

own words rather than copying from the text.
Ask: *Why did the fish look to see who was making all that noise?* (They were curious.) Help students to understand the concept of curious. **Say:** *When you're playing outside and all of a sudden, you hear a big loud noise, what do you want to do? You want to run and see what that noise is. You're curious. The story doesn't tell us that the fish were curious, but we can guess it from their behaviour, from what they did.*

3 'on the river bank.'

   Students are likely to know the word 'bank' associated with the financial institution. Explain that this is a word with more than one meaning. Show the river bank in the illustration on page 58 of the Student Book.

4 The crabs thought that losing clothes was unimportant; they think clothes are unnecessary as they don't use them. Make sure that students see the humour in this detail.

Fiction Comprehension

 What do you think?

Use phrases from the story to help with your answer.

1 Why do you think Bawang was so unhappy when she saw that the basket had gone?

2 Find three strong verbs in the story that the author has used instead of 'said'.

3 Find the phrase that describes how quickly Bawang ran along the river bank. Do you think this phrase is effective? Why?

4 Write two sentences to describe what we know about Bawang's character.

 What about you?

How would you feel if you were Bawang? What would you do?

Discussion time

Stories can sometimes make us form pictures in our minds. Work with a partner and describe the pictures this story makes you think of.

59

3 Student Book teaching notes and comprehension answers

Answers:

Ask students to look for specific phrases in the story to find the answers to these questions.

B

1 She had lost something important for the family: all their clothes; she had a responsibility and failed to do it well; she knew her mother would be angry. If students only give the part about the mother being angry, encourage them to go further. **Ask:** *Was that the only reason? Did she feel bad because she had failed in her task? Did she feel bad because she had lost something important for the whole family?*

2 'gasped', 'sobbed', 'croaked'. Ask students to read the sentences where these words appear and replace them with 'said' each time. Ask if this gives a clear picture of how Bawang felt, or what sound the frogs made.

3 'She ran … as fast as her feet would carry her.' Yes, it is effective because it gives a picture that her feet could not go any faster. Ask students if they know of a saying in their home languages that suggests fast running.

4 She is helpful. (She does the washing for the family.) She is smart. (She realizes what has happened and runs to fix the problem.) If students respond with 'She is very sweet-tempered', copied from the introduction, encourage them to find other clues.

C

Students discuss in pairs how they would feel if they were Bawang, and what they would do next. **Ask:** *If you were Bawang, how would you feel?* (Sad, cross, guilty, annoyed, etc.) Invite individuals to say what they would do next. **Ask:** *Is this a good idea?* Encourage students to join in the discussion, listening and responding appropriately.

4 Discussion time

Read aloud the Discussion time directions. Tell students to close their books, and work in pairs to describe the pictures the story created in their minds. Encourage note-taking. Invite individuals to share their ideas with the class. Point out good discussion strategies, such as listening to others before giving your own opinion, etc.

Learning objectives

Infer the meaning of unknown words from the context.

Identify different types of stories and typical story themes.

Students read the next part of Bawang's story. They continue to guess the meanings of unfamiliar words using the clues chart developed in Unit 1 (*see* page 10). They predict how the introduction of a new character, the golden bird, is going to affect the story, and consider whether Bawang deserves her reward.

Remember to display the child-friendly learning objectives to the class along with the child-friendly checklist that students can use to assess how well they achieve them.

We know that we have achieved these because:

▸ We can correctly identify typical story themes.

▸ We use all the clues available to us to understand unfamiliar words.

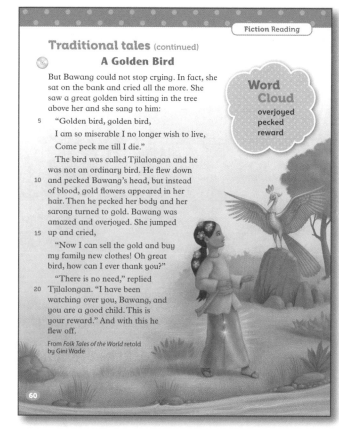

Traditional tales (continued)

A Golden Bird

But Bawang could not stop crying. In fact, she sat on the bank and cried all the more. She saw a great golden bird sitting in the tree above her and she sang to him:

5   "Golden bird, golden bird,
I am so miserable I no longer wish to live,
Come peck me till I die."

The bird was called Tjilalongan and he was not an ordinary bird. He flew down
10 and pecked Bawang's head, but instead of blood, gold flowers appeared in her hair. Then he pecked her body and her sarong turned to gold. Bawang was amazed and overjoyed. She jumped
15 up and cried,

"Now I can sell the gold and buy my family new clothes! Oh great bird, how can I ever thank you?"

"There is no need," replied
20 Tjilalongan. "I have been watching over you, Bawang, and you are a good child. This is your reward." And with this he flew off.

From *Folk Tales of the World* retold by Gini Wade

Word Cloud
overjoyed
pecked
reward

60

---

2 Fiction reading notes

Direct attention to the illustration on pages 56–57 of the Student Book. **Ask:** *Do you see something in that picture that we haven't met in our story yet?* (The bird.) Now look at the picture on pages 60–61 of the Student Book. **Ask:** *Do you see the bird there as well?* Ask students, in pairs or small groups, to predict what the bird is going to do in the story. Write these predictions on the board. Do not repeat the same or similar predictions. Now that students have had a chance to see all the predictions, ask the pairs or groups to decide which prediction they think is most likely to be the one in the story. Get a show of hands for each prediction and mark the number.

Begin reading, stopping at unfamiliar words and encouraging students to guess at their meaning with the help of the four-factor clues chart prepared in Unit 1 (*see* page 10). Make sure to point out the words in the Word Cloud.

When you reach the part about the bird, check with the predictions on the board and see which one comes closest. You can also refer to the e-book and the audio on the CD-ROM.

---

3 Word Cloud definitions

Ask students if they think that Bawang got a fair reward. **Ask:** *Is that why Bawang was such a good child? So she would get rewarded?* Remind students of what they guessed about Bawang's character in the questions on page 59 of the Student Book.

Encourage students to add new words to their New Word List (*see* Workbook) in English and their home languages. You can also refer to the audio on the CD-ROM.

overjoyed very happy, filled with great joy.

pecked hit sharply at something with the beak (birds do this).

reward some kind of payment which is given for doing something good.

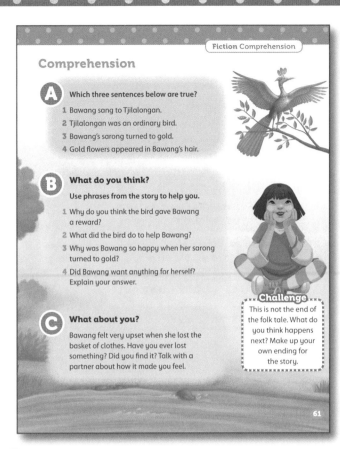

Comprehension

Fiction Comprehension

A Which three sentences below are true?

1 Bawang sang to Tjilalongan.
2 Tjilalongan was an ordinary bird.
3 Bawang's sarong turned to gold.
4 Gold flowers appeared in Bawang's hair.

B What do you think?

Use phrases from the story to help you.

1 Why do you think the bird gave Bawang a reward?
2 What did the bird do to help Bawang?
3 Why was Bawang so happy when her sarong turned to gold?
4 Did Bawang want anything for herself? Explain your answer.

C What about you?

Bawang felt very upset when she lost the basket of clothes. Have you ever lost something? Did you find it? Talk with a partner about how it made you feel.

Challenge
This is not the end of the folk tale. What do you think happens next? Make up your own ending for the story.

61

Learning objectives

④ **Answer questions with some reference to single points in the text.**

Begin to infer meanings beyond the literal, for example about motives and character.

Identify the main points or gist of a text.

Students continue to answer specific and general questions about the tale. They practise how to talk about the story, and make up their own ending.

Remember to display the child-friendly learning objectives to the class along with the child-friendly checklist that students can use to assess how well they achieve them.

We know that we have achieved these because:

▶ **We can answer specific and general questions about the text.**

▶ **We can talk about the story and make ourselves understood.**

---

⑤ **Student Book teaching notes and comprehension answers**

Answers:

A

1, 3, 4

B

1 The bird had been watching Bawang and knew that she was a good child, so he gave her a reward.
2 The bird gave Bawang something valuable (gold), so she could buy new clothes for her family and replace the ones that had been lost. He gave her the gold by pecking her, and wherever he pecked, gold appeared.
3 She was happy because gold is valuable and she could sell it to buy new clothes for her family to replace the ones that had been lost.
4 No, she was only concerned about buying new clothes for her family.

C

Model for the students what they might feel about losing something. Tell them how you lost something once, whether you found it or not, and how you felt. For beginner second language students, you may want to give them Talk Tools to help them start a conversation with their partner. *Example:* write these on the board: 'Once I lost…', 'I was so …' and give some adjectives as options: 'sad', 'happy', 'upset', 'angry', etc. Practise using these Talk Tools with the students.

---

⑥ **Challenge**

Summarize the two parts of the tale that you have read. Read the first two sentences of the challenge. **Ask:** *So what do you think happens to Bawang after the bird flies away?* Say that there are many events that could take place. Ask students to work in pairs to think of an idea for what could happen next, and then to end the story in whatever way they prefer.

Learning objectives

①

Generate synonyms for high frequency words, such as 'big', 'little', 'good'.

Collect examples of nouns, verbs and adjectives, and use the terms appropriately.

Use a dictionary or electronic means to find the spelling and meaning of words.

Students practise replacing common words with others that mean the same or nearly the same thing. They do this by looking in a thesaurus and checking spelling and definitions in a dictionary. They continue to fill in the charts of NOUNS, VERBS and ADJECTIVES (*see* Unit 1, page 16).

Remember to display the child-friendly learning objectives to the class along with the child-friendly checklist that students can use to assess how well they achieve them.

We know that we have achieved these because:

▶ We can come up with synonyms for commonly-used words by using a thesaurus.

▶ We can see the difference in intensity or interest with the use of synonyms.

▶ We can check spelling and meaning of words in a dictionary.

② Student Book teaching notes and vocabulary exercise answers

On the board, write down the three pairs of words on page 62 of the Student Book, exactly as they appear in the book. Divide the class into two groups (left and right, or front rows and back rows). Ask one group to take the words on the left, and the other group the words on the right. Tell the students to look up their words in their thesaurus. Ask students what they noticed. (The words of the other column appear as synonyms.) Read aloud the explanation of a synonym on page 62 of the Student Book. (A synonym is a word that has the same meaning or nearly the same meaning as another word.) Ask students to add the six words that they just looked up to the appropriate NOUNS, ADJECTIVES and VERBS chart (*see* Unit 1, page 16).

Answers:

Ⓐ

1 truthful **2** instruct **3** error

If a wrong answer is given, encourage students to work out whether the word they chose belongs in

---

Synonyms

A synonym is a word that has the same meaning or nearly the same meaning as another word. Synonyms can be **nouns, adjectives** or **verbs**.

Examples:
noise, sound
laugh, giggle
big, large

Top Tip

If you want to find a synonym for a word, look in a **thesaurus**. You will also find other words with similar meanings. You can use the words to make your writing more interesting.

Ⓐ Copy the following words and choose the correct synonym from the words in brackets.

1 honest (trust, truthful, believe)
2 teach (instruct, lesson, tutor)
3 mistake (wrong, error, false)

Challenge

Look up the words 'good', 'bad', 'big' and 'little' in a thesaurus. For each word, find another word with a similar meaning. Write a sentence using each of the new words you find.

Ⓑ Rewrite the following sentences, replacing the words in bold with a synonym below.

assist angry overjoyed

1 Bawang thought her mother would be **cross**.
2 The frogs could not **help** Bawang.
3 Bawang was **happy** when her sarong turned to gold.

62

---

the same chart as the word in question. ***Example:*** 'honest' is an adjective. Is either 'trust' or 'believe' an adjective? Point out that this is a clue to the correct answer.

 Ⓑ

1 angry **2** assist **3** overjoyed

③ Top Tip

When students look up their words in the thesaurus, point out synonyms that are more dramatic, acting them out in an exaggerated way. ***Example:*** 'hoot' for 'laugh'.

④ Challenge

Students replace the words 'good', 'bad', 'big' and 'little' with a synonym and write them into a sentence. On completion, invite volunteers to read their sentences, once with the original word in place and once with the synonym they found. Ask the students to vote on which version they think is better.

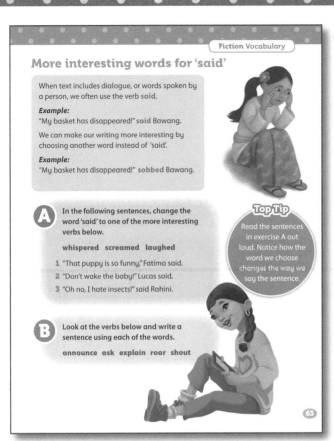

Fiction Vocabulary

More interesting words for 'said'

When text includes dialogue, or words spoken by a person, we often use the verb said.

Example:
"My basket has disappeared!" said Bawang.

We can make our writing more interesting by choosing another word instead of 'said'.

Example:
"My basket has disappeared!" sobbed Bawang.

A In the following sentences, change the word 'said' to one of the more interesting verbs below.

whispered screamed laughed

1 "That puppy is so funny," Fatima said.
2 "Don't wake the baby!" Lucas said.
3 "Oh no, I hate insects!" said Rahini.

Top Tip
Read the sentences in exercise A out loud. Notice how the word we choose changes the way we say the sentence.

B Look at the verbs below and write a sentence using each of the words.

announce ask explain roar shout

63

(6) Student Book teaching notes and vocabulary exercise answers

Focus on different ways that characters in the story say a statement. *Example:* on pages 56–57 of the Student Book, point out 'gasped', 'asked', 'replied', 'sobbed', 'croaked', and on page 60 of the Student Book, 'sang'. Invite students to think about the different feel that each of these words has. **Ask:** *Would the sentence have the same feel if the author had simply used 'said' instead of these different words? Which do you like better?*

Use the same pages to demonstrate that sometimes it isn't necessary to use the verb 'said' at all. Show them the instance on page 57 of the Student Book (lines 30–31), and then ask them to find another example of this on page 60 of the Student Book (lines 16–18).

Answers:

(A)

1 laughed **2** whispered **3** screamed

Act out the three sentences, dramatizing the verb that is used.

(B)

Accept any sentence that uses the verbs 'announce', 'ask', 'explain', 'roar' and 'shout' appropriately.

(7) Top Tip

Read the three sentences in exercise A out loud in a straightforward manner. Then act out the same three sentences as dramatically as you can, laughing as you read the first one, whispering the second sentence and screaming the third. Ask students which version they prefer, and why.

Learning objectives

(5)

Explore vocabulary for introducing and concluding dialogue, such as 'said', 'asked'.

Generate synonyms for high frequency words

Read aloud with expression to engage the listener.

Consider words that make an impact, such as adjectives and powerful verbs.

Students continue to examine different ways of writing dialogues in texts, by using synonyms for the verb 'said'. They discover that using more interesting forms of 'said' has the same impact as other powerful verbs and adjectives examined in earlier exercises.

Remember to display the child-friendly learning objectives to the class along with the child-friendly checklist that students can use to assess how well they achieve them.

We know that we have achieved these because:

▶ **We can read dramatically and see how different ways to end dialogues in a text have an effect on the listener or reader.**

▶ **We can use synonyms for the verb 'said' to make a text more powerful.**

▶ **We can point out powerful adjectives and words in the text.**

Learning objective

Learn the basic conventions of speech marks and begin to use them.

Students identify speech marks and start to use them. They also learn other conventions for laying out speech. (The use of capital letters for the first spoken word, and starting a new line when a new person speaks.)

 Remember to display the child-friendly learning objective to the class along with the child-friendly checklist that students can use to assess how well they achieve it.

We know that we have achieved this because:

▶ We can use speech marks before and after words are spoken in a text.

2 Student Book teaching notes and punctuation exercise answers

Write some speech marks on the board. Ask what they are, accepting all answers. (We use speech marks when people speak, etc.)

Ask students what the word 'punctuation' means. (Accept: full stops, commas, etc.)

Create a 'PUNCTUATION' chart. Write a definition for punctuation together on a large sheet of paper. 'Punctuation marks are signs that help to make the writer's meaning clear to the reader. They mark where sentences end and when pauses come.' Elicit examples of punctuation and write them down with their marks. Add definitions. ***Example:*** 'A full stop is used to show the end of a sentence.' and 'A comma shows a pause in a sentence or separates items in a list in a sentence.' Keep the PUNCTUATION chart on display and add to it as students learn more about its use.

Refer students to the speech marks on the board, and ask them to look back at the story on pages 56–57 of the Student Book and find where speech marks have been used. Identify together who was speaking. (In order: Bawang, Bawang, fish, Bawang, frogs, Bawang and crabs.)

Ⓐ

Copy the sentences onto the board and invite students to add speech marks. The rest of the class confirms if they are right or wrong.

⇨

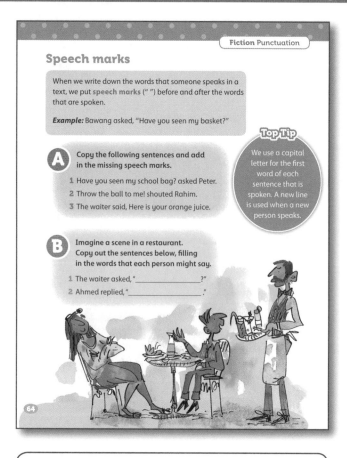

Fiction Punctuation

Speech marks

When we write down the words that someone speaks in a text, we put **speech marks** (" ") before and after the words that are spoken.

Example: Bawang asked, "Have you seen my basket?"

Top Tip

We use a capital letter for the first word of each sentence that is spoken. A new line is used when a new person speaks.

Ⓐ Copy the following sentences and add in the missing speech marks.

1 Have you seen my school bag? asked Peter.
2 Throw the ball to me! shouted Rahim.
3 The waiter said, Here is your orange juice.

Ⓑ Imagine a scene in a restaurant. Copy out the sentences below, filling in the words that each person might say.

1 The waiter asked, "_____?"
2 Ahmed replied, "_____."

64

Answers:

1 "Have you seen my schoolbag?" asked Peter.
2 "Throw the ball to me!" shouted Rahim.
3 The waiter said, "Here is your orange juice."

Ⓑ

Refer students to the picture of the restaurant. Discuss the conversation between the waiter and Ahmed, and fill in the words. ***Example:***

1 The waiter asked, "What can I get you?"
2 Ahmed replied, "A glass of orange juice, please."

You can also add what the girl might say.

Example: "Can I have a glass of water, please?" Write the conversation on the board, giving the girl a name chosen by the class. Point out the other punctuation marks in the sentences and ask for their uses, referring students to the PUNCTUATION chart.

3 Top Tip

Read the Top Tip together, and ask students to check if a new line was used every time a new character speaks in the extracts from Bawang's tale, pages 56–57 and 60 of the Student Book. See if they have done this in their own writing, too.

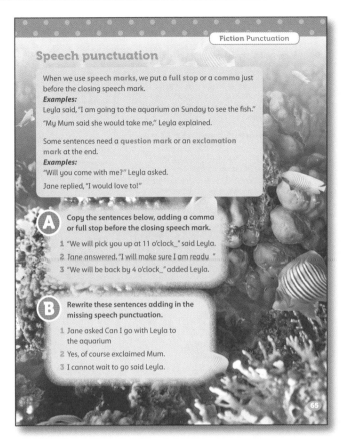

Fiction Punctuation

Speech punctuation

When we use **speech marks**, we put a **full stop** or a **comma** just before the closing speech mark.
Examples:
Leyla said, "I am going to the aquarium on Sunday to see the fish."
"My Mum said she would take me," Leyla explained.

Some sentences need a **question mark** or an **exclamation mark** at the end.
Examples:
"Will you come with me?" Leyla asked.
Jane replied, "I would love to!"

A Copy the sentences below, adding a comma or full stop before the closing speech mark.

1 "We will pick you up at 11 o'clock_" said Leyla.
2 Jane answered, "I will make sure I am ready_"
3 "We will be back by 4 o'clock_" added Leyla.

B Rewrite these sentences adding in the missing speech punctuation.

1 Jane asked Can I go with Leyla to the aquarium
2 Yes, of course exclaimed Mum.
3 I cannot wait to go said Leyla.

Learning objective

4

Use question marks, exclamation marks and commas.

Students investigate how punctuation, capitalization and interesting words make writing clear and appealing to the reader.

Remember to display the child-friendly learning objective to the class along with the child-friendly checklist that students can use to assess how well they achieve it.

We know that we have achieved this because:

▶ **We can use speech marks to show that people are talking.**

▶ **We put a comma or full stop before the closing speech mark.**

▶ **We can use capital letters, question marks and exclamation marks.**

▶ **We check our writing for punctuation.**

5 Student Book teaching notes and punctuation exercise answers

Discuss the punctuation of other languages. **Ask:** *Do you think punctuation exists in all languages?* (Yes, it exists in all written forms of language.) *Does it look the* ⟶

same in all languages? (No, speech marks may be written differently, as in Spanish and Japanese.) *Do your home languages have different speech marks?* If students aren't sure, they should ask their parents, or other home members or speakers of their home languages, and report back.

Refer students to the PUNCTUATION chart. Add definitions for a question mark (a question mark is used when we ask a question), and an exclamation mark (an exclamation mark is used at the end of a sentence to show emotion or surprise, or after a sentence that gives a strong or urgent command). Elicit examples and write them on the board.

Review the use of speech marks by reading the blue box text together. Write a sentence on the board without punctuation. ***Example:*** 'Where do you live' Together turn the sentence into direct speech. Add speaker, then speech marks, then other punctuation using different colours. ("Where do you live?" said Paolo.) Go through the same process with an exclamation mark, comma and full stop.

Ask students to copy the sentences in A, adding a comma or full stop before the closing speech mark.

Answers:

1 "We will pick you up at 11 o'clock," said Leyla.
2 Jane answered, "I will make sure I am ready."
3 "We will be back by 4 o'clock," added Leyla.

Correct together on the board.

Students work in pairs to complete exercise B.

Answers:

1 Jane asked, "Can I go with Leyla to the aquarium?"
2 "Yes, of course!" exclaimed Mum.
3 "I cannot wait to go," said Leyla.

Students check their answers with another pair, taking it in turns to explain their choice of punctuation.

6 Extension

Give students postcards with people in them. (If postcards are unavailable, use any images of two or more people, such as magazine advertisements, etc.) Ask students in pairs to write a dialogue between the people, using appropriate speech marks. Students share their dialogues with other students who say whether or not they have used punctuation correctly.

Learning objectives

①

Identify different types of stories and typical story themes.

Read a range of story books and begin to make links between them.

Students read a modernized version of the beginning of *Goldilocks and the Three Bears*, a traditional tale. They identify the main features of traditional tales and understand in what ways they are similar to and different from other story-telling genres.

Remember to display the child-friendly learning objectives to the class along with the child-friendly checklist that students can use to assess how well they achieve them.

We know that we have achieved these because:

▸ **We can tell the difference between different kinds of writing, such as stories in familiar settings, poetry, play scripts and traditional tales.**

Rewriting a traditional tale
Model writing

Traditional stories are often stories written a long time ago. Read through this modernized beginning to the traditional tale 'Goldilocks and the Three Bears.'

Glossary

bundled out
went quickly together

get a move on
hurry

hectic
busy

Goldilocks and the Three Bears

It was the usual hectic Monday morning for the Bear family at number 5 Foxhole Avenue.

"Dad, I can't find my school bag!" shrieked John Bear. John was 5 years old and had just started at the local school. He was a rather forgetful young bear.

"It's by the television, where you left it last night," Dad shouted back, while trying to put on his coat. "Come on, Mum and I are going to be late for work if you don't get a move on. We don't even have enough time to eat our porridge!"

With that, they all bundled out of the house, into the car and sped off – forgetting to lock the door behind them…

66

---

② Writing workshop teaching notes

Traditional tales are a type of narrative genre, along with adventure, fantasy, horror, epic, science fiction and romance. Their structure follows this order:

1 Introduction to the setting, situation and characters.
2 One or more problems emerge as events unfold.
3 A solution emerges (although a major problem can remain unresolved until the end of the story).
4 A message may come from the story (a moral or word of wisdom).

Refer to the multilingual BEGINNINGS AND ENDINGS poster prepared in the Unit 4 warm up (*see page 64*).
Ask: *What other features do traditional tales have in common?* Ask them to think about *Aladdin*, *The Gingerbread Man*, *Goldilocks and The Three Bears* or any other well-known traditional tale. Show copies if available.

Ask: *Can you remember any phrases from these stories?* ("Run, run as fast as you can; you can't catch me I'm the Gingerbread Man…", etc.) Write suggestions on the board. Point out that traditional tales often include repetition of phrases.

⇨

Ask students what the problem is in each of the stories and how it is resolved. Write 'Problem' and 'Solution' on the board, and collect ideas. ***Example:*** **problem:** no-one can catch the gingerbread man; **solution:** the fox tricks the gingerbread man and finally catches him. Elicit how students say 'problem' and 'solution' in their home languages.

Ask: *Are there any lessons to be learnt from the stories?* (Don't talk to strangers; don't touch things that don't belong to you, etc.) Point out that traditional tales always have a problem that is solved and that they often teach a lesson.

Tell students they are going to read the beginning of a modernized version of *Goldilocks and the Three Bears*. Read the extract, stopping to work out difficult words. Challenge students to find 'bundled out', 'get a move on' and 'hectic' from the Glossary. Give the meaning of 'shrieked' (cry loudly), local (nearby), porridge (a hot cereal made from oats).

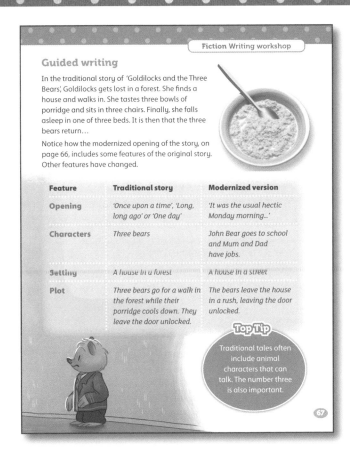

Guided writing

In the traditional story of 'Goldilocks and the Three Bears', Goldilocks gets lost in a forest. She finds a house and walks in. She tastes three bowls of porridge and sits in three chairs. Finally, she falls asleep in one of three beds. It is then that the three bears return…

Notice how the modernized opening of the story, on page 66, includes some features of the original story. Other features have changed.

Feature	Traditional story	Modernized version
Opening	'Once upon a time', 'Long, long ago' or 'One day'	'It was the usual hectic Monday morning…'
Characters	Three bears	John Bear goes to school and Mum and Dad have jobs.
Setting	A house in a forest	A house in a street
Plot	Three bears go for a walk in the forest while their porridge cools down. They leave the door unlocked.	The bears leave the house in a rush, leaving the door unlocked.

Top Tip

Traditional tales often include animal characters that can talk. The number three is also important.

67

③ Writing workshop teaching notes

Model writing

Divide the class into two: Group 1 to act out the beginning of the traditional tale *Goldilocks and the Three Bears*, Group 2 to act out the modernized version on page 66 of the Student Book. If the traditional tale of *Goldilocks and the Three Bears* is unfamiliar, you can use the opening of any traditional tale as comparison, as this is only a warm-up activity.

Ask Group 1 to consider the traditional beginning and come up with ideas. Write these on the board. (Beautiful morning in the woods, Mummy Bear makes porridge and suggests they go for a walk while it cools.) Students form groups of three to play Mummy, Daddy and Baby Bear. Ask them to think what the bears might say, and act out the conversation.

⇨

Divide Group 2 into groups of three, and ask the students to read the extract as Narrator, Dad and John Bear. Discuss how the Glossary can help them. (Understanding the hurried mood.) Tell them to emphasize the new words in the Glossary, showing the busy lifestyle of the bears in the modern version.

Encourage all students to change their voices and act. Ask for volunteers from each group to act out the beginning of their *Goldilocks and the Three Bears*. Talk about the contrast: the relaxed pace of the traditional, compared to the mad rush in the modern version; a walk in the woods versus school and work, etc.

Check vocabulary by asking individual students to explain the terms in the Glossary.

Guided writing

Refer students to the Guided writing introduction and read it aloud. Direct them to the chart of features. Ask students for the meanings of the features: opening (beginning words), characters (people in a play or a story), setting (place where story or play takes place), plot (what happens in a play or story). Instruct students to fold their notebook page in three to make columns, and copy the chart on page 67 of the Student Book into it.

④ Top Tip

Read through the Top Tip with students. **Ask:** *Can you name any tales that have animals that can talk, or where the number three is important?*

① Learning objectives

Plan main points as a structure for story writing.

Begin to organize writing in sections or paragraphs in extended stories.

Use reading as a model for writing dialogue.

Adapt tone of voice, use of vocabulary and non-verbal features for different audiences.

Students plan a modern version of a traditional tale based on their own reading. The story must be suitable for sharing with younger children. They choose their own tale or continue with the modernized *Goldilocks and the Three Bears*, used to illustrate the planning process. They learn to organize their writing into paragraphs.

Remember to display the child-friendly learning objectives to the class along with the child-friendly checklist that students can use to assess how well they achieve them.

We know that we have achieved these because:

▶ We can identify the main features of a traditional tale.

▶ We start a new paragraph when there is a change of time, place, character or action.

▶ We can use our reading to help us be better writers.

② Writing workshop teaching notes

Your writing

Ask students to bring in traditional tales from their home countries. They should practise reading the beginning in their home languages at home (*see* Guidelines re parental involvement, page 189). Display the books.

Invite a few students to share their traditional tales and give the gist in English. Tell students they are going to write their own modern version of a traditional tale, either their own or continuing the modernized *Goldilocks*. Emphasize that they are going to be sharing their stories with younger children.

Refer students to the illustration. **Ask:** *What part of the Goldilocks story is this?* (The bears are home and notice the porridge has been eaten.) In pairs, students decide where Goldilocks is and what happens next.
⇨

Fiction Writing workshop

Rewriting a traditional tale
Your writing

Write your own updated version of a traditional tale. You can either choose your own tale to update, or continue with the modernized version of the 'Goldilocks and the Three Bears' story. Whichever you choose, start by making a plan.

1 List some of the typical features of traditional stories that you plan to include.
   Example: talking animals and things that happen in threes.

2 List some modern features that you plan to include.
   Example: John Bear goes to school.

3 Make your story four to five paragraphs long. Write a sentence saying what will happen in each paragraph.
   Example: The bears return home and see that John Bear's porridge has been eaten.

4 Include some speech or dialogue.
   Example: "We don't even have enough time to eat our porridge!"

Top Tip
Remember to start a new paragraph when there is a change of time, place, character or action.

68

Elicit the features of traditional tales orally. (Talking animals, the number three, repetition of phrases, a problem, a solution, a lesson to be learnt.) Read through the plan, stopping at each point to elicit further examples. Give each student a sheet of paper folded in four. Ask students to copy point 1 in the first box, point 2 in the second, etc. If students plan to use their own tale, remind them to fill the plan in with features from it.

Establish a place where students can come to you for help. Put up a 'Do Not Disturb' sign. Tell students everyone will get a turn. Make sure you see each student.

Allow an extended period of time for independent writing.

③ Top Tip

Read the Top Tip aloud together. Refer students to the extract on page 66 of the Student Book, and discuss why the author started each new paragraph. (Paragraph 1 – introduction of place; paragraph 2 – John Bear is a new character; paragraph 3 – Dad is a new character; paragraph 4 – change of action.) Write the Top Tip on the board.

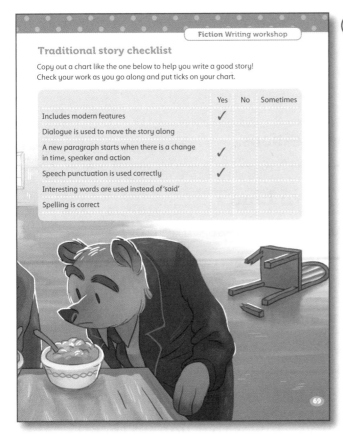

Traditional story checklist

Copy out a chart like the one below to help you write a good story!
Check your work as you go along and put ticks on your chart.

	Yes	No	Sometimes
Includes modern features	✓		
Dialogue is used to move the story along			
A new paragraph starts when there is a change in time, speaker and action	✓		
Speech punctuation is used correctly	✓		
Interesting words are used instead of 'said'			
Spelling is correct			

69

④ Learning objectives

Identify misspelt words in own writing and keep individual spelling logs.

Learn the basic conventions of speech punctuation and begin to use speech marks.

Explore vocabulary for introducing and concluding dialogue, such as 'said', 'asked'.

Students continue to work on their version of a traditional tale, using the features outlined when studying the modernized extract of *Goldilocks and the Three Bears*. They begin to self-correct errors in punctuation and spelling.

Remember to display the child-friendly learning objectives to the class along with the child-friendly checklist that students can use to assess how well they achieve them.

We know that we have achieved these because:

▶ **We can use a checklist to improve our writing.**

▶ **We can identify words we are not sure how to spell.**

▶ **We know how to find the correct spelling and record it in our spelling log.**

⑤ Writing workshop teaching notes

Traditional story checklist

At the beginning of the lesson, invite some more students to share the book they brought in, reading in their home languages and then giving the gist of how the story starts in English.

Direct students' attention to the checklist. Read through each point.

Use a large sheet of paper to prepare a chart headed: 'Instead of 'said'…' Brainstorm with students words they can use instead of 'said' and write them on the chart. Suggest that they look back at their reading to find words. Ask students to copy the chart on paper and refer to it as they write their stories.

Encourage students to underline words they think they may have misspelt, and then check them using a dictionary.

When they have finished writing, and feel they have ticked all the places they can on the chart, ask them to work with a partner to see if they agree. Confer with each student, helping them to add words to their spelling log and pointing out errors of punctuation.

Ask students to share their final copy with peers/ other classes and parents/home members.

⑥ Extension

1 Ask the students to turn their writing into a book. Each page should have a space for a picture and lines. Help them divide their writing up (illustration and paragraph). Show students some books with clear illustrations and explain how important illustrations are to a story. They can then make a cover for the book where they write the title: 'A modern version of… By …' The finished tales can be shared and displayed in the school library.

2 Ask students to write an 'About the author' page. This could be done in their home languages and glued into the cover.

End of Unit Test

Question Paper

Reading: fiction

Read the following story and answer the questions.

The Upside-down Lion

One fine day the Warthogs were walking amongst some trees.

"Remember," said Mr Warthog, "this is a dangerous place. Always stick to the paths and never go off exploring things that don't concern you."

Scarcely were the words out of his mouth when a terrible noise filled
5 the forest.

"Baby Warthog, I've warned you before," said Mrs Warthog. "Say 'pardon' when you burp!"

"That wasn't me," said Baby Warthog. "It was that lion up there!"

Sure enough, a lion was hanging upside down from the tree above
10 them. He had been caught in a trap.

"Please," said Lion, "let me down. I've been up here for three days..."

"How silly do you think we are?" asked Mr Warthog. "If we let you down, you'll eat us!"

"I promise I won't!" pleaded Lion. "I'm so weak from lack of food,
15 I'm as harmless as a kitten."

So the Warthogs undid the trap and set Lion free.

"Thank you so much," said Lion. "Dear Mr Warthog, sweet Mrs Warthog and lovely, delicious, good-enough-to-eat Baby Warthog, I am so grateful, I could just gobble you up!"

20 Mrs Warthog didn't like the sound of that...So, very quickly, she said, "How on earth did you get caught in this trap?"

From *Treetops Fables from Africa* by Timothy Knapman

Glossary

burp make a noise by letting air come up from your stomach.

exploring looking for new things in new places.

gobble eat very quickly.

> **lack** not having something.
> **trap** a device for catching and holding animals.

Comprehension

A **Give evidence from the extract to support your answers.**

1 What was the weather like when the Warthogs saw the lion?

_____ [1]

2 Where was the lion when the Warthog family first saw him?

_____ [1]

3 What did Mr Warthog think the lion would do if they let him down?

_____ [1]

B **Give evidence from the extract to support your answers.**

1 Which member of the Warthog family saw the lion first?

_____ [1]

2 How many days had it been since the lion had last eaten?

_____ [1]

3 Give an example of one powerful adjective and one powerful verb used in the extract.

_____ [2]

C **Give evidence from the extract to support your answers.**

1 Which do you think are the three main events in this story?

_____
_____ [3]

2 Why do you think the lion said he was 'as harmless as a kitten'?

_____ [1]

3 Why do you think Mrs Warthog asked the lion how he got caught in the trap?

_____ [1]

Writing: fiction

Read the extract below where the lion explains how he was caught in the trap. Notice how the writer uses a new paragraph when there is a change of time, place, speaker and action. Notice also the other features listed on the notepad on page 83.

The Upside-down Lion

"I was just wandering along, minding my own business," said Lion, "when I put my paw here," and Lion put his paw back into the trap to show them. "Then the rope went tight, and the next thing I knew I was hanging upside down from that tree."

5   "Like this?" asked Mrs Warthog, as she pulled hard so that the rope went tight and Lion was once again hanging upside down from the tree.

"What did you do that for?" said Lion.

"My family and I set you free," said Mrs Warthog, "and you were going to thank us by eating Baby Warthog here! What an ungrateful
10   scoundrel you are."

The Warthogs turned their backs and walked away with their noses in the air.

Lion hung upside down like that for another three days until Grass Mouse came by.

15   "Excuse me," said Lion, who was now so weak from lack of food that his voice was just a whisper. "Would you please be kind enough to help me down? I promise I won't hurt you."

Grass Mouse's mother had told him to steer clear of lions, but she had also said that he should always help fellow creatures in trouble.

20   "All right then," said Grass Mouse. He scampered up the tree and with his sharp front teeth he gnawed through the rope that was holding Lion.

"Thank you so much," said Lion when he was back on solid ground.

Lion wasn't going to make the same mistake twice, so instead of
25   thinking about eating Grass Mouse, he promised to help him whenever he was in trouble.

From *Treetops Fables from Africa* by Timothy Knapman

Glossary

gnawed kept biting something hard.

minding my own business not being interested in what other people are doing.

scampered ran quickly with short steps.

steer clear of stay away from.

ungrateful not thankful that someone has done something for you.

wandering walking around without trying to reach a particular place.

Write your own modern version of 'The Upside-down Lion' story.

Please use a separate sheet of paper.

Organize your story in four or five paragraphs. Use a new paragraph when there is a change of place, time, action or speaker.

Before you start, make a paragraph plan. Write a sentence saying what will happen in each paragraph. Remember to include some modern features as well as the following features:

Setting

Where is your story set? Describe the place, including details of noises and smells.

Characters

Include details that tell the reader about the characters' personalities and what they look like.

Dialogue

Use speech or dialogue to help the story move along.

Typical features of traditional tales

Include features such as animals that can talk and things that happen in threes.

[20]

Keep in touch!

① Warm-up objectives

Speak clearly and confidently in a range of contexts.

Take it in turns in discussion, building on what others have said.

Listen and respond appropriately to others' views and opinions.

Students talk about letter writing and emailing. They look at an old Chinese proverb that warns against writing a letter when angry, and discuss why this is true. Words associated with communication are explored, along with reasons for writing letters.

Remember to display the child-friendly learning objectives to the class along with the child-friendly checklist that students can use to assess how well they achieve them.

We know that we have achieved these because:

▷ We can listen to our classmates and ask questions about letter writing.

▷ We are able to talk about letters we have seen or received.

Non-fiction Speaking and listening

5 Keep in touch!

"Never write a letter while you are angry."
Old Chinese proverb

Let's Talk

1 Look at this picture. What do you think is happening? Why do you think this boy looks happy?

2 Have you ever written a letter or an email? Why did you write it?

70

② Unit warm up

Bring an email, a letter, an envelope and a stamp to class, and have the old Chinese proverb displayed on the board. Show the objects and ask students to name them, writing the words on the board.

Tell them that emailing and writing letters are ways of 'communication'. Write this on the board. **Ask:** *How do we send an email?* (By computer.) *How do we send a letter?* (In the post.) Elicit the things we need to do to send a letter. (Put it in an envelope, write the address and stamp the envelope.) Ask students for these words in their home languages.

Direct attention to the Chinese proverb: "Never write a letter while you are angry." Have this displayed in Chinese script.

永远不要在你生气时写信

If you have Chinese students, invite them to read the script first. Read the proverb together in English and ask students what they think it means. Write on the board: 'It is not a good idea to write letters while you are angry because…' Add the students' ideas. (You may say things you don't really mean, etc.)

③ Let's Talk

Refer students to the photo and discuss question 1 as a class. **Ask:** *What is the boy doing?* (Reading a letter, smiling, thinking.) *Who do you think the letter is from?* (Grandparents, friend, etc.) *How does it make him feel? How do you know?* (Happy, he is smiling.) Focus on the word 'communication' on the board. **Ask:** *What other words are similar to this word?* Write the words and definitions:

communication a way of passing news and messages to others.

community people living together or working together.

communicate to give news.

Elicit how students say these words in their home languages. Ask them to suggest other ways of communication. (Phone, radio, TV, etc.)

Ask students to answer question 2 in pairs. Brainstorm reasons for writing letters. (To say hello, thank you, sorry, etc.)

Using words

Non-fiction Speaking, listening and vocabulary

A Look at the words in the Word Cloud and match them to the meanings here.

1 A place where you buy stamps or post a letter.
2 Letters and other mail items that are sent in a plane.
3 The details of where someone lives.

Word Cloud
address
air mail
post office

B Copy the sentences below. Use the correct words to fill the gaps.

stamp envelope handwriting pen

It is fun to get a letter in the post.
I open the _____ and tear off the
_____ . I keep it for my collection.
My grandmother always uses ____ and
ink when she writes to me. Sometimes it
is hard to read her _____ !

C Do you like emails or letters best? Work with a partner and talk about what is the same and what is different about sending a letter and an email.

71

④ Learning objectives

Infer the meaning of unknown words from the context.

Develop sensitivity to ways that others express meaning in their talk.

Students work in pairs to guess the meaning of new vocabulary to do with sending letters. They explore the similarities and differences between emails and letters using a T chart (*see* Guidelines, page 193), and decide which method of communication they prefer.

Remember to display the child-friendly learning objectives to the class along with the child-friendly checklist that students can use to assess how well they achieve them.

We know that we have achieved these because:

▶ We can use the context to learn new words about sending letters.

▶ We can work well in small groups and pairs.

⑤ Word Cloud definitions

address the details of the place where someone lives.
air mail post carried by aircraft.
post office a place where you can send letters, buy stamps, etc.

⑥ Student Book teaching notes and exercise answers

If possible, bring in used, addressed envelopes, preferably with foreign stamps, or a collection of foreign stamps. You could also ask students to bring in envelopes with stamps from their home countries.

Lead a discussion on how addresses are written on envelopes. **Ask:** *Where does the house number go?* (Either before the road name as in English, or afterwards as in Italian and Spanish.)

Ask students to compare stamps in small groups, or refer to what they can see in the picture on page 70 of the Student Book. **Ask:** *Do you know anyone who collects stamps? Do you collect anything?* (Stickers, cards, etc.) Write 'collect' and 'collection' on the board, and elicit the words for these in home languages. Point out the verb (collect) and noun (collection).

Read the Word Cloud words, and ask students to repeat them. Point out the double 'd' and double 's' in 'address', and the spacing in 'post office' and 'air mail'. Ask students to identify the word type. (Noun.) Tell students to work in pairs for exercise A. Explain that 'details' in sentence 3 means 'all the information'.

Answers:

1 post office **2** air mail **3** address

Focus attention on the boy in the picture. **Ask:** *What is he doing?* (Sending a post card.) *When do we send postcards?* (When visiting somewhere new; on holiday, etc.) *Where is he putting the post card?* (In a post box.) Ask students if they have post boxes in their home countries, and to describe what they look like.

Students work individually on the exercise. Correct orally.

Answers:

1 envelope **2** stamp **3** pen **4** handwriting

Students make a T chart (*see* Guidelines, page 193) about emails and letters. In pairs, they discuss what is the same and what is different about sending emails and letters, and fill in the chart. They then decide which they like best.

Learning objectives

1

Read a range of story, poetry and information books and begin to make links between them.

Infer the meaning of unknown words from the context.

Students read a letter sent to an author by two young girls, asking questions about her previous and next books. They then explore the content of the author's response. They learn how letters are different to both stories and poetry.

Remember to display the child-friendly learning objectives to the class along with the child-friendly checklist that students can use to assess how well they achieve them.

We know that we have achieved these because:

▶ We can correctly identify texts as non-fiction.

▶ We use all the clues available to us to understand unfamiliar words.

Non-fiction Reading

Letters

The letters on this page and page 73 come from a book about a girl whose full name is Clarice Bean Tuesday. In the story, Clarice and her friend Betty write to the author of their favourite books.

Letter to Patricia Maplin Stacey

Dear Patricia F Maplin Stacey,

We are avidish readers of the Ruby Redfort series and we have read all of them at least once. What we would like to know is when is the next Ruby Redfort book coming out and what will it be called?

Also, on page a hundred and 6, chapter eight of Run for it Ruby why did the arch villain Hogtrotter not double-check that he had locked the cellar door?

And also, on page 33 you said Ruby was wearing her glasses and then later on you say she couldn't see well because she didn't have her reading glasses.

Eagerly awaiting your reply.

Betty P Moody and Clarice Bean Tuesday.

P.S. We think you should write a bit faster.

From Utterly Me, Clarice Bean *by Lauren Child*

72

> **Glossary**
>
> **arch villain**
> a bad person or chief criminal
>
> **avidish**
> quite keen
> (-ish = quite)
>
> **double-check**
> check twice
>
> **fan club**
> a club for people who admire the same person, like an author or a pop star

---

2 Non-fiction reading notes

If possible, bring a letter you have received, preferably in its envelope. Tell students that one of your favourite things is getting letters back. **Ask:** *To whom do people write letters?* (Family, friends, newspapers, etc.)

Explain that some people write to authors whose books they like. Tell students they are going to read a letter from Clarice and Betty to their favourite author. In it, they have some urgent questions. **Say:** *Let's see what they write.*

Read the letter, stopping at words that are unfamiliar to students. Refer them to the four-factor clues chart developed in Unit 1 (*see* page 10), to help them guess meanings. See the Glossary for 'arch villain', 'avidish', 'double-check' and 'fan club'. Point out the use of the suffix *–ish* to mean 'quite'. Elicit other examples. ***Example:*** 'sweetish' (quite sweet), 'greenish' (quite green), etc. You can also refer to the e-book and the audio on the CD-ROM.

Point out the four sections of Betty and Clarice's letter, and jot them down on the board:

1 Addressing the person.
2 The content of the letter.
3 Signing off.
4 The post script (P.S.).

Explain that P.S. is used when adding something to a letter after signing it. ('post' refers to 'after', 'script' to 'writing'.) Keep this information on the board for later use.

Tell students they are going to write a letter to their parents, or someone else who looks after them at home. Ask students to copy what you write and give the letter to their parents (*see* Guidelines, page 189). Write on the board, verbalizing the words. Use a different colour to highlight where to add names.

'Dear Parents,

We are studying letter writing, and I would like to know if you write letters on a regular basis and to whom. Please give this information to (Your name.) to bring to school tomorrow.

Thank you,

(Teacher's name.)

P.S. If you would like (Your name.) to show us a letter that you have received, we would love to see it, especially if it's in a language other than English.'

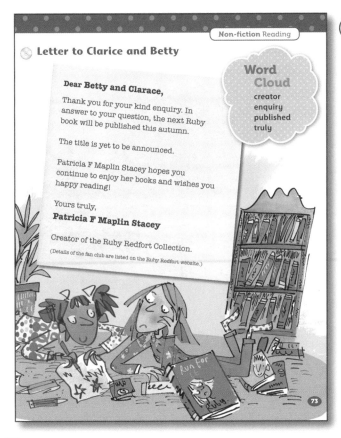

Letter to Clarice and Betty

Dear Betty and Clarace,

Thank you for your kind enquiry. In answer to your question, the next Ruby book will be published this autumn.

The title is yet to be announced.

Patricia F Maplin Stacey hopes you continue to enjoy her books and wishes you happy reading!

Yours truly,
Patricia F Maplin Stacey

Creator of the Ruby Redfort Collection.
(Details of the fan club are listed on the Ruby Redfort website.)

Word Cloud
creator
enquiry
published
truly

73

3 Learning objectives

Identify the main points or gist of a text.

Consider ways that information is set out on a page.

Students discuss their own ideas for the author's response to Betty and Clarice's letters, and create a letter following the four-section guide on page 86. They then compare this to the author's actual response.

Remember to display the child-friendly learning objectives to the class along with the child-friendly checklist that students can use to assess how well they achieve them.

We know that we have achieved these because:

▶ We are able to plan a letter.

▶ We are able to identify the main purpose of a letter.

4 Non-fiction reading notes

Before students look at the response to Betty and Clarice's letter, ask them to jot down what they would say if they were Patricia F Maplin Stacey. Direct students' attention to the four sections of a letter discussed earlier, rewriting them on the board if necessary. Tell students to use these as guides for their ideas. Students at a more advanced proficiency level could write an actual letter.

Next, read the response in the book, stopping at unfamiliar words and asking students to use their four-factor clues chart (see Unit 1, page 10) to work out their meanings. You can also look at the e-book and listen to the audio on the CD-ROM.

Ask students to compare the response to Betty and Clarice in the Student Book with their own ideas for the author's response. Draw out responses from students about similarities and differences. Ask them if the author's letter follows the same organization as the girls'. **Ask:** *Why did the author write 'Creator of the Ruby Redfort Collection' under her name?* (People sometimes write their title or what defines them after their signature.) *Why did she put the sentence about the website?* (To have more children look at it; to let people know about her fan club; to save her from having to write letters in future, etc.)

5 Word Cloud definitions

Ask students to use the four-factor clues chart developed in Unit 1 (see page 10), to guess the meaning of these words. You can also refer to the audio on the CD-ROM. Remind students to add new words to their New Word List (see Guidelines, page 192, and Workbook) in English and their home languages.

creator a person who makes something new.
enquiry a request for information.
publish produce a book for sale.
truly truthfully; with sincerity.

Learning objectives

Scan a passage to find specific information and answer questions.

Identify the main purpose of a text.

Answer questions with some reference to single points in the text.

Identify the main points or gist of a text.

Students examine the letters between Betty and Clarice and Patricia F Maplin Stacey, the author of their favourite books. They look for the meaning of specific details as well as the general idea in each of the letters.

 Remember to display the child-friendly learning objectives to the class along with the child-friendly checklist that students can use to assess how well they achieve them.

We know that we have achieved these because:

▶ **We can correctly identify specific information in the two letters.**

▶ **We can say what the letters are about in general.**

② Student Book teaching notes and comprehension answers

Ⓐ

Answers:

1 Hogtrotter.
Ask students how they worked out their answer? Direct attention to the four-factor clues chart developed in Unit 1 (*see* page 10): illustrations, context, structure of English, and structure of their home languages. Go through each one, modelling the process that they would use to guess at the answer.

2 Dear.
Tell students that this is a common way to address someone when writing to them. If you have a letter addressed to you in English to hand, show students that it begins with 'Dear'. **Ask:** *What does 'dear' mean here?* (Valued, loved.) Ask students why they think this is the way to address a person when writing to them. **Ask:** *Do the girls know Patricia Stacey in person? Do they love her? Is this a*
⇨

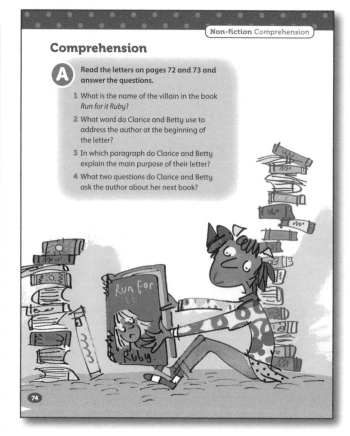

Comprehension

Ⓐ Read the letters on pages 72 and 73 and answer the questions.

1 What is the name of the villain in the book *Run for it Ruby*?

2 What word do Clarice and Betty use to address the author at the beginning of the letter?

3 In which paragraph do Clarice and Betty explain the main purpose of their letter?

4 What two questions do Clarice and Betty ask the author about her next book?

common way of addressing the recipient of letters in other languages? If you have a letter in a language other than English, show them how it addresses you. If students have brought in the letters from home requested earlier, ask them to do the same.

3 First paragraph.
The main purpose of the letter is to find out two things about Patricia F Maplin Stacey's next book. But remember, the girls also want the author to explain why she did two things in her last book.

4 When it is coming out and what it is going to be called.

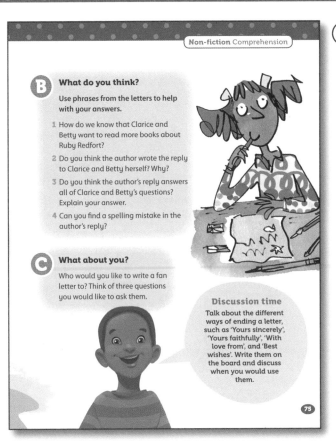

Non-fiction Comprehension

B **What do you think?**

Use phrases from the letters to help with your answers.

1 How do we know that Clarice and Betty want to read more books about Ruby Redfort?

2 Do you think the author wrote the reply to Clarice and Betty herself? Why?

3 Do you think the author's reply answers all of Clarice and Betty's questions? Explain your answer.

4 Can you find a spelling mistake in the author's reply?

C **What about you?**

Who would you like to write a fan letter to? Think of three questions you would like to ask them.

Discussion time

Talk about the different ways of ending a letter, such as 'Yours sincerely', 'Yours faithfully', 'With love from', and 'Best wishes'. Write them on the board and discuss when you would use them.

75

Learning objectives

3

Begin to infer meanings beyond the literal, for example about motives and character.

Take turns in discussion, building on what others have said.

Listen and respond appropriately to others' views and opinions.

Students begin to form an idea of Betty's and Clarice's characters. They participate in discussions about the questions asked in an appropriate way, listening to others and respecting others' opinions.

Remember to display the child-friendly learning objectives to the class along with the child-friendly checklist that students can use to assess how well they achieve them.

We know that we have achieved these because:

▶ We can form an image of who these two young girls are.

▶ We can talk to one another in an appropriate way and discuss our opinions without hurting anyone's feelings.

4 **Student Book teaching notes and comprehension answers**

B

Answers:

1 We know they want to read more Ruby Redfort books because they say they are 'avidish readers' and have read all the author's books at least once. They want to know when the next book is coming out and what it is called. They are aware of details in the last book they read. **Ask:** *How do you know all this?* (By guessing at things that are not written explicitly, and by forming an image of the two girls.)

2 No.
Ask: *How do you know the author didn't write the letter?* (Whoever wrote the response refers to the author in the third person.) *Who do you think wrote the response?* Explain that many authors and other famous people get so many letters from fans that they have people who help them answer letters.

3 No. She didn't answer their questions about the details in the last book.

4 Clarice's name is misspelt. **Ask:** *Has your name ever been misspelt? How did it make you feel? Why do they think that Clarice's name was misspelt?* (Pronunciation; confusion between Clarice and Clarace, a boy's name.)

C

Read the questions about writing a fan letter to the class, and ask individuals to offer their responses. Ask students to write a brief letter to that person, following the four-stage model for writing letters (*see* page 86).

5 **Discussion time**

Discuss different ways of ending a letter in English. Write examples on the board and discuss when to use them. ***Example:*** 'Yours sincerely' (for formal letters addressed to a known person, such as 'Dear Mrs Nayar'); 'Yours faithfully' (for formal letters addressed to an unknown person, such as 'Dear Sir'); 'With love from' (for letters to family and close friends); 'Best wishes' and 'Kind regards' (for less formal letters to people you know), etc.

Extend the discussion by looking at ways of ending letters in home languages. Look at any letters brought in. Add them to the board in the home languages and in translation to English.

Learning objectives

(1) **Read a range of information texts and begin to make links between them.**

Infer the meaning of unknown words from the context.

Make a record of information drawn from a text.

Students examine another type of letter written by the author Roald Dahl to his mother while he was at boarding school. They compare it to Betty and Clarice's letter to their favourite author, and record differences and similarities using a Venn diagram (*see* Guidelines, page 193). Students continue to use clues to guess the meaning of unfamiliar words.

Remember to display the child-friendly learning objectives to the class along with the child-friendly checklist that students can use to assess how well they achieve them.

We know that we have achieved these because:

▶ We can see differences and similarities between two letters, one from a boy to his mother and Betty and Clarice's letter to their favourite author.

▶ We can guess the meanings of unfamiliar words by using illustrations, context, structure of English and structure of home languages.

▶ We can make a record of information that we take from a text by drawing a Venn diagram.

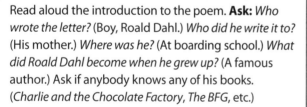

(2) Non-fiction reading notes

Read aloud the introduction to the poem. **Ask:** *Who wrote the letter?* (Boy, Roald Dahl.) *Who did he write it to?* (His mother.) *Where was he?* (At boarding school.) *What did Roald Dahl become when he grew up?* (A famous author.) Ask if anybody knows any of his books. (*Charlie and the Chocolate Factory*, *The BFG*, etc.)

Read the letter, stopping at unfamiliar words, and asking students to guess what they mean using the four-factor clues chart developed in Unit 1 (*see* page 10).

Draw a Venn diagram on the board (*see* Guidelines, page 193), labelling one side 'Boy' and the other 'Betty and Clarice'. Ask students to work in pairs and compare Boy's letter with Betty and Clarice's on page 72 of the Student Book. Ask them to jot down differences between the two. Elicit responses and record the differences on the outer areas of the Venn diagram. Now ask students to identify similarities, and record these in the overlapping centre of the diagram. ⇨

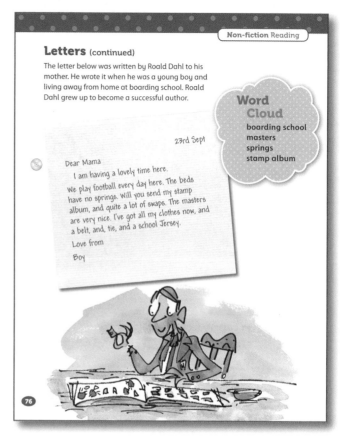

Ask students to imagine where Boy was when he wrote this letter, and gather their ideas. (In his room; in the playground; in the school library; in the park, etc.)

(3) Word Cloud definitions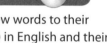

Encourage students to add new words to their New Word List (*see* Workbook) in English and their home languages.

boarding school a school where students live during the school year.

masters male teachers.

springs coils inside a bed mattress that make it bouncy.

stamp album a book where you keep stamps that you collect.

(4) Extension

Ask if any of the letters that students brought from home earlier are from family members. Are any of them written from a son/daughter to a mother? How are they similar to or different from the letter from Roald Dahl to his mother?

Comprehension

Non-fiction Comprehension

 A Which three sentences below are true?

1 Roald Dahl's mother calls him 'Boy'.
2 The beds in the school are comfortable.
3 Roald thinks the teachers at his school are nice.
4 Roald collects stamps.

Challenge
Think of a place that you have visited that you liked. Describe what you liked about it in a letter to a friend. Was there anything you didn't like about it?

B What do you think?

Use phrases from the letter to help with your answer.

1 Why do you think Roald is writing to his mother?
2 Find two sentences in the letter that show that Roald likes his school.
3 Roald asks his mother to send him some 'swaps'. What do you think these are and what will he do with them?
4 Do you think there is anything that Roald does not like about his school? Explain your answer.

C What about you?

How would you describe your school in a letter to a friend or family member?

77

---

 6 Student Book teaching notes and comprehension answers

 A

Answers:

1, 3, 4

You may have to explain that 'Boy' is a special name that Roald's mother calls him. These special names are called 'nicknames' or 'pet names'. Ask students if any of them have nicknames that family members use.

B

1 To ask for his stamp album; to tell his mother that he's all right and that he's enjoying school; to tell her that he's got all of his school uniform.

2 'I am having a lovely time here', 'The masters are very nice.'

3 'Swaps' are duplicates of stamps that he already has. He can exchange them with other boys who collect stamps for stamps that he doesn't have in his collection. Ask students if they collect anything. **Ask:** *When did you start collecting? Why do you collect that particular object? Do you do swaps with others who collect the same thing?*

4 The beds, because they have no springs and sound like they are uncomfortable.

C

Working in pairs, ask students to make notes on what they would include in their letters about school. They then complete the activity by writing individual letters. It would be ideal if students could send their letters to a real person, such as a student in another class or another school.

7 Challenge

Tell students about a place you visited. It could be another country or town, or even a place in your town. List on the board the things you liked and a couple of things you did not like. Erase your list and ask students to complete the activity, writing their own letter to a friend about a place they have visited. Sit down and write about your visit while students do the same.

Learning objectives

5 Scan a passage to find specific information and answer questions.

Identify the main purpose of a text.

Begin to infer meanings beyond the literal, for example about motives and character.

Write first person accounts and descriptions based on observation.

Students examine the letter from the young Roald Dahl to his mother, gathering specific information and the general gist of the letter. They use this to deduce the writer's purpose for sending the letter.

Remember to display the child-friendly learning objectives to the class along with the child-friendly checklist that students can use to assess how well they achieve them.

We know that we have achieved these because:

▶ We can answer specific questions about Roald Dahl's letter.

▶ We can describe the purpose of the letter.

Learning objective

①

Use effective strategies to tackle segmenting unfamiliar words to spell, including identifying known suffixes.

Students explore the suffixes –*ful* or –*less*, and add them to words to convey the correct meaning. They learn that some words can take both –*ful* and –*less*, while others can only take one of these, and a game is played to sort them out. They discover that adding –*ful* or –*less* turns a noun into an adjective.

Remember to display the child-friendly learning objective to the class along with the child-friendly checklist that students can use to assess how well they achieve it.

We know that we have achieved this because:

▶ We can use the suffixes –*ful* and –*less* appropriately.

▶ We understand that adding the suffixes –*ful* and –*less* turns a noun into an adjective.

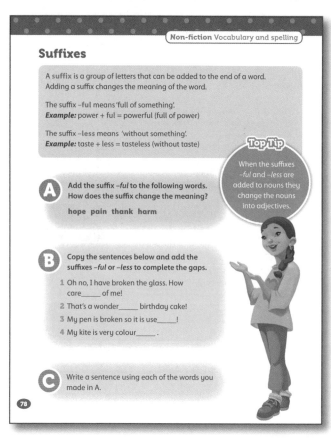

Non-fiction Vocabulary and spelling

Suffixes

A suffix is a group of letters that can be added to the end of a word. Adding a suffix changes the meaning of the word.

The suffix –ful means 'full of something'.
Example: power + ful = powerful (full of power)

The suffix –less means 'without something'.
Example: taste + less = tasteless (without taste)

Top Tip

When the suffixes –ful and –less are added to nouns they change the nouns into adjectives.

A Add the suffix –ful to the following words. How does the suffix change the meaning?

hope   pain   thank   harm

B Copy the sentences below and add the suffixes –ful or –less to complete the gaps.

1 Oh no, I have broken the glass. How care_____ of me!
2 That's a wonder_____ birthday cake!
3 My pen is broken so it is use_____!
4 My kite is very colour_____ .

C Write a sentence using each of the words you made in A.

78

---

② **Student Book teaching notes and vocabulary and spelling exercise answers**

Take two cards and write 'ful' on one and 'less' on the other. Make ten cards with root words that can only end in –*ful* (cup, hand, etc.), ten with words that can only end in –*less* (spot, sound, etc.), and ten that can carry either suffix (thought, hope, etc.).

Show the 'ful' card to the class. **Say:** *Full.* Ask what this suffix might mean. (Full of something.) Do the same with the –*less* card. (Without something.)

On the board, write 'care', 'delight', 'spoon' and other root words known to class that can take the suffix –*ful*. Put the 'ful' card at the end of each, saying it and eliciting meaning. Repeat for the suffix –*less* with 'beard', 'colour', 'pain', and any other appropriate words met recently. Explain that some words can take either suffix ('careful' – 'careless', etc.)

Choose two students, and give the card 'ful' to one and 'less' to the other. Now distribute the root words to the rest of the class. At your signal, the students have to gather words that fit their suffix. Students holding the word cards can refuse a suffix if they think it doesn't fit. See who gathers more words.

Refer students to the Top Tip. Go to the NOUNS, VERBS and ADJECTIVES charts developed in Unit 1 (*see* page 16). Ask students for words that can take the suffixes –*ful* and –*less*, and write them with and without the suffix on the charts. Direct attention to question A and complete it orally with the class. Ask students to complete B and C individually.

Point out that the suffix –*ful* turns the words (nouns) into adjectives. Add the words with and without the suffix to the NOUNS, VERBS and ADJECTIVES charts (*see* Unit 1, page 16).

Answers:

'hope' – 'hopeful', 'pain' – 'painful', 'thank' – 'thankful'. The suffix makes the words mean 'full of …'.

1 careless
2 wonderful
3 useless
4 colourful

Accept any sentence that makes sense.

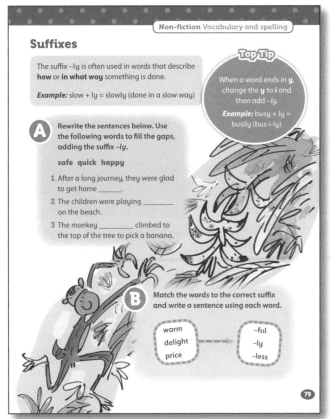

Suffixes

The suffix –ly is often used in words that describe **how** or **in what way** something is done.

Example: slow + ly = slowly (done in a slow way)

Top Tip

When a word ends in **y**, change the **y** to **i** and then add –ly.

Example: busy + ly = busily (bus-i-ly)

A Rewrite the sentences below. Use the following words to fill the gaps, adding the suffix –ly.

safe quick happy

1 After a long journey, they were glad to get home _____.
2 The children were playing _____ on the beach.
3 The monkey _____ climbed to the top of the tree to pick a banana.

B Match the words to the correct suffix and write a sentence using each word.

warm
delight
price

→

–ful
–ly
–less

79

---

④ Student Book teaching notes and vocabulary and spelling exercise answers

Tell students they are going to learn about another suffix, *–ly*. This suffix turns words into 'How' words. Write examples of root words on the board. ('nice', 'quick', etc.) Include words students know or have seen.

Write 'ly' on a card, and hold it next to each word, verbalizing it. Give an example of use. ('I went to the party dressed nicely', etc.)

Direct students' attention to the NOUNS, ADJECTIVES and VERBS charts (*see* Unit 1, page 16). Remind them that suffixes change the type of word, and illustrate it. *Example:* point to 'hope'. **Ask:** *What type of word is this?* (Noun.) *Now look at this word with the suffix –ful.* ('hopeful'.) *What type of word did it become?* (Adjective.) *Hold the 'ly' card at the end of 'hopeful'. What has it become now?* ('How' word.)

Remind students that when *–ly* is added to adjectives they become 'How' words. Give examples. ('How did I dress for the party? Nicely.')

Answers:

1 safely
2 happily
3 quickly

warmly, delightful, priceless. Accept any sentence where these words are used appropriately.

⑤ Top Tip

Read out the Top Tip: *When a word ends in –y change the 'y' to an 'i' and then add 'ly'.* Now write 'happy' and 'angry' on the board. Hold the 'ly' card next to each of them, cross out the 'y' and write 'i' instead.

Learning objective

③

Extend earlier work on suffixes.

Students look at another suffix, *–ly*. They learn that it changes words into 'How' words (adverbs), and practise using it in sentences. They also learn the spelling convention for words that end in *–y* when adding *–ly*.

Remember to display the child-friendly learning objective to the class along with the child-friendly checklist that students can use to assess how well they achieve it.

We know that we have achieved this because:

▷ We can use the suffix *–ly* appropriately.

▷ We know we must change the 'y' to an 'i' when we add *–ly* to words that end with *–y*.

① Learning objective

Understand pluralization and use the terms 'singular' and 'plural'.

Students explore the concept of singular and plural in English and their home languages, and identify how to make nouns plural. They also learn that if they use a plural noun in a sentence, they must also use a plural form of the verb.

Remember to display the child-friendly learning objective to the class along with the child-friendly checklist that students can use to assess how well they achieve it.

We know that we have achieved this because:

▸ We know that for many words in English we just add 's' to make them plural.

▸ We know that words that end in –ch, –sh, –ss and –x need 'es' to make them plural.

▸ We know that when you use a plural noun with a verb, the verb must be plural too.

Singular and plural

We can write nouns in the **singular** or the **plural**. Singular means there is just **one**. Plural means there are **more than one**.

Many singular nouns are made into plural nouns by adding an **s**. *Example:* apple→apples

We add **es** to singular nouns that end in **ch, sh, ss** or **x**. *Example:* fox→foxes

A Change the following nouns into plural nouns by adding **s** or **es**.

pencil   rabbit   book
glass   watch   dish

Top Tip

When you use a plural noun with a verb, the verb must be plural, too.

B Rewrite the sentences below. Fill the gaps using plurals of the following words.

flower dog beach

1 We visited two _____ on our holiday.
2 The _____ were barking loudly.
3 The field was full of pretty _____.

Challenge

Look at the letters on pages 72 and 73 . Find two examples of singular nouns and two examples of plural nouns. Write four sentences, using one of the nouns in each sentence.

80

---

② Student Book teaching notes and grammar and spelling exercise answers

Divide a large sheet of paper into two columns with the headings 'One' and 'More than one'.

On a table, place one object requiring an 's' to make it plural, and objects ending in –ch, –sh, –ss and –x requiring 'es'. *Example:* apple, watch, dish, dress, box. Pick up the apple and ask what it is. **Say:** *One apple.* Write 'apple' under 'One'. **Ask:** *How would the word 'apple' change if there were more than one?* Write 'apples' under 'More than one'. Highlight the 's' with another colour.

Say: *To make a word plural in English we normally just add 's'.* Add 'plural' to 'More than one'. **Ask:** *Can anyone tell me the word for 'One' thing?* Write 'singular' next to 'One'. Ask students how they say these in their home languages. If they don't know, ask them to find out by asking a parent or other home language speaker. Elicit other things for the chart that use 's' for plural.

Draw a line across and write the letters 'ch', 'sh', 'ss' and 'x' in red. Tell students that words ending in these letters make their plurals by adding 'es'. Write '+ es' next to them.

Go through the objects ending in –ch, –sh, –ss and –x in the same way. (Watch, dish, dress, box.) Elicit other examples and add them to the chart.

Ask: *Are these words verbs, nouns, adjectives or 'How' words?* (Nouns.)

⇨

A

Tell students to work in pairs to decide whether to add 's' or 'es'. Check answers orally and add words to the chart.

Answers:

pencils, rabbits, books, glasses, watches, dishes

B

Students copy and fill in the gaps individually.

Answers:

1 beaches
2 dogs
3 flowers

③ Challenge

Working individually, ask students to look at the letters on pages 72 and 73 of the Student Book, and find two examples of singular nouns and two of plural nouns. Tell them to use these in four sentences.

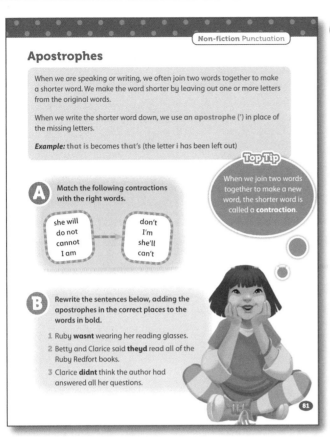

Apostrophes

When we are speaking or writing, we often join two words together to make a shorter word. We make the word shorter by leaving out one or more letters from the original words.

When we write the shorter word down, we use an **apostrophe** (') in place of the missing letters.

Example: **that is** becomes **that's** (the letter i has been left out)

Top Tip

When we join two words together to make a new word, the shorter word is called a **contraction**.

A Match the following contractions with the right words.

she will		don't
do not		I'm
cannot		she'll
I am		can't

B Rewrite the sentences below, adding the apostrophes in the correct places to the words in bold.

1 Ruby **wasnt** wearing her reading glasses.
2 Betty and Clarice said **theyd** read all of the Ruby Redfort books.
3 Clarice **didnt** think the author had answered all her questions.

81

Learning objective

(4) **Recognize the use of the apostrophe to mark omission in shortened words, such as 'can't', 'don't'.**

Students learn the meaning of contractions and the use of apostrophes. They practise contracting words using an apostrophe, and reversing the process by turning contractions into full forms. They also practise placing the apostrophe in the correct place.

Remember to display the child-friendly learning objective to the class along with the child-friendly checklist that students can use to assess how well they achieve it.

We know that we have achieved this because:

▸ We can use an apostrophe in place of missing letters to make words shorter.

(5) ## Student Book teaching notes and punctuation exercise answers

Write the following punctuation marks on the board: comma (,), full stop (.), speech marks (") and apostrophe ('). **Ask:** *What are these?* (Punctuation marks.) Elicit the word 'punctuation' in their home languages.

Point to each punctuation mark, except the apostrophe. **Ask:** *What it is this called? When do we use it?* Refer them to the PUNCTUATION chart made in Unit 4 (*see* page 74). Elicit which marks go on the line (comma and full stop) and which ones above the line (apostrophe and speech marks).

Point to the apostrophe and tell students that they are going to learn how to use apostrophes. Together, read the box introducing apostrophes on page 81 of the Student Book.

Write the example 'that is = that's' on the board. Circle the apostrophe in red and draw a line to the 'i' in 'is'. Point out that the apostrophe replaces the 'i'.

Ask students to look back at the letters on pages 72 and 76 of the Student Book, and find words with apostrophes. ('couldn't', 'didn't', 'I've'.) Tell students to write these out in full, working in pairs. (could not, did not, I have.)

Students complete exercise A and B individually and check their answers in pairs. Write the words in A and sentences in B on the board and check them together as a whole group.

Answers:

she will = she'll, do not = don't, cannot = can't, I am = I'm

1 wasn't
2 they'd
3 didn't

(6) **Top Tip**

Read aloud the definition of a contraction in the Top Tip. Tell students that contractions tend to be used more in informal speech and writing. **Ask:** *What does the word 'informal' mean?* (Relaxed, no rules, etc.) *Can you think of an example of when you'd use informal speech or writing?* (Talking or writing to a friend.)

Write 'CONTRACTIONS' on a large sheet of paper and make a list together. Write the full and short versions.

Working in pairs, ask students to write five sentences using contractions from the list.

Learning objectives

Read a range of information books and begin to make links between them.

Establish purpose for writing, using features and style based on model texts.

Students look at a formal letter written by Maria to her head teacher, requesting permission to hold a party. The main features of a formal letter are identified and discussed, and their difference to other forms of letter writing established.

Remember to display the child-friendly learning objectives to the class along with the child-friendly checklist that students can use to assess how well they achieve them.

We know that we have achieved these because:

▶ We understand the differences between formal and informal letters.

▶ We are able to plan a formal letter.

▶ We know how to begin and end formal letters.

▶ We can work out the purpose for writing a letter.

② Writing workshop teaching notes

Model writing

Refer students to the text on page 82 of the Student Book. Ask what it is. (A letter.) Ask students what helped them decide it was a letter. (Address, date, beginning 'Dear…', etc.) **Ask:** *Who is the letter to?* (Mr Lopez.) *And who is it from?* (Maria.)

Make a T chart (*see* Guidelines, page 193) headed 'Formal' and 'Informal'. **Ask:** *What does the word 'formal' mean?* (Having rules for the way things are done, official, businesslike, etc.) *What does the word 'informal' mean?* (Relaxed, no rules, etc.) Ask students how they would begin a letter to a friend. (Hi, Ciao, etc.) Write these under 'Informal'. **Ask:** *Would you write this way to the head teacher?* (No.) *How would you begin?* (Dear Mr/Mrs …) Add this under 'Formal'. Draw out other features of formal and informal letter writing. (Use/no use of contractions, etc.) Include them on the chart.

Refer students to Maria's letter to the head teacher. Tell them to read the letter and try to work out its purpose. (To ask if Class 3 can have a party.) Remind them to make a note of new words. Now read through the letter together, stopping for unfamiliar words. Make sure the following are explained:

Writing a formal letter
Model writing

Read the formal letter below from Maria to her head teacher.

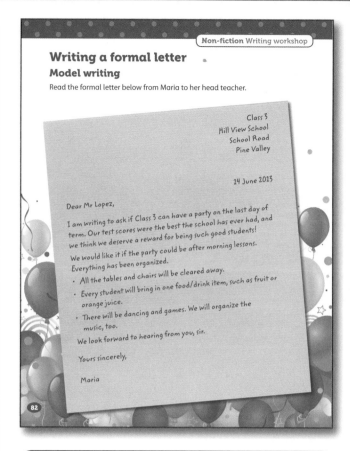

Non-fiction Writing workshop

> Class 3
> Hill View School
> School Road
> Pine Valley
>
> 14 June 2013
>
> Dear Mr Lopez,
> I am writing to ask if Class 3 can have a party on the last day of term. Our test scores were the best the school has ever had, and we think we deserve a reward for being such good students! We would like it if the party could be after morning lessons. Everything has been organized.
> - All the tables and chairs will be cleared away.
> - Every student will bring in one food/drink item, such as fruit or orange juice.
> - There will be dancing and games. We will organize the music, too.
> We look forward to hearing from you, sir.
>
> Yours sincerely,
>
> Maria

82

'deserve' (to merit something), 'reward' (something received for doing something good), 'organize' (to plan something), 'item' (one thing in a list). Write these on the board, and ask students to copy them into their New Word List (*see* Guidelines, page 192, and Workbook) in English and their home languages.

Point out the meaning of the sentence: 'We would like it if the party could be after morning lessons.' (We would like to have the party after morning lessons.)

Ask students how they begin and close a formal letter in their home languages. They may need to ask their parents, other home members or other speaker of their home languages. Encourage them to bring in samples of formal letters in their home languages and have them share how they begin and end. Remind students to ask permission from the owner of the letter before they bring it in.

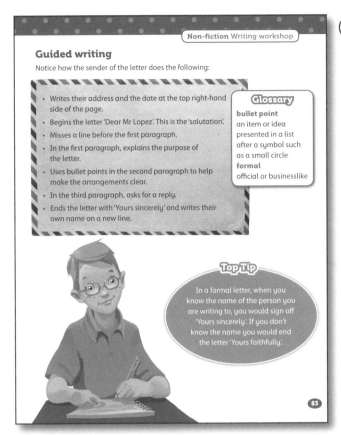

Non-fiction Writing workshop

Guided writing

Notice how the sender of the letter does the following:

- Writes their address and the date at the top right-hand side of the page.
- Begins the letter 'Dear Mr Lopez'. This is the 'salutation'.
- Misses a line before the first paragraph.
- In the first paragraph, explains the purpose of the letter.
- Uses bullet points in the second paragraph to help make the arrangements clear.
- In the third paragraph, asks for a reply.
- Ends the letter with 'Yours sincerely' and writes their own name on a new line.

Glossary

bullet point
an item or idea presented in a list after a symbol such as a small circle

formal
official or businesslike

Top Tip

In a formal letter, when you know the name of the person you are writing to, you would sign off 'Yours sincerely'. If you don't know the name you would end the letter 'Yours faithfully'.

83

③ Learning objectives

Consider ways that information is set out on a page.

Write letters, notes and messages.

Students investigate the layout of a formal letter. As a class they write a letter to their head teacher about a subject of their choice, following the main features of formal letter writing. They deliver English and home-language versions to the head teacher.

Remember to display the child-friendly learning objectives to the class along with the child-friendly checklist that students can use to assess how well they achieve them.

We know that we have achieved these because:

▶ We can identify the features of a formal letter, and write one.

▶ We can write the address and date at the top.

▶ We know to begin with 'Dear…'

▶ We explain our reason for writing in paragraph one.

▶ We do not use contractions.

▶ We end our letter with 'Yours sincerely' if we know the name of the person we are writing to, and with 'Yours faithfully' if we don't.

④ Writing workshop teaching notes

Read out Maria's letter on page 82 of the Student Book. **Ask:** *Why did Maria write the letter?* (To have a class party at the end of term.) *Where did you find this information in the letter?* (At the beginning.) Ask students if they think Class 3 deserves a party and why. (Their test scores were the best the school has ever had, etc.)

Ask: *Has Maria presented Class 3's ideas clearly?* (Yes.) *How did she present their ideas?* (Accept using dots, points, etc.) Explain that the dots are called bullet points.

Guided writing

Refer students to the Glossary and read it together. Then read through the Guided writing introduction, the list of points and the Top Tip on when to use 'Yours sincerely' and 'Yours faithfully'.

Return to Maria's letter. Tell students to work with a partner to identify each point in the list, then close their books. As a whole class, invite students to tell you the main features of formal letter writing, offering prompts where necessary. *Example: Where do you put the address/date?* (Top right-hand corner.) Continue until all points have been covered.

Ask students if they have anything they would like to write to the head teacher about. Gather ideas, such as more playtime, more multilingual books, etc. Choose an idea, and ask the class to tell you how to lay out the letter as you write it on the board. They can use the points on page 83 of the Student Book as reference. *Example:* 'Write the address and date at the top.' (You write the school address.)

Ask students to copy the letter into their notebooks and then work with their parents or other home members to write a translation of it. Deliver the dual-language letters to the head teacher, and ask that they reply. Request that the letters be displayed in their office for a period to promote multilingualism.

Learning objectives

Read a range of story, poetry and information books and begin to make links between them.

Establish purpose for writing, using features and style based on model texts.

Consider ways that information is set out on a page.

Students learn that letter writing is non-fiction. The differences between formal and informal letter writing are discussed. They imagine the head teacher's reply to Maria and work in pairs to create it, following a given plan and using the features of formal letter writing.

Remember to display the child-friendly learning objectives to the class along with the child-friendly checklist that students can use to assess how well they achieve them.

We know that we have achieved these because:

▶ We know that letter writing is a type of non-fiction (information) text.

▶ We understand the differences between writing formal and informal letters.

▶ We are able to plan a formal letter.

▶ We can work out the purpose for writing a letter.

▶ We can identify and use the features of a formal letter.

② Writing workshop teaching notes

Begin by reviewing the terms 'fiction' (stories) and 'non-fiction' (information text). Ask students how they say these words in home languages. Some languages do not have a word for non-fiction, they use a phrase to express the idea. Ask students to find out how non-fiction is expressed in their home languages. **Ask:** *Does letter writing belong to fiction or non-fiction?* (Non-fiction.) Explain that this is because they are written about factual things.

Ask: *Can you remember what kind of letter Maria wrote?* (Formal.) *When might we write a formal letter?* Gather students' ideas. (To a newspaper to give our opinion; to a company to complain, etc.)

Review the different features of informal and formal letter writing listed on the T chart. Elicit additions to the chart. *Example:* In informal letters endings include kisses 'xxx'; there are decorations, etc. None of these are in formal letters.

⇨

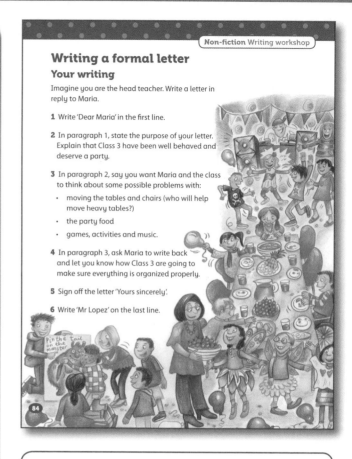

Writing a formal letter

Your writing

Imagine you are the head teacher. Write a letter in reply to Maria.

1 Write 'Dear Maria' in the first line.

2 In paragraph 1, state the purpose of your letter. Explain that Class 3 have been well behaved and deserve a party.

3 In paragraph 2, say you want Maria and the class to think about some possible problems with:
- moving the tables and chairs (who will help move heavy tables?)
- the party food
- games, activities and music.

4 In paragraph 3, ask Maria to write back and let you know how Class 3 are going to make sure everything is organized properly.

5 Sign off the letter 'Yours sincerely'.

6 Write 'Mr Lopez' on the last line.

84

Point to Maria's letter. **Ask:** *Do you think Mr Lopez wrote back? What do you think he might have said?* Elicit suggestions and write them on the board. Tell students they are going to imagine they are Mr Lopez and write a reply to Maria.

Your writing

Working in pairs, ask students to review the features of formal letter writing, and then follow the given writing plan. Encourage them to read points 1–6 carefully before they begin. Ask if there are any words that they don't understand, and check that they understand 'agree'. (To think the same as someone else.) Suggest they add another possible problem to those listed in point 3. (Not fair to single out one class to have a party, etc.)

They should each write a letter, but collaborate with their partner on points 2, 3 and 4.

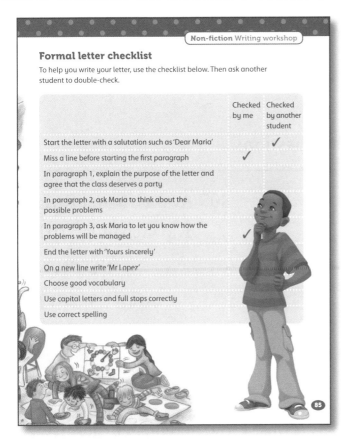

Non-fiction Writing workshop

Formal letter checklist

To help you write your letter, use the checklist below. Then ask another student to double-check.

	Checked by me	Checked by another student
Start the letter with a salutation such as 'Dear Maria'		✓
Miss a line before starting the first paragraph	✓	
In paragraph 1, explain the purpose of the letter and agree that the class deserves a party		
In paragraph 2, ask Maria to think about the possible problems		
In paragraph 3, ask Maria to let you know how the problems will be managed		✓
End the letter with 'Yours sincerely'		
On a new line write 'Mr Lopez'		
Choose good vocabulary		
Use capital letters and full stops correctly		
Use correct spelling		

85

(3) Learning objectives

Make a record of information drawn from a text.

Ensure consistency in the size and proportion of lettering and the spacing of words.

Practise joining lettering in handwriting.

Build up handwriting speed, fluency and legibility.

Students use a checklist to discuss their writing with a partner. They become more familiar with the way a letter is presented. They also practise their joined-up handwriting skills, focusing on well-proportioned letters, even spacing and legibility.

 Remember to display the child-friendly learning objectives to the class along with the child-friendly checklist that students can use to assess how well they achieve them.

We know that we have achieved these because:

▶ **We can identify letter writing from other types of text.**

▶ **We can work with a partner to check our written work.**

▶ **We can write using joined-up lettering.**

▶ **We understand that using equal-sized lettering and even spacing between words makes our writing easier to read.**

(4) Writing workshop teaching notes

Formal letter checklist

Read through the checklist with students point by point. Ask students if they can guess the meaning of 'salutation'. (Greeting.) **Ask:** *If you didn't know the word, how did you guess it?* (The words 'such as' are used to introduce an example, or to say 'of the same kind'.)

Elicit another word for 'purpose'. (Reason.) Ask students to give you another word for 'managed' (solved), 'sincerely' (truly) and 'faithfully' (trustworthy, can be trusted). Students should write all new vocabulary in their New Word List (*see* Workbook) in English and their home languages.

Tell students to review their writing using the checklist. Encourage them to underline lightly words that they think they have misspelt, and to use a dictionary to find the correct spelling, adding the word to their personal spelling log. When students have had ample time to check their work, ask them to let another student check it.

Ask students to write you a good formal letter, outlining reasons for having a night off from homework. Put students in groups of three to brainstorm reasons for needing a night off. Tell them that all students who follow the formal writing model on page 83 of the Student Book will indeed get a night off homework!

Students then work individually to write their letter to you.

Ask them to write their letters to you using their best, joined-up handwriting. Remind them to make their lettering of equal size and proportion, and to keep an even spacing between the words. If scribing for students who are not yet able to write in English, encourage them to practise forming the lettering and words by making a copy of the letter you have written for them. They can also practise writing their signature in joined-up English script. You can find useful resources for teaching the formation of lettering and handwriting skills at: http://www.tes.co.uk

(5) Extension

Create a letter-writing centre in the classroom with envelopes, lined and plain paper, glitter, glue sticks, markers, pens and pencils. Make a multilingual 'Keep in touch!' sign. To teach this idiom, focus attention on the words 'keep' and 'touch'. Point out that you cannot touch people when they are far away, but letter writing is way of being (keeping) close to them. Tell them that people also use the similar phrase 'Stay in touch.' Ask students if they have a similar saying in their home languages. Encourage students to use the centre to make greeting cards and write informal notes, messages and letters.

End of Unit Test

Question Paper

Reading: non-fiction

Read the following letter and answer the questions.

807 Avenue Santa Rosa

Rio Ceballos 5101

Argentina

April 25, 2013

Dear Francesca,

I am so happy you want to be my pen pal. That's so cool! I want to write in English so I can get better at it. I hope you don't mind.

So, tell me, what is your school like? Is it big? How do you get there?

My school is small and is in Rio Ceballos. I take the bus that comes by our house at 7:30 in the morning. I hope that you don't have to get up that early. I come home also by bus at 1:30 in the afternoon. I have two main teachers, and they're the best! Señorita Silvia teaches Maths and Natural Sciences, and Señorita Roxana teaches Language (boring!!) and Social Studies. We also have Mariana who teaches Music and Nancy who teaches Physical Education. My favourite subject is Music. I love to sing and to dance.

Aren't you almost finishing school this year? We have just begun! In Argentina, school starts in March because that's fall, and it ends in December, the beginning of summer. Yaaay!

My best friend's name is Melina. Sometimes I go to her house and she comes to my house. Who is your best friend?

I hope you can write soon and tell me about yourself.

Lots of love,

Carla

Glossary

pen pal a friend in another country to whom you write letters.

Comprehension

A Give evidence from the text to support your answers.

1 Why does Carla want to write in English?

_____ [1]

2 Who is Carla's best friend?

_____ [1]

3 Which subject does Carla like best at school?

_____ [1]

B Give evidence from the text to support your answers.

1 What is Carla's least favourite subject at school? How do you know?

_____ [2]

2 Why do you think Carla has put her address at the top of the letter?

_____ [1]

3 Is Carla looking forward to receiving a letter from Francesca? How do you know?

_____ [2]

C Give evidence from the text to support your answers.

1 In which months are the summer holidays in Argentina?

_____ [2]

2 Do you think Carla likes going to school? If yes, why? If no, why?

_____
_____ [2]

3 List two ways in which Carla's school is similar to yours, and two ways in which it is different.

_____
_____ [4]

Writing: non-fiction

Read Francesca's letter to Carla. Notice how she begins her letter, how she answers Carla's questions and how she asks for a reply in the final paragraph.

Collina International School of Rome

May 15, 2013

Dear Carla,

Thank you for your letter. I am very happy we are pen pals. I hope you can teach me some Spanish!

I go to a big international school in Rome in Italy. At my school there are children who come from all over the world who speak many different languages. I too have to get up early to go to school as we live in a village 40 km from Rome. My mum drives me to school. You are so lucky that school finishes at 1:30. We finish at 3:30. Sob sob!

My class teacher is Ms Green. She can be strict but she is very simpatico (nice). Ms Green teaches us English, Math, History and Science. We have many other teachers for art, Italian, Music, Computers and P.E. I love P.E. and we learn it in Italian, which is my language. We go on many field trips all over Italy. Next week we are going to visit a paper mill in Subiaco.

Yes, school finishes in June here, so it's nearly time for going to the beach and having fun. My best friend's name is Shihomi. She comes from Japan.

Next time tell me all about your family. Do you have a pet? We have a dog. His name is Eros.

Write back soon,

Francesca xox

Glossary

field trip a visit to somewhere with your school to study something.
paper mill a factory where paper is made.
sob a gasping noise you make when you cry.
strict demanding that people obey rules and behave well.
Subiaco an old town south of Rome.

Giorgio, Pedro, Teresa and Sofia live in Spain. They are all looking for pen pals.

- Giorgio is eight years old. He loves music.
- Pedro is seven and his favourite sport is swimming.
- Teresa is eight. She is learning to play the piano.
- Sofia is seven and her favourite sport is football.

Choose one of the children to write a letter to. In your letter describe your school. Use the letter on page 102 to help you and the notepad below.

Please use a separate sheet of paper.

Include the following features in your letter:

- Write your address and the date at the top right-hand side of the page.
- Start the letter with a salutation 'Dear …'
- Leave a line before the first paragraph.
- Ask your pen pal some questions.
- Use correct spelling and punctuation.
- End the letter in a friendly way.

Organize your letter in three paragraphs:

Paragraph 1: say something about yourself.

Paragraph 2: describe your school and ask your pen pal some questions about their school and hobbies.

Paragraph 3: ask for a reply.

Close your letter.

[20]

6

Sharing cultures

1 Warm-up objectives

Speak clearly and confidently in a range of contexts.

Take turns in discussion, building on what others have said.

Students discuss the topic in pairs, small groups and as a whole group. They look at an old Maori proverb and take turns talking about its meaning. They use the Maori culture as a context for talking about forms of greeting in other cultures and their own culture. They relate words describing greetings to those used in their home languages.

Remember to display the child-friendly learning objectives to the class along with the child-friendly checklist that students can use to assess how well they achieve them.

We know that we have achieved these because:

▸ We are able to talk about greetings in pairs, small groups and as a whole group.

▸ We are able to take turns in discussions.

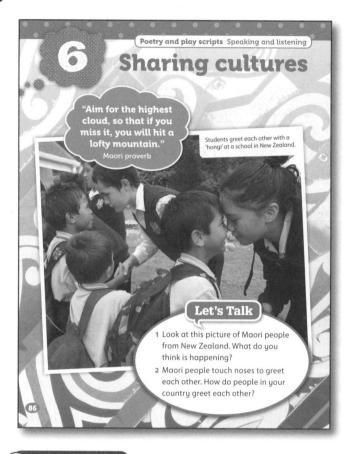

6 Sharing cultures

"Aim for the highest cloud, so that if you miss it, you will hit a lofty mountain."
Maori proverb

Students greet each other with a 'hongi' at a school in New Zealand.

Let's Talk

1 Look at this picture of Maori people from New Zealand. What do you think is happening?

2 Maori people touch noses to greet each other. How do people in your country greet each other?

86

2 Unit warm up

Read the title of the unit aloud. **Ask:** *What does 'sharing cultures' mean?* (Telling people about the way your family/community does things: festivals, food, tales and so on.) Write the students' responses on the board.

Copy the well-known whakatauki, or Maori proverb, onto a chart. 'Whāia te iti kahurangi ki te tuahu koe me he maunga teitei.' Ask students if they can recognize the language. If you have a student who can read Māori ask them to read the proverb. Tell students that the Maori people were the first people to live in New Zealand. Ask students to find New Zealand on the world map at the front of the Student Book. Point out that it is an island country in the Pacific Ocean and tell them that the Maori language is one of the official languages of New Zealand.

Read the English translation of the proverb with the students. Give the meaning of 'aim' (try) and 'lofty' (tall) to second language students. Ask students to turn to their partner and discuss what the proverb means. Listen to the students' ideas and agree that it can be interpreted as 'try your hardest and you will always do your best', or 'try your hardest to reach your goals and if you don't quite make it, you are one step closer. With perseverance comes achievement.'

3 Let's Talk

1 Focus attention on the photograph and ask students as a whole group what they think is happening in the picture (Maori children are greeting each other with a traditional hongi). Ask students to describe the greeting (touching noses and foreheads and shaking hands).

2 Ask students to describe different forms of greeting in their own cultures and other cultures. Invite them to write greeting words in their home languages on a chart. Also ask them to share words for the actions that go with the greetings. Write words for the actions on the chart (shake hands, kiss once, kiss twice, etc.).

Ask the students, as a whole group, to form two circles, one inside the other. The inner circle walks anti-clockwise and the outer circle walks clockwise. They say the following chant: 'As I was walking down the street, a friend of mine I chanced to meet.' Call out one of the class's home languages. Students should then stop and greet the person nearest to them in the other circle with the words and actions appropriate in that home language. Continue with all home languages.

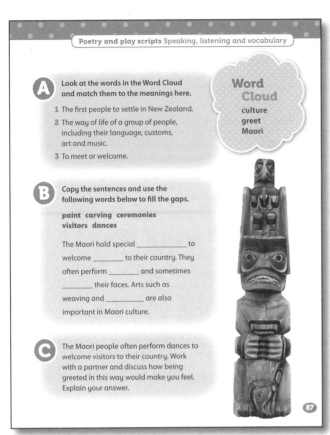

Poetry and play scripts Speaking, listening and vocabulary

A Look at the words in the Word Cloud and match them to the meanings here.

Word Cloud
culture
greet
Maori

1 The first people to settle in New Zealand.
2 The way of life of a group of people, including their language, customs, art and music.
3 To meet or welcome.

B Copy the sentences and use the following words below to fill the gaps.

paint carving ceremonies visitors dances

The Maori hold special _____ to welcome _____ to their country. They often perform _____ and sometimes _____ their faces. Arts such as weaving and _____ are also important in Maori culture.

C The Maori people often perform dances to welcome visitors to their country. Work with a partner and discuss how being greeted in this way would make you feel. Explain your answer.

87

Learning objectives

④ **Infer the meaning of unknown words from the context.**

Listen and respond appropriately to others' views and opinions.

Students guess the meaning of unknown words from the context. They discuss with a partner how they would feel if they were welcomed as a visitor to New Zealand with a performance by Maori dancers. They listen to their partner's opinions and respond appropriately.

Remember to display the child-friendly learning objectives to the class along with the child-friendly checklist that students can use to assess how well they achieve them.

We know that we have achieved these because:

▶ We can understand new words from the context and explain their meanings.

▶ We can listen and respond appropriately to others in discussions about greetings in other cultures.

---

⑤ Word Cloud definitions

Focus students' attention on the Word Cloud and ask them to work in pairs and guess the meanings from the context. Remind students to add the words to their New Word List (*see* Workbook).

culture the customs and traditions of a people.
greet say hello to or welcome someone when they arrive with words or actions.
Maori the first people to settle in New Zealand.

---

⑥ Student Book teaching notes and exercise answers

Ask students to work in pairs and match the words in the Word Cloud with their meanings.

Answers:

1 Maori
2 culture
3 greet

Students copy the sentences and fill the gaps with the correct words. Check for understanding of 'perform' (to act) 'carving' (to cut carefully or artistically) and 'weaving' (to make something by passing threads over and under other threads).

Answer:

The Maori hold special **ceremonies** to welcome **visitors** to their country. They often perform **dances** and sometimes **paint** their faces. Arts such as weaving and **carving** are also important in Maori culture.

Ask students to imagine that they have just arrived in a Maori region of New Zealand and they are being welcomed by Maori dancers. Ask them to discuss in pairs how being greeted in this way would make them feel. **Ask:** *Would it make you feel that you are very welcome? Would it make you want to learn more about Maori culture?* Remind students to take turns when speaking, to listen to each other's opinions and respond appropriately.

---

⑦ Extension

Students make a Maori bookmark or mask using traditional Maori designs. Display the bookmarks and masks in the classroom.

Learning objectives

① Identify different types of stories and typical story themes.

Read play scripts and dialogue, with awareness of different voices.

Read a range of story, poetry and information books and begin to make links between them.

Infer the meaning of unknown words from the context.

Students focus on a play script based on a traditional legend, making links with the traditional tale they read in Unit 4. They identify the features and characteristics of the play script. They read the play script aloud using expression, changing their voices as they read. They continue to guess the meaning of unfamiliar words by consulting the clues chart developed in Unit 1 (*see* page 10).

Remember to display the child-friendly learning objectives to the class along with the child-friendly checklist that students can use to assess how well they achieve them.

We know that we have achieved these because:

▶ We can recognize the text as a play script and identify its features.

▶ We are able to identify the general theme of the play and make links with a traditional tale we have previously read.

▶ We are able to read the parts of the play script with expression and different voices.

▶ We can guess the meanings of unfamiliar words from the context and other clues we have available to us.

② Play script reading notes

Introduce the general story of this play summarized at the top of page 88 of the Student Book. Remind students who the Maori people are, asking them what they learned about them from the introduction on pages 88–89. Ask students to find New Zealand again on the world map at the front of the Student Book. When you read the statement that the play script is based on a well-known Maori legend, remind them that a legend is a traditional tale, like the story about Bawang and the golden bird in Unit 4. Remind students that traditional tales are often stories that were originally written a long time ago. ⇨

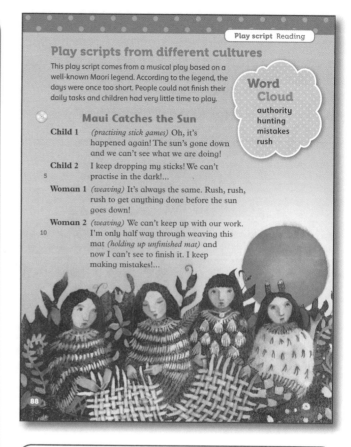

Play script Reading

Play scripts from different cultures

This play script comes from a musical play based on a well-known Maori legend. According to the legend, the days were once too short. People could not finish their daily tasks and children had very little time to play.

Word Cloud
authority
hunting
mistakes
rush

Maui Catches the Sun

Child 1 *(practising stick games)* Oh, it's happened again! The sun's gone down and we can't see what we are doing!

Child 2 I keep dropping my sticks! We can't
5 practise in the dark!...

Woman 1 *(weaving)* It's always the same. Rush, rush, rush to get anything done before the sun goes down!

Woman 2 *(weaving)* We can't keep up with our work.
10 I'm only half way through weaving this mat *(holding up unfinished mat)* and now I can't see to finish it. I keep making mistakes!...

88

Read the play script aloud or refer to the CD-ROM. Stop at words in the Word Cloud and any other unfamiliar words, asking students to guess the meanings from the clues chart created in Unit 1 (*see* page 10).

③ Word Cloud definitions

Read the words in the Word Cloud or refer to the CD-ROM. Ask students to work in pairs and match the meanings from the context. Ask students to write the cloud words in their home languages. If they are unsure they can use bilingual dictionaries, check on online translators or ask a parent or other speaker of their home language. Remind students to write all new vocabulary in their New Word List (*see* Workbook).

authority the power to give orders to other people.
hunting chasing and killing animals for food.
mistakes things that are done wrongly.
rush hurry.

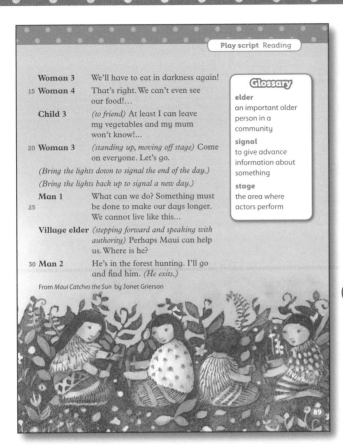

Woman 3	We'll have to eat in darkness again!
15 Woman 4	That's right. We can't even see our food!...
Child 3	*(to friend)* At least I can leave my vegetables and my mum won't know!...
20 Woman 3	*(standing up, moving off stage)* Come on everyone. Let's go.
	(Bring the lights down to signal the end of the day.)
	(Bring the lights back up to signal a new day.)
Man 1	What can we do? Something must
25	be done to make our days longer. We cannot live like this...
Village elder	*(stepping forward and speaking with authority)* Perhaps Maui can help us. Where is he?
30 Man 2	He's in the forest hunting. I'll go and find him. *(He exits.)*

From *Maui Catches the Sun* by Janet Grierson

Glossary

elder
an important older person in a community

signal
to give advance information about something

stage
the area where actors perform

89

4 Play script reading notes

Continue reading the play script aloud (or refer to the CD-ROM), stopping at unfamiliar words. Draw attention to the Glossary words 'elder', 'signal' and 'stage'. Ask students to read the words and definitions aloud. Challenge students to be the first to find these words in the play script. Remind students about the characteristics of plays that they learned about in Unit 3: there are different characters and each character has something to say; the names of the characters are written on the left and the words spoken are on the right; and stage directions, telling the actors how to speak their words and what to do on stage, are written in brackets.

Ask students to skim the text on the two pages and find the characters in the play. Make a list on the board as students call out the different characters (two children, four women, village elder and two men).

Ask students to find examples of stage directions in the play script. ***Examples:*** practising stick games, to friend, etc. Write the stage directions on the board. Turn the lights off in the classroom (or close the shutters or curtains) to make the room as dark as possible. Some students may complain that they cannot see anything. Turn the lights back on and discuss the similarity with the situation in the play.

Discuss the main theme in the play script. **Ask:** *Why are the characters complaining?* (Because the sun does not shine for long enough each day and there aren't enough hours of daylight.) Elicit the three actions that characters in the play have difficulty with because of the darkness (practising stick games, weaving, eating). Write down the verbs on the board and ask one of the students to add them to the VERBS chart (*see* page 17).

Using a flow chart graphic organizer (a diagram with boxes connected by arrows to show the links between events), list the main events in the play so far.

5 Extension

Draw attention to the list of characters you have written on the board. Ask for volunteers or assign students to read the lines of each character. Give them a little time to prepare. Then begin the reading, with you reading the stage directions. Encourage students to read their parts with expression, changing their voices as they read, saying the words with feeling and taking account of the stage directions.

(1) Learning objectives

Answer questions with some reference to single points in the text.

Begin to infer meanings beyond the literal.

Take turns in discussion, building on what others have said.

Listen and respond appropriately to others' views and opinions.

Students answer questions about the play script focusing on specific points in the text. They also answer questions that show their understanding of points that are not directly stated in the text. They take turns in a discussion with a partner, listening and respecting each other's opinions about the importance of learning about other cultures.

 Remember to display the child-friendly learning objectives to the class along with the child-friendly checklist that students can use to assess how well they achieve them.

We know that we have achieved these because:

▶ We can correctly answer questions about specific points in the text.

▶ We can deduce things from the extract that are not written down explicitly in the text.

▶ We are able to take turns in discussions.

▶ We can listen to and respond appropriately to the opinions of others.

(2) Student Book teaching notes and comprehension answers

(A)

Students read the play with a partner before answering the questions. They answer the questions individually or in pairs. When they have finished, check the answers with the whole class.

Answers:

1 The characters are complaining about the days being too short, being left in darkness and not being able to see what they are doing. The children cannot practise their stick games. The women cannot finish their weaving. The characters have to eat in darkness. Accept any suitable sentence as an example that shows a character is complaining about the sun going down too soon or not being able to see what they are doing. *Example:* lines 2–3.

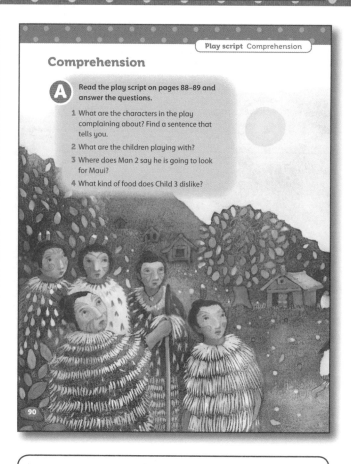

Play script Comprehension

Comprehension

(A) Read the play script on pages 88–89 and answer the questions.

1 What are the characters in the play complaining about? Find a sentence that tells you.

2 What are the children playing with?

3 Where does Man 2 say he is going to look for Maui?

4 What kind of food does Child 3 dislike?

90

2 The children are playing a game with sticks. (This game was traditionally used to train young men in how to handle their spears.)

3 Man 2 says he will go to the forest to find Maui.

4 Child 3 does not like to eat vegetables. Ask students how they worked out the answer to this question. Sometimes the answer to a question is not given directly in the text but can be derived from clues in the text. The text does not say explicitly that this child does not like vegetables, but we can deduce this from the fact that the child plans to leave his vegetables and can get away with it because his mother won't know in the dark. Ask students for a show of hands for liking/disliking vegetables. Ask and list students' favourite and least favourite vegetables.

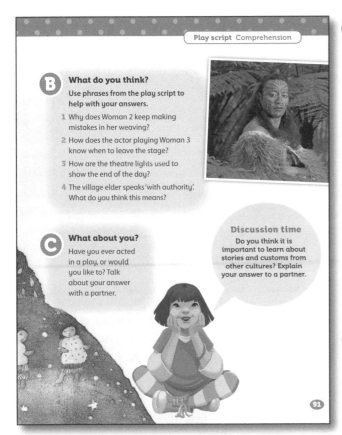

Play script Comprehension

B **What do you think?**

Use phrases from the play script to help with your answers.

1 Why does Woman 2 keep making mistakes in her weaving?

2 How does the actor playing Woman 3 know when to leave the stage?

3 How are the theatre lights used to show the end of the day?

4 The village elder speaks 'with authority'. What do you think this means?

C **What about you?**

Have you ever acted in a play, or would you like to? Talk about your answer with a partner.

Discussion time

Do you think it is important to learn about stories and customs from other cultures? Explain your answer to a partner.

91

④ Discussion time

Tell students about a cross-cultural experience you had. ***Examples:*** you are or were in a country other than your home country; you had guests from another country; you helped tourists from another country find what they were looking for; you have friends who are from another country. Tell them one or two things you learned from that experience.

Ask students to discuss with a partner anything they know about the traditions and customs of other cultures. Ask them to compare these with their own culture. Walk around the classroom and help students carry on the discussion in an appropriate way. Help beginner second language students with words or expressions.

⑤ Extension

Darken your classroom again, either by turning the lights off or by closing the shutters or curtains. Elicit the things students would not be able to do well because of the darkness. Ask them to imagine what their world would be like if we had very few hours of light. Ask students if we experience fewer hours of light at some times of year than others (for those who live far from the equator, you can talk about shorter days in the winter).

③ Student Book teaching notes and comprehension answers

 B

Encourage students to check the text of the play to find their answers. However, encourage them to use their own words to write the answers rather than copy word for word from the play script.

Answers:

1 Woman 2 keeps making mistakes because she cannot see what she is weaving in the dark.

2 The person who is acting the role of Woman 3 knows she has to leave the stage because the stage directions in line 19 tell her to stand up and move off the stage.

3 The theatre lights are brought down (turned down and perhaps even completely off) to indicate the end of the day.

4 'Authority' means power to make decisions, so speaking 'with authority' means speaking without hesitation, with self-confidence and with power.

 C

Tell students a story about yourself that involves a play (when you went to see a play at a theatre and wanted to act; if you ever acted in a play; if you have a friend who is an actor; if you ever saw a famous actor). Then ask students to think about the question in this section, to make notes about their thoughts, and to talk to a partner.

1 ## Learning objectives

Read a range of story, poetry and information books.

Identify different types of stories and typical story themes.

Infer the meaning of unknown words from the context.

Students read the continuation of the play *Maui Catches the Sun*. They continue to identify the features of the play script and guess the meaning of unknown words from the clues available to them (*see* page 10).

 Remember to display the child-friendly learning objectives to the class along with the child-friendly checklist that students can use to assess how well they achieve them.

We know that we have achieved these because:

▸ We are able to read the text and correctly identify it as a play script.

▸ We are able to say what the play is about.

▸ We use all the clues available to us to understand unfamiliar words.

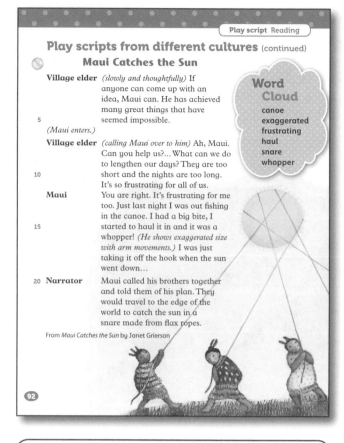

Play scripts from different cultures (continued)
Maui Catches the Sun

Village elder *(slowly and thoughtfully)* If anyone can come up with an idea, Maui can. He has achieved many great things that have
5   seemed impossible.
(Maui enters.)

Village elder *(calling Maui over to him)* Ah, Maui. Can you help us?... What can we do to lengthen our days? They are too
10   short and the nights are too long. It's so frustrating for all of us.

Maui   You are right. It's frustrating for me too. Just last night I was out fishing in the canoe. I had a big bite, I
15   started to haul it in and it was a whopper! *(He shows exaggerated size with arm movements.)* I was just taking it off the hook when the sun went down...

20 **Narrator**   Maui called his brothers together and told them of his plan. They would travel to the edge of the world to catch the sun in a snare made from flax ropes.

From *Maui Catches the Sun* by Janet Grierson

Word Cloud

canoe
exaggerated
frustrating
haul
snare
whopper

92

Ask for three volunteers, or assign students to play the three roles in this part of the play (Village elder, Maui and Narrator). Give them a little time to prepare and have them act out the play.

2 ## Play script reading notes

With the help of the students, and by looking at the flow chart graphic organizer that you worked on earlier (*see* page 107), summarize the events in the first part of the play on pages 88–89 of the Student Book. Ask the students whether they think that Maui will be able to come up with a solution to the villagers' problem. **Ask:** *What do we know about Maui already?* (From the extract on page 89, we know that the village elder thinks highly of Maui because he thinks he might be able to help them.) Ask the students what they think Maui is going to suggest as a solution for getting more hours of light into their days. Direct the students' attention to the illustration, and ask what students think the Maori men are doing. Write down on the board the different predictions given by the students.

Begin reading the play or refer to the CD-ROM. Stop at unfamiliar words and focus on the words in the Word Cloud. Make the movements (entering, calling to come over, moving arms to make an exaggerated size) as you get to the stage directions. When you get to the solution that Maui has (described in the words spoken by the Narrator), compare it to the students' predictions.

⇨

3 ## Word Cloud definitions

Read out the words in the Word Cloud or refer to the CD-ROM. Ask students to locate the words in the text. Remind students to add the words to their New Word List (*see* Workbook) in English and their home language.

canoe a light, narrow boat driven with paddles.

exaggerated made to seem bigger, better or worse than it really is.

frustrating annoying because you cannot do what you want to do.

haul pull with a lot of power or strength.

snare a trap for catching something.

whopper something unusually large.

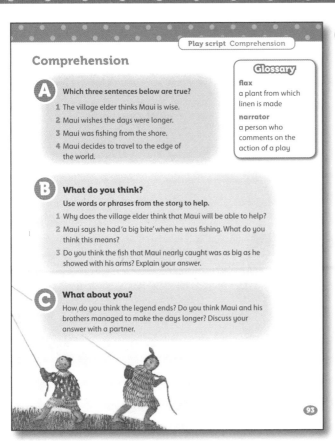

Comprehension

A Which three sentences below are true?

1 The village elder thinks Maui is wise.
2 Maui wishes the days were longer.
3 Maui was fishing from the shore.
4 Maui decides to travel to the edge of the world.

Glossary

flax
a plant from which linen is made

narrator
a person who comments on the action of a play

B What do you think?
Use words or phrases from the story to help.

1 Why does the village elder think that Maui will be able to help?
2 Maui says he had 'a big bite' when he was fishing. What do you think this means?
3 Do you think the fish that Maui nearly caught was as big as he showed with his arms? Explain your answer.

C What about you?
How do you think the legend ends? Do you think Maui and his brothers managed to make the days longer? Discuss your answer with a partner.

93

Learning objectives

4

Answer questions with some reference to single points in the text.

Begin to infer meanings beyond the literal, for example about motives and character.

Identify the main points or gist of a text.

Students answer questions by focusing on specific points in the play script. They also answer questions that show understanding of points that are not explicitly given in the text. They discuss the main points of the text and possible endings for the legend.

Remember to display the child-friendly learning objectives to the class along with the child-friendly checklist that students can use to assess how well they achieve them.

We know that we have achieved these because:

▶ We can correctly answer specific questions about the text.

▶ We can answer questions relating to points about characters and events that are not written explicitly in the text.

▶ We can identify the main events in the play script and say what it is mainly about.

5 **Student Book teaching notes and comprehension answers**

 A

Students read the text and decide which three statements are true.

Answers:

1, 2 and 4

 B

Encourage students to check the play script for answers but ask them to put the answers in their own words rather than copying word for word from the text.

Answers:

1 The village elder says that Maui has achieved many great things, even when they have seemed impossible. So, Maui has shown that he can do things even when others cannot.

2 A big fish nibbled at Maui's line and was caught on his hook.

3 No, the fish that he nearly caught was smaller than Maui was showing with his arms. We know this because the play script says that he was showing the size of the fish with exaggerated movements. Many people exaggerate things they have done or seen. Ask students to think of examples (how much they ate; how they fell; how fast a car was going; how big a storm was). **Ask:** *Can people exaggerate when the real thing is in front of everyone?* (No, it's only when whatever we are exaggerating is absent that we can exaggerate. Maui's fish got away, and that's why he can exaggerate its size.)

 C

Students discuss how they think the legend ends. Ask students to jot down notes to use when they talk to a partner. Start a whole class discussion by getting ideas for the end of the legend and writing them down on the board.

6 **Extension**

In pairs, students pick an ending to the legend and write it out as a play script, with Maui and three or four men at the edge of the earth, then the men returning to the village.

Learning objectives

Know irregular forms of common verbs.

Continue to improve consistency in the use of tenses.

Students identify and use different forms of the irregular verb 'to be' in the present and past tense.

Remember to display the child-friendly learning objectives to the class along with the child-friendly checklist that students can use to assess how well they achieve them.

We know that we have achieved these because:

▶ We can use the verb 'to be' correctly in its present and past forms.

▶ We can identify if verbs are in the present or past tense from the context and from the way they are written.

Student Book page

Poetry and play scripts Grammar

Irregular verbs

Top Tip

Remember: A verb in the **present tense** tells us what is happening **now**. Verbs in the **past tense** tell us what happened in the **past**. Many verbs in the past tense end with **ed**.

Some verbs are **irregular**. The means they do not follow the usual pattern when we use them in different tenses. One of the most common irregular verbs is the verb to be.

Present tense	Past tense
I am	I was
You are	You were
He is	He was
She is	She was
We are	We were
They are	They were

A Rewrite the following sentences, choosing the correct verb to fill the gaps.

1 The village elder _____ an important man. (are, is, were)

2 Maui _____ in the forest. (am, was, were)

3 Maori carvings _____ often made from wood. (are, was, is)

B Rewrite the following sentences in the past tense.

1 I am on my way to see a play.

2 The actors are ready to begin.

3 The play is based on a Maori legend.

94

---

② Student Book teaching notes and grammar exercise answers

Display the VERBS chart created in Unit 2 (*see* page 38). Review the meaning of 'verb' and 'tense' (verb is a doing or action word, and the tense of the verb tells us the time of the action). Elicit the endings that show the action is in the present (–s, –ing) and the action happened in the past (–ed).

Tell students that some verbs are irregular – they do not end in –ed in the past tense. Ask them to work with a partner and think of five verbs that do not take –ed in the past tense (speak, eat drink, go, run, etc.).

Tell students that one of the most common irregular verbs is the verb 'to be'. Refer them to the chart on page 94 of the Student Book. Read through this together. In pairs, students take turns to say a sentence in the present using 'to be' and changing it to the past.

Students complete exercises A and B individually. Correct on the board, with students giving correct responses chorally.

A

Students rewrite the sentences, choosing the correct form of the verb 'to be' to fill the gaps.

Answers:

1 is

2 was

3 are

B

Students rewrite the sentences in the past tense.

Answers:

1 was

2 were

3 was

③ Top Tip

Read through the Top Tip with the students. Ask students to fold a page in their notebooks in two. Ask them to write 'present tense' on the left side, and 'past tense' on the right. Ask them to record irregular verbs here. To get them started, refer them to page 92 of the Student Book and ask them to find four verbs in the past tense that do not end in –ed (was, had, went, told). Ask them to write these in the 'past tense' column and write what the present form would be in the 'present tense' column (am, have, goes, tells).

④ Extension

Students work in pairs and turn the statements in exercise A and B into questions.

Example: Is the village elder an important man?

Alphabetical ordering

A dictionary lists words in **alphabetical order**. Words beginning with a come first, followed by words beginning with b. Words beginning with z come last.

Many words start with the letter a, so we also need to look at the second letter.

Example:
agree comes before **arrive** in a dictionary because g comes before r in the alphabet.

A Rewrite the words in alphabetical order.
1 tiger lion monkey zebra fish
2 yellow blue orange green pink
3 apple melon banana lemon peach

B Look at these groups of words. For each group, write the word that would come first in a dictionary.
1 friend feel fish football
2 alligator adventure animal art
3 plant pencil paint present

C Look up these words in a dictionary. Which comes first and why?

tonight today tomorrow

95

Learning objectives

⑤ Organize words or information alphabetically using first two letters.

Use a dictionary to find the spelling and meaning of words.

Students focus on the features of dictionaries and the Roman alphabet. They put words in alphabetical order using the first two letters. They find words that begin with the same two letters in a dictionary and say which comes first and why.

Remember to display the child-friendly learning objectives to the class along with the child-friendly checklist that students can use to assess how well they achieve them.

We know that we have achieved these because:

▶ We are able to put words in alphabetical order using the first two letters.

▶ We can find words that begin with the same two letters in a dictionary.

⑥ Student Book teaching notes and spelling exercise answers

It is a good idea for emergent bilinguals to have a bilingual dictionary in the classroom for reference (see Guidelines). Collect bilingual dictionaries in the home languages of the classroom. Invite all the children to take a look at them and notice similarities and differences. Elicit information from the students (they all have two languages; in some cases the scripts look different; there is information about grammar and punctuation, etc.). Ask students how they say 'dictionary' in their home languages.

Refer children to the Roman alphabet on page 95 of the Student Book. **Ask:** *How many letters are there?* (26.) *How many consonants and how many vowels?* (5 vowels, 21 consonants.) On a chart, write the home languages of the class and ask students how many letters/vowels characters, etc. there are. (They may need help from a parent or other home language speaker.)

Hand out English dictionaries. Read the information on page 95 with the students. Use the first and last page in their dictionaries to emphasize alphabetical order and demonstrate the rule of looking at the second letter to help with finding words.

Students work in pairs to complete exercises A, B and C.

Students rewrite the words in alphabetical order.

Answers:

1 fish, lion, monkey, tiger, zebra
2 blue, green, orange, pink, yellow
3 apple, banana, lemon, melon, peach

Students write the word that would come first in a dictionary. Correct as a whole group and ask students to articulate how they made their decision.

Answers:

1 feel
2 adventure
3 paint

Students look at a group of words, each beginning with the same two letters. They decide which comes first in a dictionary and explain why.

Answer:

Today comes first because the third letter of 'today' is 'd', which comes before the third letter of 'tomorrow' (m) and 'tonight' (n) in the alphabet.

Learning objectives

1

Read a range of story, poetry and information books and begin to make links between them.

Students discuss different kinds of weather and listen to a poem about the wind. They then read the poem in pairs. They discuss the features of the poem, comparing them with features of letters, and exploring the patterns in the verses.

Remember to display the child-friendly learning objective to the class along with the child-friendly checklist that students can use to assess how well they achieve it.

We know that we have achieved this because:

▶ We are able to identify the text as a poem.

▶ We can compare the features of the poem with other forms of text.

▶ We are able to identify the patterns in the verses.

Poetry Writing workshop

Writing a poem
Model writing

In the play script on pages 88–89 and 92, the Maori people want the sun to shine for longer each day. This poem describes what happens when the wind does not blow strongly enough.

Dear Mr Wind

Dear Mr Wind,
Could you please blow much harder
As we cannot
Sail our boats,
Dry our clothes,
Fly our kites!

Dear Mr Wind,
Could you please blow much harder
As we have
No breeze cooling us gently on a hot day
No waves crashing hard on the beach
No aeroplanes flying high in the sky!

Dear Mr Wind,
Please BLOW and BLOW
and BLOW and BLOW!

Moira Brown

96

② Writing workshop teaching notes

Model writing

Ask students to name the four seasons (spring, summer, autumn, winter). Write these words on a chart. Ask students how they say 'season' and each of the seasons in their home languages and ask whether there are four distinct seasons in their own countries. Elicit words that describe the weather in each season and put them on a chart. *Examples:* summer: warm; autumn: windy, etc. Ask students to turn to a partner and tell them what their favourite type of weather is and why.

Ask: *What did Maui want the sun to do each day?* (Shine for longer.) Tell the students you are now going to read them a poem and ask them to listen and make a note of the weather word and what happens if this type of weather is not strong enough. Read the poem (Student Books closed) emphasizing the question in the poem (Could you please blow much harder) and what you cannot do and have not got. The students share what they have understood. Now ask them to open their Student Books and read the poem in pairs, one verse each and the last verse together. See if they can add anything more to the list.

Ask: *Does the poem look like a letter?* (Yes, because it begins with 'Dear', but no because there is no date, address, etc.) See if the students can identify what punctuation is missing (question marks at the end of

the question in line 2 of verses 1 and 2). Point out that this is okay in poetry as we can use our voice to express a question.

Ask students to identify other features of the poem that make it different from a letter. *Examples:* the lines in the poem are broken up into short lines, while a letter would have full lines that are not broken up; in the poem each new line starts with a capital letter; the poem includes repetition of particular words to create an effect.

Ask: *How many verses are there?* (Three.) **Ask:** *Can you see a pattern in verses 1 and 2?* (Verse 1 has verbs at the beginning of lines 4, 5 and 6; verse 2 has 'No' at the beginning of lines 4, 5 and 6.)

Check for understanding of new words and encourage students to write them in their New Word List (*see* Workbook). Read the poem chorally, emphasizing the rising tone in the questions at the beginning of verses 1 and 2.

⇨

Poetry Writing workshop

Your writing

Write a poem that asks the sun to shine for longer. Use the same number of verses as the 'Dear Mr Wind' poem. The first four lines of the first two verses have been done for you.

Look at the notebook below and use the following ideas to help you write your poem:

- Write two more lines for the first verse shown below. Start each line with a verb.
- Then write two more lines for the second verse. Start each line with the word 'No'.
- Put an exclamation mark at the end of each verse.

How should you write verse 3?

Top Tip

When you have written your poem read it aloud to a partner. Can your partner suggest any way that you can improve it?

Dear Mr Sun,
Could you please shine for much longer
As we cannot
Grow our vegetables,
....
....

Dear Mr Sun,
Could you please shine for much longer
As we have
No gentle warmth heating our cold land
....
....

97

Learning objective

Write and perform poems, attending to the sound of words.

Students write a poem following the pattern of the 'Dear Mr Wind' poem they have read. They read and perform their poems, focusing on the tone and sound of words.

Remember to display the child-friendly learning objective to the class along with the child-friendly checklist that students can use to assess how well they achieve it.

We know that we have achieved this because:

▶ We can recognize how poetry is different from other writing.

▶ We know how to use our voice to make poetry understood and come to life.

---

④ Writing workshop teaching notes

Your writing

Tell students they are to write a 'Dear Mr Sun' poem following the pattern of the 'Dear Mr Wind' poem. Before they start, brainstorm why the students would like the sun to shine for longer.

Ask students to close their eyes and think of summer, then turn to their partner and share the picture that came into their mind.

Remind students of the pattern their poem needs to follow. Students work in pairs to create their own poems. (Every student should write their own poem.) Encourage partners to offer each other help and advice on word choice and state things that are good about the poem and things that could be improved. Circulate, making sure they follow the pattern.

Beginner second language students can write a poem in their home language. Work individually with children who can speak English but who are not yet ready to write, and scribe for them. When they have finished, they can illustrate their poem.

Model reading the 'Dear Mr Wind' poem aloud as a two-voice poem with a colleague. Both read the first three lines of verses 1 and 2 and take turns in reading lines 4, 5 and 6. Say the final verse together emphasizing 'Please BLOW and BLOW and BLOW and BLOW!' Ask students to practise reading their poems in the same way. Let them choose the lines they want to say together and the lines they want to say alone. Ask for volunteers to perform for the rest of the class.

⑤ Extension

1 Ask students to bring in poems about the weather in their home languages. They share the poems and give the gist of the poems in English.

2 If possible, play a section from Vivaldi's *The Four Seasons*. Ask the students to close their eyes and try to imagine the season as they listen. Elicit their ideas and accept all answers.

End of Unit Test

Question Paper

Reading: play script

Read the extract and answer the questions.

> ### The Camel, The Wolf and The Fox
>
> *(The wolf and the fox crawl close to the ground, while the camel stands high. They are walking around and come across a piece of bread on the ground.)*
>
> **Camel** Look, here is a piece of bread!
>
> 5 **Fox** We're so lucky!
>
> **Wolf** But what are we to do?
>
> **Fox** What do you mean?
>
> **Wolf** This bread is not enough for all three of us.
>
> **Fox** There is just enough for one of us. Let the oldest have it all.
>
> 10 **Wolf** *(smiling)* I am the oldest. I have been around over ten years!
>
> **Fox** Oh, my friend, my grandson is the same age as you! I have been here much longer than ten years! So, I am the oldest.
>
> *(As the wolf and the fox are arguing, the camel bends down and picks up the bread quietly and starts to chew on it happily.)*
>
> 15 **Camel** That's a lot of talking for little animals like you. Do you think that I was born yesterday, with legs so tall?
>
> *(The wolf and the fox circle around the camel while he keeps chewing, but can't reach his mouth. They get tired and walk away. The camel pats his stomach happily and walks the other way.)*
>
> Adapted from an Armenian fable.
>
> ---
>
> **Glossary**
>
> **arguing** having a discussion or debate.
>
> **come across** find.
>
> **crawl** move slowly on hands and knees, close to the ground.
>
> **pats** beats or taps gently.

Comprehension

(A) Give evidence from the text to support your answers.

1 What does the camel find?

_____ [1]

2 Which of the three animals does the fox think is the oldest?

_____ [1]

3 Which of the three animals eats the bread?

_____ [1]

(B) Give evidence from the text to support your answers.

1 What does the camel do while the wolf and fox are arguing?

_____ [1]

2 What does the wolf mean when he says, "What are we to do?"

_____
_____ [2]

3 Why do the fox and the wolf try to reach the camel's mouth?

_____ [1]

(C) Give evidence from the text to support your answers.

1 List the three main points in this play script.

_____
_____
_____ [3]

2 Why does the fox suggest that the oldest have the bread?

_____ [1]

3 Which animal do you think deserved to eat the bread? Give reasons for your answer.

_____
_____ [2]

Writing: poetry

Read the poem below about our world. Notice the repeated pattern:

- Verses 1 and 2 begin with the line 'Our world'.
- The second line in each verse is the same and has three adjectives.
- The third lines in each verse are the same except 'can' changes to 'must' in verse 2.
- Lines 4, 5 and 6 begin with a verb.
- The last line of verse 2 is repeated.

Our World

Our world
Is big, bright and beautiful
We are so lucky we can
Grow beautiful plants
5 Swim in oceans, rivers and seas
Play with animals of every kind

Our world
Is big, bright and beautiful
We are so lucky we must
10 Protect our trees
Take care of our seas
Look out for endangered animals
To keep our world big bright and beautiful
To keep our world big bright and beautiful

Glossary

endangered at risk of extinction.

grow plant in the ground and look after.

lucky having good things happening to you.

protect keep someone or something safe.

Write a poem about your family or your language.

Please use a separate sheet of paper.

Organize your poem in two verses like this and refer to the poem on page 118 to help you:

My ....

My ....
Is **(write three adjectives)** ....
I am so lucky I can ....
(Begin the next three lines with a verb)
Verb ....
Verb ....
Verb ....

My ....
Is **(write three adjectives)** ....
I am so lucky I must ....
(Begin the next three lines with a verb)
Verb ....
Verb ....
Verb ....
Last line ....
Repeat last line ....

[20]

7 It's a mystery!

(1) Warm-up objectives

Speak clearly and confidently in a range of contexts.

Take turns in discussion, building on what others have said.

Listen and respond appropriately to others' views and opinions.

Students talk about mystery and adventure stories in small groups and pairs. They take turns in discussion, listening to their classmates' views and responding appropriately.

Remember to display the child-friendly learning objectives to the class along with the child-friendly checklist that students can use to assess how well they achieve them.

We know that we have achieved these because:

▶ We can talk about a mystery setting and mystery stories in small groups and pairs.

▶ We are able to take turns in discussion, listening to and responding appropriately to the views of others.

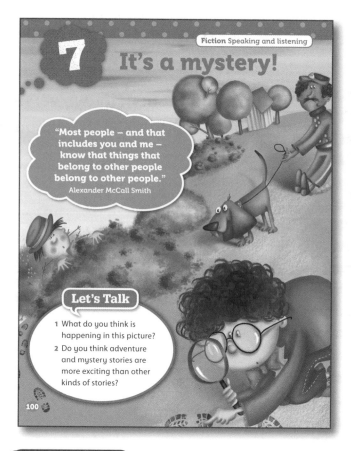

Fiction Speaking and listening

7 It's a mystery!

"Most people — and that includes you and me — know that things that belong to other people belong to other people."
Alexander McCall Smith

Let's Talk

1 What do you think is happening in this picture?
2 Do you think adventure and mystery stories are more exciting than other kinds of stories?

100

(2) Unit warm up

Bring a bunch of flowers or other treat to class. On a card, write 'For Class 3 and their teacher.' Place the treat in the centre of the room. Make a couple of muddy footprints on the floor or leave a window or door ajar that is not usually open. As the class is settling down, pick up the treat and ask lots of questions. **Ask:** *What's this? Who could have left it? When did they do it? How did they come in?* Discover the footprints or the open door or window. **Say:** *It's a mystery!*

Books open. Focus students' attention on the title of this unit on page 100 of the Student Book and elicit the meaning of the word 'mystery' (something strange or puzzling). At this point, some students may begin to realize you left the treat. Do not confirm. Write the word 'mystery' on a chart.

Read the quote bubble together. Discuss the quote and elicit words for people who take things that belong to other people (robber, thief, burglar). Ask if any of the students has heard of Alexander McCall Smith. Tell them he has written many children's books and make a point of looking for them next time the class visits the library.

(3) Let's Talk

1 Focus attention on the illustration. Elicit words to describe the different characters in the illustration (detective, police officer, thief, etc.). Write the words on the chart. Ask students to work in small groups to identify what they think is happening. **Ask:** *What is the detective doing?* (Looking at footprints.) *What is the detective holding?* (A magnifying glass.) *What is the character behind the bush doing?* (Hiding from the detective and police officer.)

2 Point out that an adventure story is a story about something exciting that someone does. In pairs, students discuss whether they prefer mystery and adventure stories to other kinds of stories. Encourage students to take turns in the discussion and listen to their partner's opinions.

(4) Extension

Students write a short story describing the mystery of the flowers/treat in the classroom. Point out that mystery stories often involve crimes but not always. They always, however, try to solve something that is unexplained. Ask the students to solve the mystery of the flowers/treat in the classroom. What clues did they have that it was you, etc? Have fun!

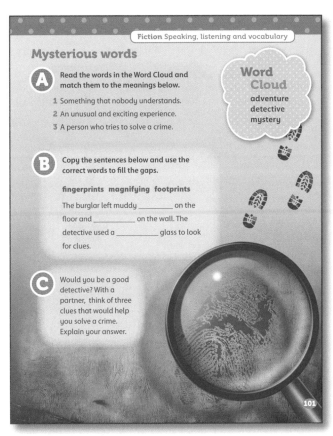

Fiction Speaking, listening and vocabulary

Mysterious words

A Read the words in the Word Cloud and match them to the meanings below.

1 Something that nobody understands.
2 An unusual and exciting experience.
3 A person who tries to solve a crime.

B Copy the sentences below and use the correct words to fill the gaps.

fingerprints   magnifying   footprints

The burglar left muddy _____ on the floor and _____ on the wall. The detective used a _____ glass to look for clues.

C Would you be a good detective? With a partner, think of three clues that would help you solve a crime. Explain your answer.

Word Cloud
adventure
detective
mystery

101

⑤ Learning objectives

Infer the meaning of unknown words from the context.

Develop sensitivity to ways that others express meaning in their talk.

Students work in pairs to guess the meanings of new words from the context. They work in pairs discussing clues that would help them solve a crime, responding sensitively to their partner.

🔘 Remember to display the child-friendly learning objectives to the class along with the child-friendly checklist that students can use to assess how well they achieve them.

We know that we have achieved these because:

▸ We can guess the meanings of mystery words from the context.

▸ We can listen and respond sensitively to our partner.

⑥ Word Cloud definitions

Focus students' attention on the Word Cloud. Ask them to work in pairs and match the meanings from the context. Remind students to write all new vocabulary in their New Word List (*see* Workbook).

adventure something exciting or interesting that someone does.

detective a person who investigates crimes.

mystery something strange or puzzling.

⑦ Student Book teaching notes and exercise answers

Add the word 'crime' to the chart of mystery words. Elicit a definition (an action that breaks the law). **Ask:** *What is the name for someone who breaks the law?* (Criminal.) Add this word to the chart. Elicit how to say 'crime' and 'criminal' in students' home languages. Write 'break the law' on the board and ask students to turn to their partner and think of three actions that break the law. ***Examples:*** driving too fast, stealing, hurting someone, etc.

Students match the words in the Word Cloud to their meanings.

Answers:

1   mystery
2   adventure
3   detective

Correct on the board. Do a syllable count and point out that we say 'a detective,' 'a mystery' but 'an adventure'. **Ask:** *Why is this?* (The words 'detective' and 'mystery' begin with consonants and 'adventure' begins with a vowel.)

Students copy the sentences and use the correct word to fill the gaps.

Answer:

The burglar left muddy **footprints** on the floor and **fingerprints** on the wall. The detective used a **magnifying** glass to look for clues.

Correct the exercise orally. Elicit from students what words helped them guess the answer (floor: footprint, wall: fingerprint, glass: magnifying).

Students discuss with a partner whether they would be a good detective and think of clues that they would use to solve a crime. Ask students to share their clues with the class.

Learning objectives

Read a range of story, poetry and information books and begin to make links between them.

Infer the meaning of unknown words from the context.

Students read a story and begin to make comparisons with other genres. They continue to guess the meaning of unfamiliar words from the context and other clues available to them.

Remember to display the child-friendly learning objectives to the class along with the child-friendly checklist that students can use to assess how well they achieve them.

We know that we have achieved these because:

▶ We can recognize similarities and differences between stories, poems and information books.

▶ We can correctly guess the meanings of unfamiliar words by trying the different clues we have available to us.

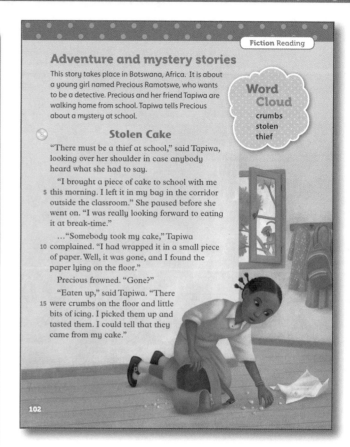

Adventure and mystery stories

This story takes place in Botswana, Africa. It is about a young girl named Precious Ramotswe, who wants to be a detective. Precious and her friend Tapiwa are walking home from school. Tapiwa tells Precious about a mystery at school.

Word Cloud
crumbs
stolen
thief

Stolen Cake

"There must be a thief at school," said Tapiwa, looking over her shoulder in case anybody heard what she had to say.

"I brought a piece of cake to school with me
5 this morning. I left it in my bag in the corridor outside the classroom." She paused before she went on. "I was really looking forward to eating it at break-time."

…"Somebody took my cake," Tapiwa
10 complained. "I had wrapped it in a small piece of paper. Well, it was gone, and I found the paper lying on the floor."

Precious frowned. "Gone?"

"Eaten up," said Tapiwa. "There
15 were crumbs on the floor and little bits of icing. I picked them up and tasted them. I could tell that they came from my cake."

102

② Fiction reading notes

Introduce the story by telling students that this is a special kind of story: one that is an adventure and a mystery. Remind students that an adventure is when something exciting and unexpected happens, and a mystery is when something that you cannot explain happens. Read the introduction to the story. Ask students to find Botswana on the world map at the front of the Student Book.

Ask students to look at the two illustrations and to try to guess what the story might be about. **Ask:** *Who do we see in the illustration on page 102?* (Tapiwa.) *What is she doing? Who do we see in the illustration on page 103? What are they doing?* (Precious and Tapiwa, walking home from school.) Do not bring up the monkeys in the illustrations unless one of the students mentions them. Write down on the board some of the ideas that students have about the story.

Begin reading the story or refer to the CD-ROM. Stop at unfamiliar words and direct students' attention to the clues chart created in Unit 1 (*see* page 10). Focus on the words in the Word Cloud. When you reach the appropriate section of the story, ask students whether they bring anything to school to eat at break-time. Ask them if they have ever brought something to eat from home that disappeared.

Point to the illustration on page 102 of the Student Book. **Ask:** *Was it a good strategy for Tapiwa to pick up the crumbs that were left on the floor and eat them to see if it was her cake?* (Yes, because that way she was sure it was her cake, but no, because she could have also been eating dirt off the floor and she is eating the evidence.)

③ Word Cloud definitions

Read aloud the words in the Word Cloud or refer to the CD-ROM. Can students guess the meanings from the context?

crumbs very small pieces of cake or bread.
stolen taken without permission.
thief someone who steals.

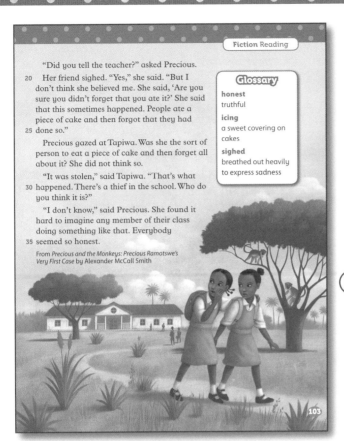

Write the elements of a mystery on a chart:

1 Something mysterious or bad happens.

2 Someone tries to explain the mystery.

3 We don't know if the explanation is true.

4 Someone looks for clues to solve the mystery.

5 Someone finds out what the truth is.

Ask students whether they think Precious and Tapiwa will solve the mystery. Elicit ideas about what happened to the cake and how students would go about solving the mystery. Point out that you will read the last part of this mystery later in the unit.

⑤ Extension

In groups of three, students read and act out the story up to this point, changing their voices to suit the roles of the narrator, Precious, Tapiwa and the teacher. Ask for volunteers to read and act out the story to the whole class.

④ Fiction reading notes ⊙

Continue to read the story or refer to the CD-ROM. Stop at unfamiliar words. When you get to the appropriate point in the text, ask students what they think the teacher thought had happened to the cake. Ask students whether they have ever eaten something and forgotten they had eaten it. **Ask:** *Why does Precious think that Tapiwa is not the kind of person who would forget that she had eaten a piece of cake? What kind of person would steal a cake that a student had brought to school to eat at break-time?*

Remind students of another thief that they have read about in an earlier unit ('The Sound Collector' in Unit 3). Remind students that the story of the sound thief was in the form of a poem. Ask students how this text differs from a poem. **Ask:** *What kind of things were stolen in the poem?* (Sounds.) *Did anyone catch that thief?* (No.)

Point out the mystery in this story: we don't know where the cake went; Tapiwa thinks that the cake was stolen and there is a thief in school; we don't know who would steal a cake; Precious thinks it does not make sense for someone to have stolen the cake because no one in class is a thief.

⇨

Learning objectives

Answer questions with some reference to single points in the text.

Identify the main points or gist of a text.

Students review the story that they have read so far and answer questions that require understanding of the gist of the text as well as specific points.

 Remember to display the child-friendly learning objectives to the class along with the child-friendly checklist that students can use to assess how well they achieve them.

We know that we have achieved these because:

▶ We can answer questions about events in the story correctly.

▶ We can find words that represent a specific idea in the story.

▶ We can answer questions that show we understand what the main points of the story are.

② **Student Book teaching notes and comprehension answers**

Ⓐ

Students re-read the story on pages 102–103 of the Student Book and answer the questions.

Answers:

1 The phrase 'in the corridor outside the classroom' tells us where Tapiwa left her cake.

2 Tapiwa found three clues on the floor: the paper that her cake had been wrapped in; cake crumbs that tasted like her cake; and pieces of icing that tasted like her cake (but no cake).

3 The teacher thought that Tapiwa had eaten the cake herself but forgotten that she had eaten it. Ask students if they think this is a good explanation for what had happened to the cake.

4 The word that describes what Precious thought of her classmates is 'honest'. Ask students whether they think Precious is on the right track to finding the thief because she thinks that it was not likely that one of her classmates had stolen the cake.

⇨

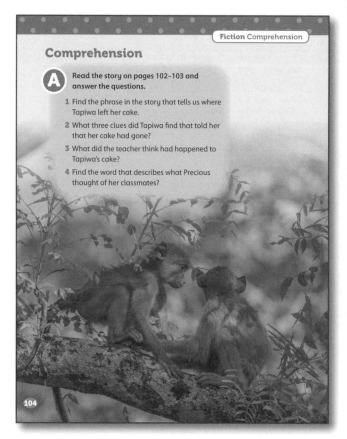

Fiction Comprehension

Comprehension

Ⓐ Read the story on pages 102–103 and answer the questions.

1 Find the phrase in the story that tells us where Tapiwa left her cake.

2 What three clues did Tapiwa find that told her that her cake had gone?

3 What did the teacher think had happened to Tapiwa's cake?

4 Find the word that describes what Precious thought of her classmates?

104

Direct students' attention to the picture on page 104 of the Student Book. Why do they think that the picture is of two monkeys? Do not give away the ending of the story. If no one says that it might be the monkeys who stole the cake, just leave it at that. If one of the students says it might be the monkeys who stole the cake, then just leave it as a possibility but do not confirm that they are right.

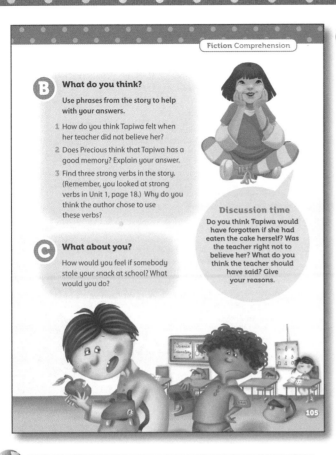

Fiction Comprehension

B What do you think?

Use phrases from the story to help with your answers.

1 How do you think Tapiwa felt when her teacher did not believe her?

2 Does Precious think that Tapiwa has a good memory? Explain your answer.

3 Find three strong verbs in the story. (Remember, you looked at strong verbs in Unit 1, page 18.) Why do you think the author chose to use these verbs?

C What about you?

How would you feel if somebody stole your snack at school? What would you do?

Discussion time

Do you think Tapiwa would have forgotten if she had eaten the cake herself? Was the teacher right not to believe her? What do you think the teacher should have said? Give your reasons.

105

3 Learning objectives

Begin to infer meanings beyond the literal, for example about motives and character.

Consider how choice of words can heighten meaning.

Take turns in discussion, building on what others have said.

Students answer questions about the mystery story and focus on the use of powerful verbs. They participate in a discussion, following the appropriate rules of conversation, using what others have said to develop and build on their own ideas.

Remember to display the child-friendly learning objectives to the class along with the child-friendly checklist that students can use to assess how well they achieve them.

We know that we have achieved these because:

▶ We can answer questions about the characters and events in the story that are not explicitly stated in the text.

▶ We can discuss whether the teacher was right not to believe Tapiwa, building on others' ideas to help develop our own opinions.

4 Student Book teaching notes and comprehension answers

B

Students use phrases from the text to help with their answers. Encourage students to use their own words to write the answers rather than copy word for word from the play script.

Answers:

1 Tapiwa felt sad and disappointed. **Ask:** *How do you know this?* (Because Tapiwa sighed as she told Precious about the teacher's response.)

2 Yes, because she didn't think that Tapiwa would forget eating her cake.

3 Accept any three of 'complained', 'frowned', 'sighed', and 'gazed'. The author chose these words because they carry more meaning than plainer words such as 'said' and 'looked'.

C

Tell students about a time when you had something stolen from you, how you felt about it and what you did. Then ask students the questions in this section. Ask them to jot down their ideas as to what they would do if their snack were stolen at school. Elicit responses from students, and write them down on the board. Read through the responses and ask for a show of hands for each one of the responses.

5 Discussion time

Divide the class into two groups: those who think that Tapiwa could have forgotten that she had eaten the cake and those who think this wasn't possible. Each group gives reasons for their opinions and writes them down as notes. One student from each group defends their point of view and a discussion follows. Ask students if any of them have changed their opinion after hearing the views of others.

Next, ask the second question. If anyone thinks that the teacher was right, ask them to defend their point of view and note it. Elicit from students other possible responses that the teacher could have given. Try them out in the form of a short scene of a play between Tapiwa and the teacher, with Tapiwa informing the teacher of her loss and the teacher responding. Vote on the best response.

Learning objectives

Read a range of story, poetry and information books and begin to make links between them.

Infer the meaning of unknown words from the context.

Students read the second part of the story in which the mystery is resolved. They identify the features of mystery stories and continue to guess the meanings of unfamiliar words from the context and other clues available to them.

 Remember to display the child-friendly learning objectives to the class along with the child-friendly checklist that students can use to assess how well they achieve them.

We know that we have achieved these because:

▶ We can identify the different ways that a story can be told.

▶ We can correctly guess the meanings of unfamiliar words by using the different clues we have available to us.

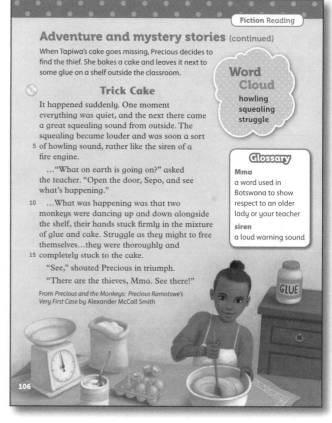

Fiction Reading

Adventure and mystery stories (continued)

When Tapiwa's cake goes missing, Precious decides to find the thief. She bakes a cake and leaves it next to some glue on a shelf outside the classroom.

Trick Cake

It happened suddenly. One moment everything was quiet, and the next there came a great squealing sound from outside. The squealing became louder and was soon a sort
5 of howling sound, rather like the siren of a fire engine.

…"What on earth is going on?" asked the teacher. "Open the door, Sepo, and see what's happening."
10 …What was happening was that two monkeys were dancing up and down alongside the shelf, their hands stuck firmly in the mixture of glue and cake. Struggle as they might to free themselves…they were thoroughly and
15 completely stuck to the cake.

"See," shouted Precious in triumph.

"There are the thieves, Mma. See there!"

From Precious and the Monkeys: Precious Ramotswe's Very First Case *by Alexander McCall Smith*

Word Cloud

howling
squealing
struggle

Glossary

Mma
a word used in Botswana to show respect to an older lady or your teacher

siren
a loud warning sound

106

2 Fiction reading notes

Before you begin to read the introduction, ask students again for their own ideas on how they would solve the mystery and catch the thief. Write the different suggestions on the board. Read the introduction and see if any of the students' suggestions comes close. Ask students how they think leaving the cake on a shelf next to some glue might help to catch the thief.

Begin reading the story or refer to the CD-ROM. Stop at unfamiliar words and ask students to guess the meanings. When you get to the end of the first paragraph, stop and ask for predictions from the students. **Ask:** *Where was the squealing and howling coming from?* Direct students' attention to the illustration on page 107 of the Student Book.

Bring out the chart on which you listed elements of mysteries and, pointing to the last element, ask students to summarize what happened.

3 Word Cloud definitions

Read aloud the words in the Word Cloud or refer to the CD-ROM. Ask whether students can work out their meanings from the context or from the other clues available to them (*see* page 10).

howling making a long sad sound like that of an animal in pain.

squealing a long, sharp piercing cry.

struggle try with great effort.

4 Extension

Look through the two parts of this mystery and list all the characters in it (Tapiwa, Precious, teacher, Sepo, two monkeys, other students in the classroom.) Divide the story into four or five parts and ask small groups of students to write one of the parts as a play script. Help the groups refine their work and put the pieces together to form a play. Make copies of the text and distribute it to students. Ask them to observe differences and similarities in the two forms of the story. Assign roles and act out the play.

6 Student Book teaching notes and comprehension answers

A

Students read the text on page 106 of the Student Book and find the three sentences that are true.

Answers:

1, 3 and 4

B

Students use phrases from the text to help with their answers. Encourage students to use their own words to write the answers rather than copy word for word from the play script.

Answers:

1   Precious put glue on the shelf so that whoever tried to eat the cake would get stuck to the glue and they would be caught.

2   Accept answers that give any reasonable reason why the monkeys started to squeal. *Examples:* because they couldn't get their hands unstuck; they were afraid; they were very surprised to be stuck; they were angry because they couldn't eat the cake; they couldn't run away.

3   The monkeys sounded like the siren of a fire engine. **Ask:** *Does the siren of a fire engine in your country sound like squealing?* In some countries fire engines have a low and very loud honk instead.

4   Yes. She shouted 'in triumph'.

C

Students can work in pairs to talk about whether Precious was right to do what she did. Ask students to list the reasons why Precious was right to do what she did (she solved the mystery; she helped her friend; she got rid of doubts in Tapiwa's mind about the honesty of her classmates). Also suggest that students think of some possible negative results of her actions (the monkeys could have become very frightened or eaten the glue and become ill).

5 Learning objectives

Answer questions with some reference to single points in the text.

Begin to infer meanings beyond the literal, for example about motives and character.

Identify the main points or gist of a text.

Students answer questions about specific points in the mystery and give answers to questions relating to characters and events that are not explicitly given in the text. Students answer questions that require an understanding of the main points or gist of the text.

Remember to display the child-friendly learning objectives to the class along with the child-friendly checklist that students can use to assess how well they achieve them.

We know that we have achieved these because:

▶ **We can correctly answer questions about specific points in the text.**

▶ **We understand points about characters and events that are not explicitly written about in the text.**

7 Challenge

Help students understand what a detective is (someone who solves mysteries such as crimes). Write on the board the characteristics that make a good detective. *Examples:* creative (can think of different solutions to problems), energetic, works hard, intelligent, wants to help people, wants to find out the truth, wants to be fair. Ask students, in pairs, to decide whether Precious had these characteristics. Ask students how they know.

Learning objectives

Extend earlier work on prefixes.

Use a dictionary to find the spelling and meaning of words.

Students build on what they already learned about the use of prefixes. They learn about the prefixes *non–*, *mis–*, *anti–*, *co–* and *ex–* and consider how these prefixes change the meanings of words. They use a dictionary to find words that begin with these prefixes.

 Remember to display the child-friendly learning objectives to the class along with the child-friendly checklist that students can use to assess how well they achieve them.

We know that we have achieved these because:

▶ We can use the prefixes *non–*, *mis–*, *anti–*, *co–* and *ex–* correctly.

▶ We can find the correct spellings of words in a dictionary.

Fiction Vocabulary and spelling

Prefixes, non- and mis-

A **prefix** is a group of letters added to the beginning of a word. When you add a prefix to a word, you change the meaning of the word.

Top Tip

When we add a **prefix** to a word, we sometimes need to add a **hyphen** (-) between the **prefix** and **root word**.

Example: non- + stick = non-stick

A The prefix *non-* means 'not' or 'opposite of'. Rewrite the following sentences, adding the prefix *non-* to fill the gaps.

1 The detective thought what the burglar said was _____sense.

2 The author wrote _____-fiction books.

3 We booked a _____-stop flight from London to Cairo.

Challenge

With a partner, use a dictionary to find as many words as you can that begin with the prefixes *mis-* and *non-*. Can you work out the meanings before you read the definitions?

B The prefix *mis-* means 'wrong' or 'false'.

1 Rewrite the following words, adding the prefix *mis-*.

behave judge take lead

2 How does the prefix change the meaning of the words?

3 Write a sentence using each of the words you made in 1.

108

---

2 Student Book teaching notes and vocabulary and spelling exercise answers

Review the use of the prefixes that students learned in Unit 3. Tell them that there are other prefixes that also attach to words and change their meaning. Make a chart on the board with five columns. At the top of the first write 'non–', with 'dairy', 'essential' and 'existent' below. In the next column, write 'mis–' at the 'top', with 'print', 'place' and 'lay' below. Have the prefixes *non–* and *mis–* written on strips of paper. Place the strips of paper with the prefixes next to the word it belongs to on the chart and read the words aloud. Encourage students to join you. Explain the meaning of the word without the prefix and with the prefix.

A

Students rewrite the sentences, adding the prefix *non–* to the words to fill the gaps.

Answers:

1 nonsense
2 non-fiction
3 non-stop

⇨

B

1 Students rewrite the words adding the prefix *mis–*.

Answers:

misbehave, misjudge, mistake, mislead

2 Students state how the prefix *mis–* changes the meaning of the words.

Answer:

The prefix *mis–* makes the words mean 'not like that' or 'badly' (misbehave: behave badly; misjudge: judge wrongly; mistake: something wrong; mislead: lead in the wrong way).

---

3 Top Tip

Point out the three words in exercise A. Ask students to observe how one of the words (nonsense) does not need a hyphen whereas the other two do.

---

4 Challenge

Students look in a dictionary for as many words as they can find that begin with the prefixes *mis–* and *non–*. If different pairs of students work with different dictionaries, you can see whether all the dictionaries have the same number of words with each prefix. To help students work out the meaning of a word, direct their attention to the clues chart created in Unit 1 (*see* page 10).

Prefixes, anti-, co- and ex-

Prefix	Meaning	Example
anti-	against	antifreeze
co-	joint, together	coordinate
ex-	out of, away from	export

A Match the following words to the meanings below.

exhale anticlockwise coexist

1 In the opposite direction to the way the hands of a clock move round.
2 To breathe out.
3 To live together or at the same time.

B Copy the following sentences and fill the gaps with the words below, adding the prefix *anti-*, *co-* or *ex-*.

1 "A monkey has eaten my cake!" ___claimed Tapiwa.
2 The detective ___operated with the policeman.
3 The nurse gave the patient an ___biotic to make him feel better.

C Look up the meaning of the following words in a dictionary. Then make up three sentences of your own, using each of the words.

explode antidote coincidence

MEDICINE

109

C

Students look up the words in a dictionary and write a sentence using each of the words. Allow students to work in pairs for this exercise. Accept any sentence in which the words are used appropriately (explode: blow up; antidote: remedy to counteract poison; coincidence: two things happening at the same time by accident).

6 Extension

1 Give pairs of students (or groups of three) all five prefixes on strips of paper, and two words for each of the prefixes, also on strips of paper. Ask them to match the prefixes with the appropriate words. The group that finishes first gets to pick students to read aloud to the rest of the class the words with the prefixes attached.

2 Tell students that you will be solving a mystery called 'The Stolen Prefixes'. Prepare a pile of words, some with the five prefixes that students have just learned, and some without their prefixes, such as 'take'. Hide or place around the classroom strips of paper with one of the five prefixes on each strip. Tell students that someone stole the prefixes from some of the words. Hold up a word from the pile, and ask students to read it aloud. If it's a word with a stolen prefix, students go searching for the correct prefix and bring it to the teacher.

3 Tell students that the Prefix Monster came into the classroom and mixed up the prefixes of some words and that they have to help to put the words back so that they are correct. Prepare a pile of strips with a word on each strip. The words should have the wrong prefix. ***Examples:*** 'antitake' instead of 'mistake', 'co-fiction' instead of 'non-fiction'. Pull out a word and read it yourself. If students think that the word has the wrong prefix on it, they try to find the correct prefix on a strip of paper, hidden or placed around the classroom.

---

5 Student Book teaching notes and vocabulary and spelling exercise answers

At the top of the third column of the chart on the board, write 'anti–', with 'freeze' and 'slip' below. In the fourth column, put 'co–' at the top and '-worker' and 'operate' below. In the fifth column, write 'ex–' at the top and 'port' and 'tend' below. Show the use of these three prefixes in the same way as you did with *non–* and *mis–*.

A

Students match the words to the meanings.

Answers:

1 anticlockwise
2 exhale
3 coexist

B

Students copy the sentences and fill the gaps.

Answers:

1 exclaimed
2 cooperated
3 antibiotic

Learning objective

①

Identify pronouns and understand their function in a sentence.

Students learn that pronouns are words we use instead of nouns.

Remember to display the child-friendly learning objective to the class along with the child-friendly checklist that students can use to assess how well they achieve it.

We know that we have achieved this because:

▶ We can identify and use pronouns instead of nouns in sentences.

② ## Student Book teaching notes and grammar exercise answers

Write the word 'Pronouns' on a chart and ask students if they can recognize a word within the word (noun). Elicit the meaning of 'noun' (a word that names a person, place or thing). Ask them if they can name the group of letters before the beginning of the word noun (prefix). Tell them that the prefix 'pro' means 'taking the place of', and a 'pronoun' is a word that takes the place of a noun in a sentence. Direct students' attention to the pronouns box and read the pronouns aloud.

Take sample sentences from students' writing and show them how they have used pronouns already in their writing. Choose examples that link the pronoun to the noun it replaces and circle both noun and pronoun, demonstrating the link. Explain that they know how to do this already and they are only learning the name for this kind of word.

Students copy the sentences individually replacing the noun with a pronoun. Correct as a group with students reading chorally.

Answers:

1 it
2 she

Students copy the sentences and fill the gaps with the missing pronoun.

Answers:

1 you
2 we
3 I

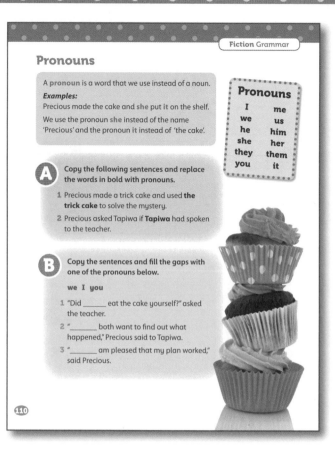

Pronouns

A **pronoun** is a word that we use instead of a noun.
Examples:
Precious made the cake and she put it on the shelf.
We use the pronoun she instead of the name 'Precious' and the pronoun it instead of 'the cake'.

Pronouns	
I	me
we	us
he	him
she	her
they	them
you	it

A Copy the following sentences and replace the words in bold with pronouns.

1 Precious made a trick cake and used **the trick cake** to solve the mystery.
2 Precious asked Tapiwa if **Tapiwa** had spoken to the teacher.

B Copy the sentences and fill the gaps with one of the pronouns below.

we I you

1 "Did _____ eat the cake yourself?" asked the teacher.
2 "_____ both want to find out what happened," Precious said to Tapiwa.
3 "_____ am pleased that my plan worked," said Precious.

110

③ ## Extension

1 Copy the pronouns in the pronouns box on page 110 of the Student Book onto a chart. Ask students to close their eyes and while their eyes are shut, cover a couple of pronouns with sticky notes. Students call out the missing pronouns. Ask them to fold a page in two in their notebooks and copy the pronouns box. Hand out sticky notes and let the students play the game in pairs.

2 Tell students they are detectives and their job is to look at pages 102 and 103 of the Student Book and find as many pronouns as they can. They can then report back to the whole group. Together students identify the noun that relates to the pronoun.

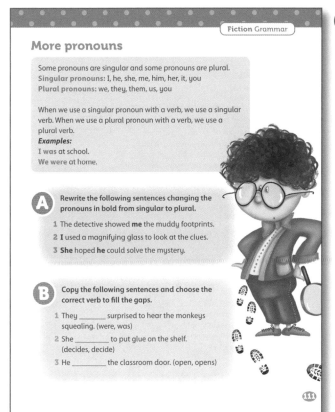

Fiction Grammar

More pronouns

Some pronouns are singular and some pronouns are plural.
Singular pronouns: I, he, she, me, him, her, it, you
Plural pronouns: we, they, them, us, you

When we use a singular pronoun with a verb, we use a singular verb. When we use a plural pronoun with a verb, we use a plural verb.
Examples:
I was at school.
We were at home.

A Rewrite the following sentences changing the pronouns in bold from singular to plural.

1 The detective showed **me** the muddy footprints.
2 **I** used a magnifying glass to look at the clues.
3 **She** hoped **he** could solve the mystery.

B Copy the following sentences and choose the correct verb to fill the gaps.

1 They _____ surprised to hear the monkeys squealing. (were, was)
2 She _____ to put glue on the shelf. (decides, decide)
3 He _____ the classroom door. (open, opens)

111

(4) Learning objectives

Understand pluralization and use the terms 'singular' and 'plural'.

Ensure grammatical agreement of pronouns and verbs in using standard English.

Students identify singular and plural pronouns. They learn that when we use a singular pronoun we use a singular verb and when we use a plural pronoun we use a plural verb.

 Remember to display the child-friendly learning objectives to the class along with the child-friendly checklist that students can use to assess how well they achieve them.

We know that we have achieved these because:

▶ We are able to identify singular and plural pronouns and use them correctly in sentences.

▶ We know that singular and plural pronouns replace nouns and that the verbs that go with them must agree (singular or plural).

(5) Student Book teaching notes and grammar exercise answers

Review the meaning of 'singular' and 'plural'. Elicit how we say these words in home languages. Point to the chart with 'One' and 'More than one' created in Unit 5 (*see* page 94) to reinforce these concepts. Tell students that when we use a singular pronoun with a verb we must use a singular verb and when we use a plural pronoun the verb must also be in the plural.

Write the singular pronouns (I, he, she, me, him, her, it) on a chart and elicit sentences from students. Underline the pronoun and the verb. Do the same with plural pronouns (we, they, them, us).

Read aloud the box at the top of page 111 of the Student Book. Ask second language students to translate this with the help of a parent or other speaker of their home language.

Students complete A and B individually.

Students rewrite the sentences, changing the singular pronouns to plural.

Answers:

1 us
2 we
3 They/they

Students copy the sentences and use the correct verb to fill the gaps.

Answers:

1 were
2 decides
3 opens

(6) Extension

Write the pronouns listed in the box on page 110 of the Student Book on four individual index cards. Divide students into four groups. Write a sentence on the board and challenge a group one at a time to find the right pronoun to replace the noun in the sentence.

Learning objectives

①

Read a range of story, poetry and information books and begin to make links between them.

Identify different types of stories and typical story themes.

Students read an adventure story and identify its features and themes.

Remember to display the child-friendly learning objectives to the class along with the child-friendly checklist that students can use to assess how well they achieve them.

We know that we have achieved these because:

▶ **We can identify the features and themes of an adventure story.**

▶ **We can feel the sense of excitement in an adventure story and see how the writer has created this.**

② Writing workshop teaching notes

Model writing

Tell the students they are going to read the beginning of an adventure story. Refer them to the picture on page 112 of the Student Book and ask them to turn to their partner and say what the story will be about. (The children are lost.) Ask what they think the children can see and hear. Write students' ideas on the board. Ask them whether they have ever been lost and if so, ask them to explain how they felt.

Read the Glossary with the students and ask them to listen to how you read the words as you read the story.

Read the story, changing your voice to act out the anger and fear in the children's voices, ending with a loud and frightening ROAR! Ask students to turn to their partner and say who or what made the roar. Listen to their ideas.

Ask students to find the word 'retorted' in the story. **Ask:** *How was Stefania feeling when she retorted "No"?* (Angry.) *What helped you guess this?* (She was stamping her feet.) Tell them the word retort means to reply quickly or angrily.

Next ask students to find the word 'quiver' in the story. **Ask:** *Do you remember how my voice sounded when I read this word?* (Shaky, as if you were about to cry.) Tell students that 'to quiver' means to shake or tremble and Stefania's voice was shaking with fear.

⇨

Writing an adventure story
Model writing

Read the story below about Stefania and Ivan's adventure in a forest.

Glossary

quivered
trembled

retorted
replied

The Adventure in the Forest

"It's your fault!" shouted Ivan, his small, round face red and angry.

"No," retorted Stefania, stamping her feet, "it's yours. You asked mother if we could play in the forest, and now we're lost and..." Her voice quivered, "no one is ever going to find us!"

Fearfully, they both looked around. The hundreds and hundreds of tall trees blocked out the light from the sky so that there was not a path to be seen, anywhere.

"What was that?" whispered Stefania.

"What?"

"That noise. Can't you hear it?"

"No, don't be silly..."

But at that point Ivan stopped. There was a noise. And it was the loudest noise he had ever heard. A roar, in fact – and whoever (or whatever) was making it, it seemed to be coming towards them. ROAR...!

112

Ask: *How do we recognize the dialogue in the extract?* (Speech marks.) Tell them to put everything in speech marks in a box and identify who is speaking.

Ask students to read the extract in groups of three (narrator, Ivan and Stefania). Give the gist of the extract to beginner second language students, using the picture to help you tell the story. Remind them to put new vocabulary in their New Word List (*see* Workbook).

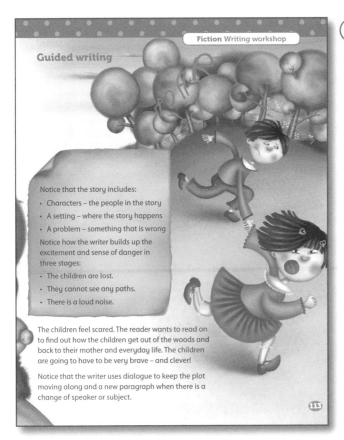

Fiction Writing workshop

Guided writing

Notice that the story includes:
- Characters – the people in the story
- A setting – where the story happens
- A problem – something that is wrong

Notice how the writer builds up the excitement and sense of danger in three stages:
- The children are lost.
- They cannot see any paths.
- There is a loud noise.

The children feel scared. The reader wants to read on to find out how the children get out of the woods and back to their mother and everyday life. The children are going to have to be very brave – and clever!

Notice that the writer uses dialogue to keep the plot moving along and a new paragraph when there is a change of speaker or subject.

113

Learning objective

③

Use reading as a model for story writing.

Students read the beginning of an adventure story as a model for their own story writing. They identify the main features of the story that they will use in their own writing.

🔘 Remember to display the child-friendly learning objective to the class along with the child-friendly checklist that students can use to assess how well they achieve it.

We know that we have achieved this because:

▶ We can see how the writer has created a sense of excitement and danger.

▶ We identify the main features of model writing that we will use to finish the adventure story.

④ Writing workshop teaching notes

Guided writing

The purpose and social function of an adventure narrative is to project a world in which unexpected things happen to the characters.

Ask: *Did Ivan and Stefania want to get lost?* (No, it just happened.) Ask students if their parents would give them permission to play in a forest by themselves. Elicit why not. (Because it's dangerous.) **Ask:** *What is the danger in this story?* (We don't know, but we can imagine something terrible and dangerous because of the loud roar.)

Direct the students to the picture showing the characters running out of the forest, looking scared. Ask them to turn to their partner and say what they think Ivan and Stefania might be shouting to each other. Students call out their ideas.

Read out the features included in an adventure story. Ask students to identify the characters in the story, describe the setting and say what the problem is. Ask them if they agree that the writer built up a sense of excitement. Go through the three points, asking the students to find them in the extract. Elicit how the writer created an eerie atmosphere (trees blocking out the light; the on-going dialogue between the children). Ask them if they felt scared as they read the extract. Explain to them that if they felt scared it was because the writer built up suspense. Write this word on the board and say that it means an uncomfortable or anxious feeling as you wait for an event to happen. Elicit how this happens in films (music, creaking doors, etc.). Explain that when a writer builds up suspense, the reader wants to read on to find out what happens.

Learning objectives

1

Write portraits of characters.

Develop descriptions of settings in stories.

Choose and compare words to strengthen the impact of writing.

Students finish the adventure story they read on page 112, using features of the adventure story genre. They understand the importance of choosing the right adjectives to describe characters and setting.

 Remember to display the child-friendly learning objectives to the class along with the child-friendly checklist that students can use to assess how well they achieve them.

We know that we have achieved these because:

▶ We are able to describe the characters and setting in an adventure story.

▶ We understand that careful choice of adjectives helps to show what characters look like and what kinds of personalities they have.

▶ We understand the importance of creating an image that the reader can see.

2 Writing workshop teaching notes

Your writing

Tell the students they are going to finish writing 'The Adventure in the Forest' story. Ask students to name the characters, describe the setting and give the main points of the plot so far.

Refer students to the chart on page 114. Read the 'characters' box and ask them to think back to the story. **Ask:** *What words does the writer use to help us learn about the characters?* (Ivan is angry; his face is small, round and red. We can guess that Stefania has a quick temper by the way she retorted "no" and stamped her feet.)

Next read the 'setting' box and ask the students how well the writer created a dangerous setting. **Ask:** *How was this achieved?* (Trees blocking out the light, etc.)

Point out how the writer has used a strong image that we can see clearly in our minds.

Finally refer them to the 'dialogue' box. Ask them to think back to the story. **Ask:** *Do you think the dialogue helps to create a sense of urgency/panic?* (Yes, we can sense the fear in the characters' voices.)

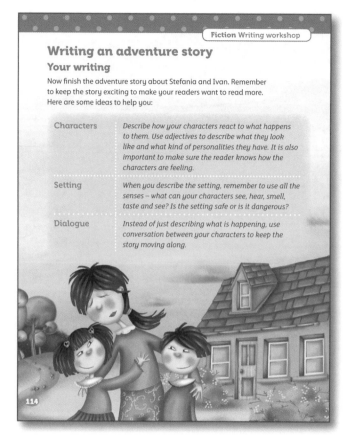

Fiction Writing workshop

Writing an adventure story

Your writing

Now finish the adventure story about Stefania and Ivan. Remember to keep the story exciting to make your readers want to read more. Here are some ideas to help you:

Characters	*Describe how your characters react to what happens to them. Use adjectives to describe what they look like and what kind of personalities they have. It is also important to make sure the reader knows how the characters are feeling.*
Setting	*When you describe the setting, remember to use all the senses – what can your characters see, hear, smell, taste and see? Is the setting safe or is it dangerous?*
Dialogue	*Instead of just describing what is happening, use conversation between your characters to keep the story moving along.*

114

Ask students to raise their hands if they think the writer has made the story exciting so far. If a student does not raise their hand, ask them to defend their point. Tell them you think the writer has helped us to understand the characters and their situation in this short piece of writing. Tell them that after reading it we want to know what happened to Ivan and Stefania and what caused the roar. Explain that this is what we want to do in adventure story – give the reader a sense of excitement from the very beginning.

Tell the students it is now their turn to finish the story. Ask them to look at the picture of the children coming out of the forest and think about what happened and how the story ended. **Ask:** *How did they find their way out? What made the roar? How are they feeling now?*

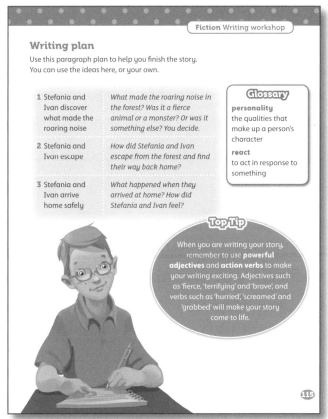

Writing plan

Use this paragraph plan to help you finish the story.
You can use the ideas here, or your own.

1	Stefania and Ivan discover what made the roaring noise	*What made the roaring noise in the forest? Was it a fierce animal or a monster? Or was it something else? You decide.*
2	Stefania and Ivan escape	*How did Stefania and Ivan escape from the forest and find their way back home?*
3	Stefania and Ivan arrive home safely	*What happened when they arrived at home? How did Stefania and Ivan feel?*

Glossary

personality
the qualities that make up a person's character

react
to act in response to something

Top Tip

When you are writing your story, remember to use **powerful adjectives** and **action verbs** to make your writing exciting. Adjectives such as 'fierce', 'terrifying' and 'brave', and verbs such as 'hurried', 'screamed' and 'grabbed' will make your story come to life.

115

(3) Learning objectives

Plan main points as a structure for story writing.

Consider how choice of words can heighten meaning.

Students will use a paragraph plan to organize their story and choose words that will make their story more exciting.

 Remember to display the child-friendly learning objectives to the class along with the child-friendly checklist that students can use to assess how well they achieve them.

We know that we have achieved these because:

▶ We can choose words that make our story exciting.

▶ We can use a paragraph planner to organize our ideas.

(4) Writing workshop teaching notes

Writing plan

Refer students to the Glossary and read through it. Write 'personality' on a chart and underneath it 'I am...' Ask each student to think of an adjective that describes their personality, and write it on chart. ***Examples:*** kind, helpful, cute, sweet, bad-tempered, friendly, tidy, untidy, naughty, etc.

Read through the paragraph plan point by point. Ask students to copy it. Read the Top Tip together.

Write the following headings at the top of three columns on a chart: Action verbs, Powerful adjectives, Instead of 'said'. Students work in pairs to find examples from their reading and writing. Set a time limit for the exercise. The pairs report back to the class. Record the words on the chart and include words from the Top Tip. Remind students to record new words in their New Word List (*see* Workbook). Encourage students to be creative with their choice of words.

When students have completed their first draft, ask them to share their story with a partner who has to check for the use of action verbs, powerful adjectives and other ways of saying 'said'. The partner should also focus on how well they have been pulled into the story and whether they kept wondering what will happen next.

Students should do a final copy and illustrate it. They can write a brief synopsis of their story in their home languages and this can be displayed next to the English version.

(5) Extension

Students write their own adventure stories from scratch to share with younger students. Encourage them to use illustrations. They can write these as dual language stories.

Make a collection of dual language writing. This can be a source of reading material for new arrivals. They will be very happy to see things written in a language/script that is familiar to them.

End of Unit Test

Question Paper

Reading: fiction

Read the extract and answer the questions.

Precious and the Monkeys

IT MIGHT HAVE BEEN EASY for her to forget about it – after all, it was only a piece of cake – but the next day it happened again. This time it was a piece of bread that was stolen – not an ordinary piece of bread, though: this one was covered in delicious red jam. You can lose
5 a plain piece of bread and not think twice about it, but when you lose one spread thickly with red jam it's an altogether more serious matter.

The owner of this piece of bread (with jam) was a small boy called Sepo. Everybody liked this boy because he had a habit of saying funny things. And people like that, because there are enough sad things in the
10 world as it is. If somebody can say something funny, then that often makes everybody feel a bit better. Try it yourself: say something funny and see how pleased everybody is...

Sepo had brought his piece of bread and jam in a brown paper bag. While Big Mma Molipi served lunch, he had left the bag in the
15 classroom, tucked away safely under his desk. He was sure that this is where he left it, and so when he went back in and saw that it had disappeared he was very surprised indeed.

"My bread!" he wailed. "Somebody's taken my bread!"

From *Precious and the Monkeys: Precious Ramotswe's Very First Case* by Alexander McCall Smith

Glossary

disappeared gone.
habit something you do often and almost without thinking.
jam a food made by boiling fruit and sugar.
ordinary common, not special in any way.
pleased happy.
serious important.
tucked away hidden in a safe place.

Comprehension

A Give evidence from the text to support your answers.

1 Where did Sepo leave his piece of bread?

_____ [1]

2 Why did people like Sepo?

_____ [1]

3 How did Sepo feel when he saw his bread had gone?

_____ [1]

B Give evidence from the text to support your answers.

1 Why was this piece of bread so special?

_____

_____ [2]

2 What did Sepo think had happened to his bread?

_____ [1]

3 When did Sepo find out that his bread had gone?

_____ [1]

C Give evidence from the text to support your answers.

1 What do you think the author means by 'it's an altogether more serious matter'?

_____

_____ [2]

2 What does the author think happens when someone says something funny?

_____ [1]

3 Why does the author suggest that you say something funny?

_____ [1]

Writing: fiction

Read the extract below from *Precious and the Monkeys*. Notice how the writer builds up the excitement in three stages.

- Precious and Poloko are walking down a dangerous path.
- They hear a noise in the rocks.
- They hear a noise again.

Precious and the Monkeys

They set off, following the path that wound down the hill. It was a narrow path and a winding one – here and there great boulders had rolled down the hill thousands of years ago and the path had to twist around these. In between the boulders, trees had grown up, their roots working their way
5 through gaps in the stone. These trees made the places in between the rocks a cool refuge from the heat of the sun, and sometimes Precious would sit down there and rest on her way home. But these places were also good hiding places for snakes, and so you had to be careful…

There was a noise off among the rocks, and they both gave a start.

10 "A snake?" whispered Poloko.

"Perhaps," said Precious. "Should we look?"

Poloko nodded. "Yes, but we must be careful."

They heard the noise again. This time Precious thought that it might be coming from the tree, and she looked up into the branches.

15 "There!" she said, pointing into the tangle of leaves.

Poloko looked up. He had expected to see a snake wound round one of the branches, but that was not what he spotted.

From *Precious and the Monkeys: Precious Ramotswe's Very First Case* by Alexander McCall Smith

---

Glossary

boulders large rocks.

gaps openings or breaks in something.

hill a piece of ground that is higher than the ground around it.

narrow not wide.

refuge a place where you are safe.

twist to turn round.

wound turned or twisted.

Finish Precious and Poloko's adventure story.

Please use a separate sheet of paper.

Remember to include the following features:

Characters

Describe how your characters react to what happens to them.

Setting

Use the senses when you describe the setting – what can your characters hear, see, smell, etc.?

Dialogue

Use dialogue to keep the plot moving along.

Paragraphs

Remember to use a new paragraph when there is a change of place, time, action or speaker. Organize your description in three paragraphs:

Paragraph 1:

What did Precious and Poloko see in the tree?

Paragraph 2:

How did they react, what did they do?

Paragraph 3:

What happened when they arrived home? How did they feel?

[20]

8 Our world

1 Warm-up objectives

Speak clearly and confidently in a range of contexts.

Take turns in discussion, building on what others have said.

Listen and respond appropriately to others' views and opinions.

Students talk in pairs and in whole-group discussions about where they live and what it is like to live in a remote place. They take turns in discussion, listening to their classmates and responding appropriately.

Remember to display the child-friendly learning objectives to the class along with the child-friendly checklist that students can use to assess how well they achieve them.

We know that we have achieved these because:

▶ We can talk clearly about where we live and what it is like to live somewhere remote.

▶ We are able to take turns in conversation.

▶ We can listen carefully to what our partner says and respond appropriately.

2 Unit warm up

In this unit, students will focus on the features of different countries and landscapes. Ask students if they have ever lived in or visited a place that is remote, far from a city or isolated in the wilderness. Students share their experiences as a whole class.

Read the quote together and point out that 'at hand' means 'nearby' and 'one' is a pronoun for 'friend'. Ask the students to work together in pairs and say what the quote means in their own words. (Sometimes our best friends are far away in terms of distance, but they may be closer to us or help us more than friends who live nearer to us, so distance is not an obstacle in friendship.)

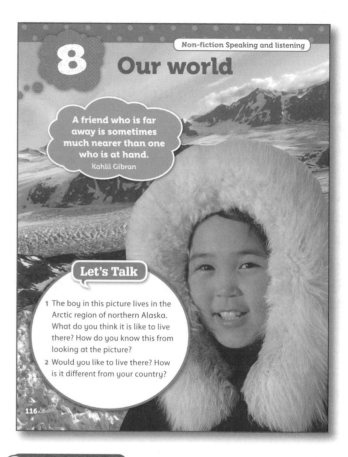

8 Our world

> A friend who is far away is sometimes much nearer than one who is at hand.
> Kahlil Gibran

Let's Talk

1 The boy in this picture lives in the Arctic region of northern Alaska. What do you think it is like to live there? How do you know this from looking at the picture?

2 Would you like to live there? How is it different from your country?

116

3 Let's Talk

1 Focus attention on the picture and ask students to share what they know about Alaska. Ask students to locate Alaska on the world map at the front of their Student Book and on the small map on page 117. Explain that most of Alaska is very isolated, with very few roads. Discuss the meaning of 'Arctic region' (the northernmost part of the earth) and tell students that Alaska is one of the coldest regions in the world. Refer students to the landscape in the picture and ask them to take turns describing it to their partner. Students share their descriptions as a class (no trees, lots of rocks, snow and ice, no houses or roads, etc.). Write what they say on the board.

2 Students discuss in pairs what they think it would be like to live in Alaska. Ask them to take turns to discuss the advantages and disadvantages of living in a remote place and how it would be similar and different from where they live. Students report their ideas back to the whole group.

Non-fiction Speaking, listening and vocabulary

A Look at the words in the Word Cloud and match them to the meanings here.

1 Very far away and isolated.
2 Very cold.
3 The regions around the North Pole.

Word Cloud
Arctic
frozen
remote

B Read about Michael, who is describing where he lives. Copy the sentences and use the words to fill the gaps.

warm neighbours summers region

I live on a farm in a remote _____ of Australia. We live hundreds of kilometres from our nearest _____. It is _____ all year round here and the _____ are hot and dry.

C Find out more about Alaska and Australia on the Internet. Work with a partner and talk about how the countries are similar to your own country and how they are different.

ALASKA North America · Europe · Asia · Africa · South America · Oceania · AUSTRALIA · Antarctica

117

Learning objectives

④ **Infer the meaning of unknown words from the context.**

Use ICT sources to locate simple information.

Develop sensitivity to ways that others express meaning in their talk.

Students guess the meanings of new words from the context. In pairs, they find out about Alaska and Australia on the Internet. They compare their own country with these parts of the world, responding sensitively in a discussion with their partner.

⊙ Remember to display the child-friendly learning objectives to the class along with the child-friendly checklist that students can use to assess how well they achieve them.

We know that we have achieved these because:

▶ **We can guess the meanings of words from the context.**

▶ **We can find out information about Alaska and Australia on the Internet.**

▶ **We can respond sensitively to our partner in conversation.**

⑤ Word Cloud definitions

Focus students' attention on the Word Cloud. Ask them to guess the meanings from the context. Ask students to write the cloud words in their home languages. Point out the pronunciation of new words and remind students to write the new vocabulary in their New Word List (*see* Workbook).

Arctic the area around the North Pole.
frozen covered with ice.
remote very far away.

⑥ Student Book teaching notes and exercise answers

Students match the words to the meanings.

Answers:

1 remote
2 frozen
3 Arctic

Ask students if they have ever been to Australia. Allow them to share their experiences. Tell students that they are going to read about a child who lives in a remote part of Australia. Students rewrite the sentences and fill in the missing words.

Answer:

I live on a farm in a remote **region** of Australia. We live hundreds of kilometres from our nearest **neighbours**. It is **warm** all year round here and the **summers** are hot and dry.

Students find Australia and Alaska on the map at the bottom of page 117 of the Student Book. Ask them to find out more about these places on the Internet and talk to their partner about how the two parts of the world are similar to and different from their own country. Remind them to listen to each other, ask questions appropriately and respond sensitively.

⑦ Extension

Make a chart with three columns, with the headings 'Home countries', 'Languages' and 'The weather'. Ask students to share information about their home countries.

Fun fact: The Alsaska region has 22 indigenous languages.

Learning objectives

①

Understand and use the terms 'fact', 'fiction' and 'non-fiction'.

Read a range of story, poetry and information books and begin to make links between them.

Infer the meaning of unknown words from the context.

Students read a non-chronological report, understanding that it describes facts about a real person and a real place. They learn that this type of text is non-fiction. Students guess the meanings of unfamiliar words from the clues available to them.

Remember to display the child-friendly learning objectives to the class along with the child-friendly checklist that students can use to assess how well they achieve them.

We know that we have achieved these because:

▶ We know what the terms 'fact', 'fiction' and 'non-fiction' mean.

▶ We can recognize similarities and differences between stories, poems and information books.

▶ We can correctly guess the meanings of unfamiliar words by using the different clues available to us.

② Non-fiction reading notes

Ask students if they remember the fictional stories that they have read about Abdullah in Unit 1, Bawang in Unit 4 and Precious in Unit 7. Tell them that in this lesson, they will read about a boy named Michael, who lives in Australia. Michael is a real boy, rather than a fictional character, and what they will read about him and his home are facts. Tell students that this type of text is called non-fiction. Ask students if they remember reading other pieces of non-fiction (instructions in Unit 2 and letters in Unit 5).

Refer students to the title 'Non-chronological reports'. Explain that the word 'chronological' is used to describe things in the order in which they happen. Remind students that the prefix *non*– means 'not'. Elicit the meaning of non-chronological.

Begin reading the text on page 118 of the Student Book or refer to the CD-ROM. Stop to clarify concepts that may be unfamiliar to students. When you get to the word 'chooks', ask students what language they think the word is (Australian English). Direct students' attention to the fact that the word is in italics, followed by an explanation of the word in brackets. Explain that italics ⇨

Non-fiction Reading

Non-chronological reports

Here is some more information about Michael. It is not a story (fiction). It is true (non-fiction).

. **Michael**

A sheep and cattle station in the South Australian outback is home to Michael, his sister and their parents. Because he lives so far from a school, Michael does his
5 schoolwork alone and talks to his teacher over a two-way radio.

Animals

As well as cattle and sheep, there are other animals on the station. The family keep *chooks*,
10 (chickens) for their eggs and ducks for their meat. There are dogs and also horses used for *mustering* (rounding up) the cattle.

Word Cloud
ranch
sheared
two-way radio
windmills

"I help feed and water the dogs, chooks, ducks, horses and cattle. When I grow up I would like my own cattle station so I could be like Dad."

Australia
Australia's population is small in relation to its size. Some farming families live hundreds of kilometres from their neighbours.

Australia

118

are sometimes used when a word might be unfamiliar to the readers. The word 'chooks' is Australian English, so may not be familiar to speakers of other forms of English. For many students, Michael's home setting may be very different from their own. It will be helpful for students to compare what they are reading with their own home and school throughout the text. For example, when you read about living on a farm with cattle and sheep, ask if students can relate to that. Ask students whether their family has any pets or other animals.

Talk a little about population density. Australia is the third least populated country in the world, with three people per square kilometre (seven people per square mile). If possible, ask students to look up information about population density on the Internet (www.worldatlas.com).

③ Word Cloud definitions

Read aloud the words in the Word Cloud or refer to the CD-ROM. Ask students to guess the meanings with the help of the factors on the chart (*see* page 10).

ranch a large farm where cattle and other animals are raised.

sheared cut off a sheep's wool.

two-way radio a radio made to send and receive messages over a distance.

windmills machines with arms called sails that turn in the wind, used for pumping water, grinding grain or producing electrical power.

Outdoors

Michael spends a lot of time outdoors. He loves
15 taking the dogs for a run and riding his bike
around the station. Twice a year he goes to
camp where he meets other children his age.

Sheep

There are 1,200 sheep and 550 cattle on the
20 ranch. Once a year, the sheep are sheared for
their wool. Even Michael and Rebecca [his
sister] get involved, although most of the work
is done by hired sheep hands.

*"The best thing about living in the outback are the
windmills, the open spaces and sunsets. The worst
thing is not being able to see my friends."*

Toys and games

25 Michael plays on his own with his toys – trucks,
tractors and a motorbike. He loves reading
Outback Magazine, and he also watches
television and plays games on his computer.

*From A Life Like Mine: How children live around
the world, Dorling Kindersley*

Glossary

outback
a remote region of
Australia

**sheep and cattle
station**
a large farm that
raises sheep and
cattle

sheep hands
farm workers who
look after sheep

*"I talk to my friend,
Naish, on the school
radio after lessons. He
lives on Bulgunnia
Station, 630 km (390
miles) from here."*

119

---

④ Learning objectives

**Consider ways that information is set out
on page.**

Identify the main purpose of a text.

Students continue to read a report about a
young boy who lives in Australia, focusing on
the way that the information is laid out on the
page. They recognize the key features and the
main purpose of the text.

Remember to display the child-friendly
learning objectives to the class along with the
child-friendly checklist that students can use to
assess how well they achieve them.

We know that we have achieved these because:

▶ **We are able to identify key features of a
report, including how the information is laid
out on the page.**

▶ **We understand the main purpose of
the text.**

---

⑤ Non-fiction reading notes

Continue to read the report or refer to the CD-ROM.
Ask: *What is the main purpose of this text?* (To give
information about the life of a boy called Michael who
lives in the Australian outback.) Point out the features
of the non-chronological report, including the
subheadings and the different fonts used for different
types of text on the page. **Ask:** *What is the purpose of
the subheadings?* (To indicate what the main topic of
each paragraph is.) *How do you know which text is a
heading and which is main text?* (The headings are in
bold and a larger font than the main text.)

Ask students to look at the photographs and consider
how they help us understand what Michael's life on
the farm is like. **Ask:** *Does the land around where you
live look like the land in the photograph on page 119 of
the Student Book? How is it different? Are the toys that
Michael plays with different from the toys you play with?*

Direct students' attention to the three quotes. **Ask:**
Are these words part of the report? (Yes, but they are
quotes, things that someone has said.) *How do you
know that they are words that someone has said?*
(There are speech marks before and after the words.)
Who said the words? (Michael.) *How do you know?*
(Michael is the focus of the report, and also because
of the placement of the first quote above Michael's
photograph.)

Tell students that the first quote is about the tasks
that Michael does around the ranch and what he'd
like to be when he grows up. Ask students to work
in pairs and tell each other the same things about
themselves.

Look at the second quote and ask students to write
down what the best things and the worst things are
about living where they live. Elicit responses from
students and write them down on the board. Mark
the replicate ideas to see the most liked and the least
liked things in students' settings.

Using a Venn diagram (*see* Guidelines), ask students
in pairs to list similarities and differences between
themselves and Michael (family members, where he
lives, what he plays with, age, pets, how he helps at
home, etc.).

Learning objectives

Scan a passage to find specific information and answer questions.

Answer questions with some reference to single points in the text.

Students scan the text on pages 118–119 to find specific information. They answer questions focusing on single points in the text.

 Remember to display the child-friendly learning objectives to the class along with the child-friendly checklist that students can use to assess how well they achieve them.

We know that we have achieved these because:

▶ We are able to scan the text to find specific information.

▶ We can answer questions about single points in the text correctly.

② Student Book teaching notes and comprehension answers

Ⓐ

Students scan the text on pages 118–119 of the Student Book and answer the questions. Encourage students to use their own words to answer the questions rather than copying word for word from the text. Correct orally with the class.

Answers:

1 Accept any four of cattle, sheep, chickens, ducks, dogs and horses. (Make sure that students understand that 'cattle' refers to cows.)

2 Michael does his schoolwork at home. He gets help from his teachers by using a two-way radio to talk to them.

3 The three things that Michael likes most about living in the outback are the windmills, the open spaces and the sunsets. (Direct students' attention to the photograph on page 120 of the Student Book. **Ask:** *How many of Michael's favourite things do you see?* (All three.)

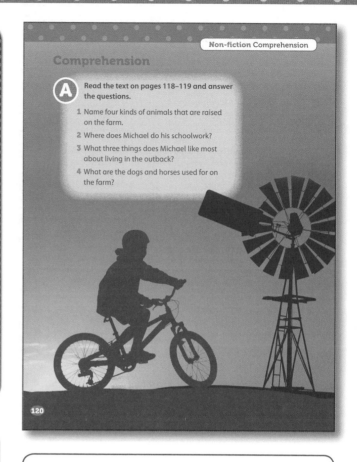

Non-fiction Comprehension

Comprehension

Ⓐ Read the text on pages 118–119 and answer the questions.

1 Name four kinds of animals that are raised on the farm.

2 Where does Michael do his schoolwork?

3 What three things does Michael like most about living in the outback?

4 What are the dogs and horses used for on the farm?

120

4 The dogs and horses are used for rounding up the cattle (to bring the cattle in or move the cattle around the farm). Ask students to think of other uses for dogs (pets, guarding the house) and horses (racing, carrying things, transportation) in other countries, particularly in their own country.

To extend the exercise and ensure that students understand, ask them to compare the responses from the text with their own experiences. **Ask:** *Would you like to do your schoolwork at home? What three things do you like most about the place where you live?*

Non-fiction Comprehension

B **What do you think?**

Use phrases from the text to help with your answers.

1 Why do you think it is difficult for Michael to see his friends?

2 Find four subheadings in the text. Why do you think these are included?

3 Do you think Michael is helpful on the farm? Explain your answer.

4 Find the three examples of quotes (words spoken by Michael). How do these help you understand more about Michael's life?

Discussion time

Discuss with a friend three reasons why you think it is important for children who live on farms in the outback to meet at camp twice a year?

C **What about you?**

How would you feel if you lived on a remote farm and had to do your schoolwork at home? Discuss your answer with a partner.

121

Learning objectives

③

Begin to infer meanings beyond the literal, for example about motives and character.

Speak clearly and confidently in a range of contexts.

Listen and respond appropriately to others' views and opinions.

Students answer questions that require understanding of points that are not explicitly described in the text. They participate in discussions, expressing their ideas and opinions clearly and following the accepted rules of conversation.

 Remember to display the child-friendly learning objectives to the class along with the child-friendly checklist that students can use to assess how well they achieve them.

We know that we have achieved these because:

▶ **We are able to answer questions about points that are not explicitly stated in the text.**

▶ **We are able to speak clearly in discussions with a partner.**

▶ **We can discuss our views and opinions with each other, listening and responding in a way that is considerate to others.**

④ Student Book teaching notes and comprehension answers

B

Students refer to phrases in the story to help with their answers. Ask students how they reached their conclusions.

Answers:

1 It is difficult for Michael to see his friends because they live too far away. The friend with whom he talks on the radio lives 630 km (390 miles) away.

2 The four subheadings are 'Animals', 'Outdoors', 'Sheep' and 'Toys and games'. Subheadings give us an idea of what each section of text is about.

3 Yes, Michael is helpful on the farm. He says that he helps to feed and water the animals. We also know that both Michael and his sister help to shear the sheep's wool once a year. Point out to students that they are making guesses about Michael's character based on other things we know about him. Remind students that they made these kinds of guesses about a character in texts in other units (about Bawang in the fictional story in Unit 4 and about Precious in Unit 7). Discuss whether there is a difference in making these guesses about characters in fiction versus non-fiction.

4 The quotes help us understand more about how Michael feels about his life on the farm because they tell us directly what Michael thinks in his own words. They are not the writer's words or the writer's opinion about what Michael thinks.

C

Students imagine what it would be like to live on a remote farm and do their schoolwork at home. They share their ideas with a partner.

⑤ Discussion time

Students participate in a discussion with a partner or small group. Help students wait for their turn, and make sure they are listening to each other's opinions in a respectful way. Encourage students to think about how going to camp benefits Michael and other children in his situation.

Learning objectives

Read a range of story, poetry and information books and begin to make links between them.

Infer the meaning of unknown words from the context.

Students read a non-chronological report and consider the kinds of information that non-fiction texts give us as compared to fictional stories. They continue to guess the meanings of unfamiliar words using the clues available to them.

Remember to display the child-friendly learning objectives to the class along with the child-friendly checklist that students can use to assess how well they achieve them.

We know that we have achieved these because:

▶ We can identify the different ways that information can be written: fiction and non-fiction.

▶ We can correctly guess the meanings of unfamiliar words by using the different clues we have available to us.

2 Non-fiction reading notes

Tell students that this is another text that deals with information that is true or factual. It gives us information about animals called meerkats. Tell students that meerkats live in Africa. Ask them to find where Africa is on the world map at the front of the Student Book.

Begin reading the extract aloud or refer to the CD-ROM. Stop at unfamiliar words and the words in the Word Cloud. Ask students to guess their meanings based on the four factors that will help them: illustrations, context, the structure of English and the structure of their home language (*see* page 10).

Remind students that information in non-fiction texts is supposed to be real or true. Discuss the possibility that it might not be, and how important it is for the reader to determine whether information is true or not. When we write fiction, we can invent what we want to say, but when we write non-fiction, we must gather information from trustworthy sources.

Non-fiction Reading

Non-chronological reports (continued)
Desert Meerkats

Meerkats are desert animals that live in groups called gangs. Meerkats dig underground burrows. The burrows are safe places where they give birth to their young. They sleep in
5 their burrows at night. In the daytime they leave their burrows and set off in search of food. When meerkats are in danger, they run to their burrows to keep safe.

Meerkats eat worms, grasshoppers, lizards,
10 snakes, scorpions, eggs and fruit. Most of all they love grubs!

When it's really hot, they have a nap. One meerkat stays awake and looks out for danger.

From Going Underground (Project X) by John Malam

Word Cloud

burrows
grubs
underground

Africa

Meerkats live in the Kalahari Desert, which is in Africa.

Africa

Kalahari Desert

122

3 Word Cloud definitions

Read aloud the words in the Word Cloud or refer to the CD-ROM. Ask students if they can see a prefix (one they have not studied yet) in one of the words in the Word Cloud ('under' in the word 'underground'). Ask students to think of other examples of this prefix. *Examples:* undercover, underwater, underarm.

burrows holes in the ground made by animals for shelter.
grubs tiny creatures that will become insects.
underground below the surface of the ground.

4 Extension

In pairs or groups of three, students write a fictional story about a meerkat, based on the information that they have in this text. For beginner second language students, you can give them lead sentences such as: 'It was a hot day and a meerkat named Morrie went… When he got to his burrow, he…'

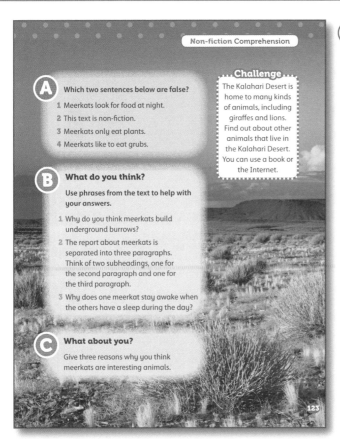

Non-fiction Comprehension

A Which two sentences below are false?

1 Meerkats look for food at night.
2 This text is non-fiction.
3 Meerkats only eat plants.
4 Meerkats like to eat grubs.

Challenge

The Kalahari Desert is home to many kinds of animals, including giraffes and lions. Find out about other animals that live in the Kalahari Desert. You can use a book or the Internet.

B What do you think?

Use phrases from the text to help with your answers.

1 Why do you think meerkats build underground burrows?
2 The report about meerkats is separated into three paragraphs. Think of two subheadings, one for the second paragraph and one for the third paragraph.
3 Why does one meerkat stay awake when the others have a sleep during the day?

C What about you?

Give three reasons why you think meerkats are interesting animals.

123

Learning objectives

⑤

Scan a passage to find specific information and answer questions.

Begin to infer meanings beyond the literal.

Use ICT sources to locate simple information.

Students look over the text they just read about meerkats and find specific facts about them. They show an understanding of the text beyond what is said explicitly. They find more information about the Kalahari Desert by consulting books or websites.

Remember to display the child-friendly learning objectives to the class along with the child-friendly checklist that students can use to assess how well they achieve them.

We know that we have achieved these because:

▶ We can answer the questions about specific facts correctly.

▶ We are able to answer questions about things that are not explicitly stated in the text.

▶ We can locate information about the Kalahari Desert from appropriate books or websites.

⑥ Student Book teaching notes and comprehension answers

A

Students scan the story again to find the two false statements.

Answers:

1 and 3

B

Encourage students to write the answers in their own words rather than copying word for word from the text.

Answers:

1 Meerkats build burrows so that they have a safe and cool place to sleep and to have babies.

2 Accept any answers that make sense as subheadings for the two paragraphs. *Examples:* 'Food', 'What do meerkats eat?', 'On guard', 'Staying safe'.

3 The meerkat that stays awake will guard the gang that is sleeping. If a dangerous animal comes close, the meerkat that is awake can warn his companions so that the whole gang can defend itself.

C

Students can work in pairs or individually. Suggest that they first jot down some of the characteristics of meerkats that they see in the text as well as in the photograph on page 122 of the Student Book. Write down students' responses on the board, marking the ones that are repeated. See which reasons are given more often than others.

⑦ Challenge

Ask students to brainstorm ideas about where to find the information requested in the challenge. **Ask:** *What kinds of books would you look in?* (Non-fiction, information books or reference books.) *Where would they find such books?* (In a library.) *What words would you put in a search engine on the Internet?* (Kalahari Desert animals.) If any students come from a country that contains a desert, ask them to find information about that desert instead of the Kalahari. When all the information is in, you can do a comparison of the Kalahari with the deserts in students' home countries.

⑧ Extension

Students collect the information on the Kalahari Desert individually. Then, in small groups of four or five, they make their own book about the Kalahari Desert (or deserts more generally if some students have gathered information about other deserts). Exhibit the books in the classroom.

Learning objectives

Know irregular forms of common verbs.

Continue to improve consistency in the use of tenses.

Students review the concept of the present and past tense and learn the past tense forms of the irregular verbs 'to have' and 'to go'. Students find verbs that have regular past tense forms and irregular past tense forms among words that they have encountered.

Remember to display the child-friendly learning objectives to the class along with the child-friendly checklist that students can use to assess how well they achieve them.

We know that we have achieved these because:

▶ We can identify the irregular past tense of the verbs 'to have' and 'to go'.

▶ We can use the present and past tense of these verbs correctly.

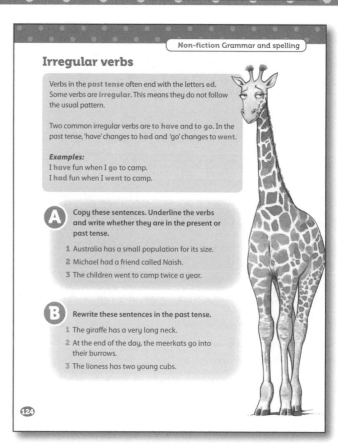

Non-fiction Grammar and spelling

Irregular verbs

Verbs in the **past tense** often end with the letters **ed**. Some verbs are **irregular**. This means they do not follow the usual pattern.

Two common irregular verbs are **to have** and **to go**. In the past tense, 'have' changes to **had** and 'go' changes to **went**.

Examples:
I **have** fun when I **go** to camp.
I **had** fun when I **went** to camp.

A Copy these sentences. Underline the verbs and write whether they are in the present or past tense.

1. Australia has a small population for its size.
2. Michael had a friend called Naish.
3. The children went to camp twice a year.

B Rewrite these sentences in the past tense.

1. The giraffe has a very long neck.
2. At the end of the day, the meerkats go into their burrows.
3. The lioness has two young cubs.

124

② Student Book teaching notes and grammar and spelling exercise answers

Review the endings that show a verb is in the present tense (–*s*, –*ing*) and that it is in the past tense (–*ed*). Ask students to find examples of verbs that have a regular past tense in the 'Stolen Cake' story on page 102 of the Student Book in Unit 7. ***Examples:*** 'paused' (line 6), 'complained' (line 10), 'frowned' (line 13), 'picked' (line 16). Remind students that some verbs are irregular and have past tense forms that do not end with –*ed*. Tell students that two common irregular verbs are the verbs 'to have' and 'to go'. Ask students to look for these verbs in the 'Stolen Cake' extract on page 102 of the Student Book. ***Examples:*** 'had' (line 3), 'went' (line 7).

 A

Students rewrite the sentences underlining the verbs and writing whether the verb is in the present or past tense.

Answers:

1 has: present tense
2 had: past tense
3 went: past tense

 B

Students rewrite the sentences in the past tense.

Answers:

1 The giraffe **had** a very long neck.
2 At the end of the day, the meerkats **went** into their burrows.
3 The lioness **had** two young cubs.

To ensure understanding, ask questions that would require the past tense of the verbs 'to have' and 'to go' in their answers. ***Examples:*** 'Where did you go for your holidays, Juan?' 'What did you have for lunch, Jeanette?' Give beginner second language students leads such as: 'I went to…' and 'I had…'

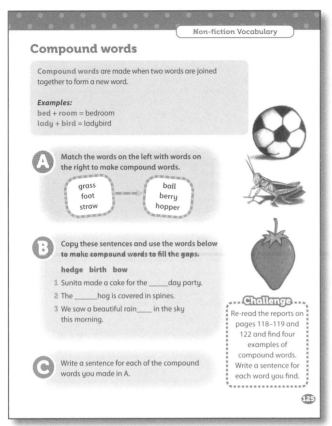

(4) Student Book teaching notes and vocabulary exercise answers

Write on the board the following words in one column: bed, lady, home, house, ball. Prepare strips of paper with the following words written on them: room, bird, work. Hold them up one by one next to the words on the board and ask students whether the two words make another real word when they are joined together (possible words: bedroom, ballroom, ladybird, homework, housework). Tell students that words that are made up of two other words are called 'compound words'.

Students match the words on the left with words on the right to make compound words.

Answers:
grasshopper, football, strawberry

Students copy the sentences and make compound words to fill the gaps.

Answers:
1   Sunita made a cake for the **birthday** party.
2   The **hedgehog** is covered in spines.
3   We saw a beautiful **rainbow** in the sky this morning.

Accept any sentence that makes sense.

(5) Challenge

Ask students to work in pairs and look through the reports on pages 118–119 and 122 of the Student Book to see if they can find some compound words. *Examples:* outback, outdoors, windmills, motorbike, underground, daytime, grasshoppers. Compare answers as a whole class and read the words aloud. You can do the same activity with the other text in this unit or other texts that students have read in earlier units.

Learning objective

(3)

Use and spell compound words.

Students learn that some words are made up of two separate words that are joined to form a new word.

Remember to display the child-friendly learning objective to the class along with the child-friendly checklist that students can use to assess how well they achieve it.

We know that we have achieved this because:

▶ We can recognize compound words in some of the texts that we have read so far.

▶ We can spell these words correctly.

(6) Extension

1   Ask students to find out from a parent or other speaker of their home language if compound words exist in their language. Ask them to bring in examples and to translate the words literally. For example, airplane in Armenian is also a compound word (otanav) but it means 'airship'. Umbrella in Spanish is 'paraguas' and it means 'stopwaters'.
2   Create a chart with compound words in English and their equivalent, if they are also compound words, in the class home languages.

Learning objectives

(1)

Use a wider variety of sentence types including simple and compound sentences.

Understand that verbs are necessary for meaning in a sentence.

Students learn that sentences are made up of clauses and that all clauses must contain a verb. They join two simple sentences with connectives to form compound sentences.

 Remember to display the child-friendly learning objectives to the class along with the child-friendly checklist that students can use to assess how well they achieve them.

We know that we have achieved these because:

▶ We understand the difference between a phrase and a clause.

▶ We can join two clauses together to form a compound sentence.

▶ We know how to use words like 'so', 'and' and 'but' to join two clauses together.

(2) Student Book teaching notes and grammar exercise answers

Tell students they are going to take a closer look at sentences. Elicit parts of a sentence they are familiar with (verbs, adjectives, nouns, punctuation). Tell students that today they are going to learn how sentences are divided up into groups of words.

Read through the introductory text box together.

Make a list of simple sentences together on the chart. On a separate sheet write a list of connectives: and, but, so. In pairs, students extend the simple sentences, using the connectives.

Students do A and B individually. Check answers together on the board.

(A)

Students copy the sentences and choose the correct connective to fill the gaps in the compound sentences.

Answers:

1 and/but
2 so

⇨

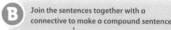

Clauses and connectives

Sentences are made up of one or more **clauses**. A **simple** sentence is just one clause that makes sense on its own.
Examples: Meerkats sleep in burrows. They look for food during the day.

Some sentences are made up of two simple clauses joined together. These are called **compound** sentences.
Example: Meerkats sleep in burrows and they look for food during the day.

We join clauses together in a sentence using **connectives**.
Examples: and, but, so

Top Tip

A **clause** is a group of words that includes a **verb**. If a group of words does not contain a verb, it is called a **phrase**.

 A Copy these compound sentences adding a connective to fill the gaps.

1 Meerkats love to eat insects _____ they also eat lizards and snakes.
2 It was very hot ___ the meerkats had a nap.

 B Join the sentences together with a connective to make a compound sentence.

1 Michael has a two-way radio. He uses it to talk to his friends.
2 Michael lives a long way from school. He does his schoolwork at home.

126

(B)

Students join two simple sentences together using a connective to form a compound sentence.

Answers:

1 Michael has a two-way radio and he uses it to talk to his friends.
2 Michael lives a long way from school so he does his schoolwork at home.

(3) Top Tip

Read through the Top Tip aloud. Write 'Phrase' and 'Clause' on the board and generate some examples.

(4) Extension

Students make a 'My Grammar Book' in which they record key aspects of grammar learnt, and with the help of a parent or other speaker of their home language they can translate the grammar point into their home languages. They should write the explanation of the point and a sentence showing it in use. They can also illustrate their sentence. This will serve as a revision of all the main language points covered in the book.

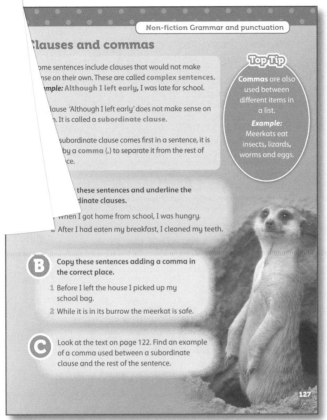

Non-fiction Grammar and punctuation

Clauses and commas

Some sentences include clauses that would not make sense on their own. These are called **complex sentences**. Example: **Although I left early,** I was late for school.

The clause 'Although I left early' does not make sense on its own. It is called a **subordinate clause**.

When a subordinate clause comes first in a sentence, it is followed by a comma (,) to separate it from the rest of the sentence.

Top Tip

Commas are also used between different items in a list.
Example: Meerkats eat insects, lizards, worms and eggs.

A Copy these sentences and underline the subordinate clauses.
1 When I got home from school, I was hungry.
2 After I had eaten my breakfast, I cleaned my teeth.

B Copy these sentences adding a comma in the correct place.
1 Before I left the house I picked up my school bag.
2 While it is in its burrow the meerkat is safe.

C Look at the text on page 122. Find an example of a comma used between a subordinate clause and the rest of the sentence.

127

Learning objectives

(5) **Use a wider variety of sentence types including some complex sentences.**

Use commas in lists.

Students identify and use complex sentences and understand that subordinate clauses do not make sense on their own. They learn how commas are used to separate subordinate clauses from the rest of a sentence and how they are used in lists.

Remember to display the child-friendly learning objectives to the class along with the child-friendly checklist that students can use to assess how well they achieve them.

We know that we have achieved these because:

▶ We understand the difference between simple and complex sentences.

▶ We know how to use commas to separate subordinate clauses from the rest of a sentence and also in lists.

(6) **Student Book teaching notes and grammar and punctuation exercise answers**

Remind students that simple sentences are made up of just one clause. *Example:* The children lined up. Compound sentences contain more than one clause, but each of the clauses makes sense on its own. *Example:* The bell rang and the children lined up. A complex sentence has more than one clause and includes a clause that does not make sense on its own. *Example:* When the bell rang, the children lined up. Explain that the clause that does not make sense on its own is called a subordinate clause. Explain that when a subordinate clause comes first in a sentence, it is followed by a comma.

Students copy the sentences and underline the subordinate clauses.

Answers:

1 When I got home from school,
2 After I had eaten my breakfast,

Students copy the sentences adding a comma in the correct place.

Answers:

1 Before I left the house, I picked up my school bag.
2 While it is in its burrow, the meerkat is safe.

Students look at the text on page 122 of the Student Book and find an example of a comma used between a subordinate clause and the rest of the sentence. *Example:* 'When meerkats are in danger, they run to their burrows to keep safe.'

(7) **Top Tip**

Explain that commas are used to separate the different items in a list. In pairs, students write two sentences containing lists.

(8) **Extension**

Give students a list of subordinate conjunctions. *Examples:* after, although, as, before, even, if, while. Ask them to make complex sentences starting with these words. Students read out their sentences. Correct as a whole group, identifying the subordinate clause and checking for commas.

Learning objectives

①

Read a range of story, poetry and information books and begin to make links between them.

Identify the main purpose of a text.

Students will read a non-chronological report about lions. They will continue to recognize the features of this genre, and how they differ from other kinds of writing. They will identify the main purpose of the text.

🔘 Remember to display the child-friendly learning objectives to the class along with the child-friendly checklist that students can use to assess how well they achieve them.

We know that we have achieved these because:

▶ We know that factual reports are different from other types of writing.

▶ We can identify the main purpose of a non-chronological report.

② Writing workshop teaching notes

Model writing

The purpose of a non-chronological report is to provide factual information about the way things are. The structure of this genre begins with a general statement, often including a definition. Then a sequence of facts follow grouped logically through paraphrasing and subheadings. Illustrations and labels may support the written text. Facts are presented in the present tense. Connectives are used to make links between ideas.

Refer students to the title 'Writing a non-chronological report'. Remind students what 'non-chronological' means: chronological means 'the order in which things happen', the prefix *non–* means 'not', so non-chronological means 'not in the order in which things happen'. **Ask:** *Is a non-chronological report fiction or non-fiction?* (Non-fiction.)

Ask students to look at the picture of lions on page 152 of the Student Book. Elicit the name of the animal. Ask how you say this in home languages. Ask children whether lions live in any of their countries. Elicit what countries/regions of the world lions live in and what lions eat. Write all their answers on the board.

⇨

Non-fiction Writing workshop

Writing a non-chronological report
Model writing

Lions

How big are lions?
Lions are the second largest cat species in the world. The average male lion weighs around 180 kg (400 lb) while the average female lion weighs around 130 kg (290 lb).

Where do lions live?
Lions mostly live in the grasslands, savanna and open woodlands of Africa, but they also live in the Gir Forest in India.

Do lions live on their own?
No, lions live in groups called prides. Sometimes, a pride can contain as many as 40 lions, but they can also have as few as three!

What do lions eat?
Lions are carnivorous animals, which means they eat meat. The animals they eat include deer, zebras, giraffes and hippos. Believe it or not, the female lions are the hunters. However, it is the male who will eat first, then the females and the cubs last.

Glossary
cub
a young lion
savanna
a grassy plain in a hot country with few trees

128

Tell students they are going to read a non-chronological report about lions and you want them to check if the information on the board is correct. Ask them to take turns reading the paragraphs aloud with their partners. Remind them to use the Glossary to help them understand.

Once students have finished reading, check the information in the report against the information elicited in the pre-reading activity. Is the information on the chart correct? Does anything need to be changed? What else can be added?

Establish what the main purpose of the report is (to give factual information about lions). **Ask:** *In what ways is the report different from an adventure story?* (It is factual, describing things that are true rather than fictional; there is no beginning, middle and end.)

Make sure everyone understands the following vocabulary and encourage students to write new words in their New Word List (*see* Workbook): male/female, species, average, hunters, carnivorous.

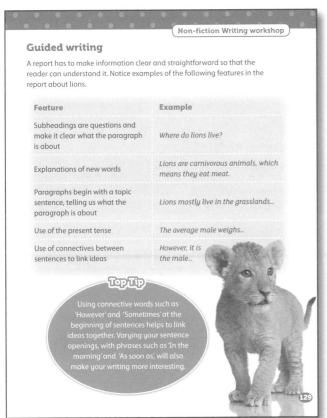

Non-fiction Writing workshop

Guided writing

A report has to make information clear and straightforward so that the reader can understand it. Notice examples of the following features in the report about lions.

Feature	Example
Subheadings are questions and make it clear what the paragraph is about	*Where do lions live?*
Explanations of new words	*Lions are carnivorous animals, which means they eat meat.*
Paragraphs begin with a topic sentence, telling us what the paragraph is about	*Lions mostly live in the grasslands...*
Use of the present tense	*The average male weighs...*
Use of connectives between sentences to link ideas	*However, it is the male...*

Top Tip

Using connective words such as 'However' and 'Sometimes' at the beginning of sentences helps to link ideas together. Varying your sentence openings, with phrases such as 'In the morning' and 'As soon as', will also make your writing more interesting.

129

(3) Learning objectives

Establish purpose for writing, using features and style based on model texts.

Begin to organize writing in sections or paragraphs.

Begin to vary sentence openings.

Students continue to learn that different genres serve different purposes. They identify the purpose, features and style of the model non-chronological report they have read. They recognize that text that is organized in paragraphs is easier to read and that the present tense is used when giving factual information in writing. They learn how the use of connectives can help to link ideas and how they can help to make their sentence openings more varied.

 Remember to display the child-friendly learning objectives to the class along with the child-friendly checklist that students can use to assess how well they achieve them.

We know that we have achieved these because:

▶ We know how to use the features of a factual report to make our writing clear.

▶ We are able to organize our writing in paragraphs.

▶ We understand that we can link our ideas and vary our sentence openings by using connectives.

(4) Writing workshop teaching notes

Guided writing

Refer students to the report on lions on page 128 of the Student Book and ask them if they thought it was easy to read. Ask them to identify the features that helped to make it easy to read. Write their answers on the board (paragraphs, writing in bold, questions, short, clear sentences, new words explained).

Explain that these are indeed the features of this kind of report writing. Read through the Guided writing chart together, stopping after each feature and pointing out words such as 'subheadings' and 'topic sentence'. Ask students to find the topic sentence in each paragraph of the report. Ask them to point out verbs in the present tense. **Ask:** *Are there any verbs written in the past tense?* (No.) Explain that when we write facts we use the present tense. Ask students to find the word 'connectives' in the last row of the Guided writing chart. Ask whether they can see a word they know in this word (connect). Elicit the meaning (to join together). Point out this is the job of connectives such as 'however'. They join ideas and sentences together. Ask students to find out how you say 'however' in their home languages.

Ask children to bring in factual books about animals in their home languages, if possible (send a note to parents about this).

(5) Top Tip

Read through the Top Tip with the students. Remind students about the connectives they learnt about on page 126 of the Student Book. Explain that, as well as joining clauses together in sentences, connectives can be used at the beginning of sentences. *Examples:* 'Although', 'Because', 'First', 'Then', 'After that', 'Finally', 'While', 'As soon as'. Explain that they can use words such as 'then' and 'finally' in their writing to show when something happened. They can also begin their sentences with words that explain how, where or how often something happened. *Examples:* 'Quickly', 'Carefully', 'Behind the door', 'At the top of the tree', 'Usually', 'Twice a year'. (Adverbs are dealt with in more detail in Level 4.) Explain that if they vary their sentence openings in this way their writing will be more interesting and they will keep the attention of the reader.

① Learning objectives

Use ICT sources to locate simple information.

Locate books by classification.

Locate information in non-fiction texts using contents page and index.

Make a record of information drawn from a text, for example by completing a chart.

Begin to organize writing in sections or paragraphs.

Students use the Internet as well as books available in the classroom and the library to research information on animals. They understand that books in a library are organized by subject, and identify tools such as the contents page and index. They record the information they find on a chart. They plan and write a non-chronological report, using a chart showing the topic of each paragraph.

Remember to display the child-friendly learning objectives to the class along with the child-friendly checklist that students can use to assess how well they achieve them.

We know that we have achieved these because:

▷ We can use the Internet to find information.

▷ We know how to read the contents and index pages to help us find information.

▷ We can record information we find from our research on a chart.

▷ We are able to organize our writing using subheadings and separate paragraphs for each topic.

② Writing workshop teaching notes

Your writing

Tell students they are going to write a factual report on an animal of their choice. Invite students to share the animal books they have brought in. Take students to the library and explain that information books are organized and grouped together on the shelves according to the subject. Ask them to find the section where they will find information books on animals. Show them how to use the contents page and index while in the library.

Ask students to do some research on the Internet to find out about the animal they have chosen to write about. The National Geographic website is a ⇨

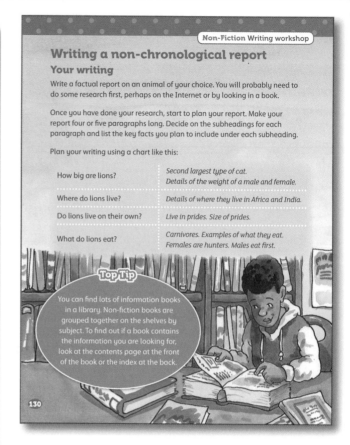

great resource for finding information reports for animals: http://kids.nationalgeographic.co.uk/kids/animals/creaturefeature/

Ask students to record the facts they find on a chart. Refer them to the chart on page 130 of the Student Book and ask them to copy it into their notebooks changing the word 'lion' to the animal they have chosen to write about. Encourage more advanced students to come up with other subheadings. *Examples:* How long do they live? How do they reproduce?

Tell students their report will be four or five paragraphs long. Remind them that each paragraph needs a subheading.

Look at the chart for guessing the meanings of new words (*see* page 10) and review the four points. Remind students to record new words in their New Word List (*see* Workbook) in their home languages and English.

Allow students who have chosen the same animal to work together and share information but the writing of the report should be done independently.

Beginner second language students can use books in their home languages for research and can also write their reports in their home languages.

Circulate, giving help and advice where needed.

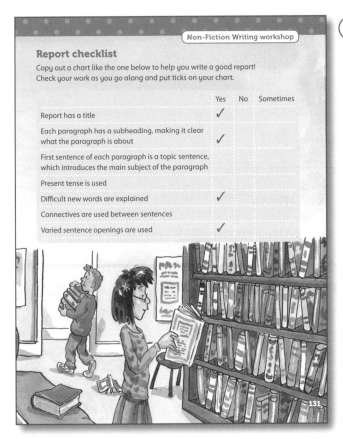

Non-Fiction Writing workshop

Report checklist

Copy out a chart like the one below to help you write a good report!
Check your work as you go along and put ticks on your chart.

	Yes	No	Sometimes
Report has a title	✓		
Each paragraph has a subheading, making it clear what the paragraph is about	✓		
First sentence of each paragraph is a topic sentence, which introduces the main subject of the paragraph			
Present tense is used			
Difficult new words are explained	✓		
Connectives are used between sentences			
Varied sentence openings are used	✓		

131

④ Writing workshop teaching notes

Report checklist

Write 'Report checklist' on a chart and ask the children to work in pairs and think up criteria for checking a factual report. Elicit the criteria and write them on the chart.

Ask students to look at the chart on page 131 of the Student Book. Read through the checklist with students point by point. Compare the points with the criteria elicited earlier and add any further points to the chart.

Students use the criteria to check their writing individually and then have a partner check their report to make sure no features have been left out.

When students have finished their writing tell them to draw a picture or some pictures of their animal to illustrate the text. Point out that cartoon drawings are not appropriate for this kind of written text. Their drawings must be as lifelike as possible. Display all the students' work in the classroom and label it 'Factual animal reports'.

⑤ Extension

Tell the class they are going to make an 'Animal Facts Book', which will be displayed in the school library. Brainstorm a list of animals. Write the names of the animals on cards, one for each child. Ask the children to pull names out of a hat to decide who will write about which animal. Each child is responsible for a page in the book. They should write the name of their animal at the top of the page in their home language and in English. Beginner second language students can write their page in their home language. Allow any other children who would like to write in their home language to write it as a dual language text. Together with the class, write a contents page and a glossary. Make a cover with the title written in all the home languages. Display the book in the school library.

Learning objectives

③

Establish purpose for writing, using features and style based on model texts.

Begin to vary sentence openings.

Students use the model non-chronological report to establish the purpose, features and style of their own report. They use a checklist to ensure that their writing includes the necessary features, including subheadings, present tense and connectives to link ideas.

Remember to display the child-friendly learning objectives to the class along with the child-friendly checklist that students can use to assess how well they achieve them.

We know that we have achieved these because:

▶ We know the purpose of the factual report we are writing and how it should differ from a story, a poem, a play script, a letter and a set of instructions.

▶ We can write a non-chronological report that includes the features and style of this genre.

▶ We are able to use connectives to link ideas in our writing and make the openings of our sentences more varied.

End of Unit Test

Question Paper

Reading: non-fiction

Read the extract and answer the questions.

A Serious Business

Playing is actually very important. You don't need expensive toys, just a good imagination. Kids don't need to speak the same language to play together. Sports exercise your body, team games teach you to work with other people, and play that involves pretending lets you use your
5   imagination.

What's the point of playing?

- **Playing on your own** teaches you to think for yourself and to enjoy your own company.

- **Playing with others** teaches you to get along with other people and
10 work well in a group.

- **Playing allows you** to be creative and enables you to explore the world around you safely.

- **Playing trains you** to be resourceful and to use your imagination.

How many different ways to play can you think of?

15 - **You can play by yourself** by reading a book or keeping a diary.

- **You can make things** by drawing or painting, building a model aeroplane, baking a cake, or making a monster.

- **You can take part in sports.** Team sports like football or netball teach you how to get along with others. Gymnastics, running, and
20 swimming teach you to rely on yourself. All sports keep you fit and healthy.

- **You can have a hobby** like collecting stickers or rocks, playing an instrument, or looking after a pet.

- **You can play with others** in the playground, in the park, using
25 board games, or by inventing your own games.

From *A Life Like Mine: How children live around the world,* Dorling Kindersley

Glossary

expensive costing a lot of money.

fit in good physical condition.

get along with work well with or be friendly with someone.

imagination an ability to form pictures and ideas in your mind.

rely on yourself trust and have confidence in yourself.

resourceful able to find clever ways to overcome difficulties.

team a group of people who play or work together.

Comprehension

A Give evidence from the extract to support your answers.

1 What does playing train you to do?

_____ [2]

2 List two hobbies that are mentioned in the extract.

_____ [2]

3 Which sports teach you how to get along with others?

_____ [2]

B Give evidence from the extract to support your answers.

1 What kind of play helps you to stay fit and healthy?

_____ [1]

2 List two reasons why you think playing is important.

_____

_____ [2]

C Give evidence from the extract to support your answers.

1 The extract includes two subheadings. What is the main subject of the text in each section?

_____

_____ [2]

2 Write two sentences explaining why you do not need expensive toys in order to play.

_____

_____ [2]

Writing: non-fiction

Read the report below about moles. Notice the subheadings that ask questions. They tell us what the paragraph is about. Notice also that the report is written in the present tense.

The Mole

What does a mole look like?

The mole has a long, furry body. It has big hands which are good for digging and a tail that sticks up. Moles grow between 15 to 20 cm (6 to 8 inches) long.

5 ### Where do moles live?

The mole eats, sleeps and lives in underground tunnels. They dig many tunnels and build nests deep underground called a fortress.

Do moles live on their own?

The mole digs its tunnel just for itself. If another mole tries to come
10 into the tunnel the mole attacks it.

What do moles eat?

The mole eats mostly worms. However, they also eat beetles, ants and other animals that live in the soil. The tunnels trap hundreds of worms. The mole checks the tunnel three times a day. If a mole collects too
15 many worms to eat in one go, it collects them up. Believe it or not, the mole nips off the worms' heads, so they cannot creep off. Then on days when it does not catch very much the mole goes back and eats them.

Glossary
beetles insects with hard, shiny covers over their wings.
digging making a hole in the ground.
fortress a strongly built castle, or the name for a mole's nest.
nips bites something quickly.
tunnels long holes made underground.

Choose an animal that you have not written about before and write an information report on it.

Please use a separate sheet of paper.

Remember:

- Include a title.
- Use questions as subheadings, making it clear what each paragraph is about.
- Explain new words.
- Begin each paragraph with a topic sentence, which introduces the main subject of the paragraph.
- Use the present tense.
- Use connectives between sentences to link ideas.
- Vary your sentence openings with words that say how, when, where or how often something happens or something is done.

Organize your description in four paragraphs. Include:

Paragraph 1: General information about the animal.

Paragraph 2: Where the animal lives.

Paragraph 3: Does the animal live in a group or alone?

Paragraph 4: What the animal eats.

[20]

9

Why do we laugh?

1 Warm-up objectives

Speak clearly and confidently in a range of contexts.

Take turns in discussion, building on what others have said.

Listen and respond appropriately to others' views and opinions.

Students discuss the importance of laughter and take turns to talk about what makes them laugh. They listen and respond to the opinions of others, agreeing and disagreeing in an appropriate manner.

Remember to display the child-friendly learning objectives to the class along with the child-friendly checklist that students can use to assess how well they achieve them.

We know that we have achieved these because:

▷ We can talk clearly and confidently in discussions about what makes us laugh.

▷ We are able to take turns in discussions.

▷ We can listen to the opinions of others and respond appropriately.

2 Unit warm up

Read the title of this unit aloud and tell students that the focus of this unit will be poems that are humorous or funny. Write on the board 'Laughter is good for you.' Read the statement aloud to the students. Ask students to turn to their partner and discuss whether they agree with the statement or disagree. Ask for a show of hands to see who agrees and disagrees, and discuss the students' ideas as a class.

Write the word 'laugh' on a chart and ask the students what kind of word it is (it can be a noun or a verb). Ask the students how to say 'to laugh' in their home languages. Ask them to write the words in the different scripts of the classroom on the chart. Divide the class into groups of three and ask them to write down any words they associate with laugh.

Read the title of the unit again and elicit answers to the question. Write all responses on the board. Encourage students to take turns in the discussion. Tell students that the latest medical research tells us that laughing is very good for our health. It helps us relax and makes us feel happy.

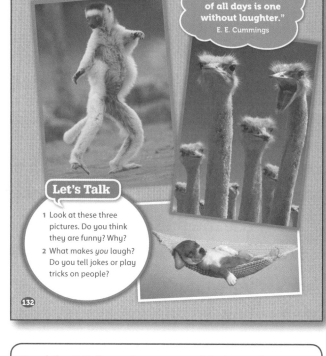

9 Why do we laugh?

"The most wasted of all days is one without laughter."
E. E. Cummings

Let's Talk

1 Look at these three pictures. Do you think they are funny? Why?

2 What makes *you* laugh? Do you tell jokes or play tricks on people?

132

Read the E. E. Cummings quote with the students. Ask students if they agree or disagree with this. Allow plenty of time for discussion. Ask students if they know who E. E. Cummings was (a famous American poet who started writing poetry when he was eight years old). If possible, show students a copy of a poetry collection by E. E. Cummings and read them a snippet from one of his poems.

3 Let's Talk

1 Focus on the three pictures on page 132 of the Student Book and ask students whether they find the pictures funny. Students share their opinions about each picture orally with the whole group.

2 Students answer in pairs, taking turns to tell their partner about things they find funny, including any jokes they know. If possible, hand out age-appropriate joke books and ask students to find a joke that they like. Ask them to copy the joke out and illustrate it. As a whole class, have a joke-telling session. Ask students to translate their favourite joke. Does it translate well? Why/why not? (They may need help from a parent or other speaker of their home language to do this.)

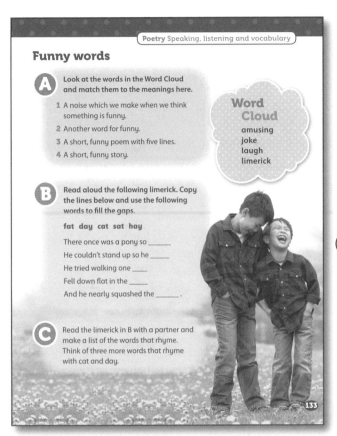

Poetry Speaking, listening and vocabulary

Funny words

A Look at the words in the Word Cloud and match them to the meanings here.

1 A noise which we make when we think something is funny.
2 Another word for funny.
3 A short, funny poem with five lines.
4 A short, funny story.

Word Cloud
amusing
joke
laugh
limerick

B Read aloud the following limerick. Copy the lines below and use the following words to fill the gaps.

fat day cat sat hay

There once was a pony so _____
He couldn't stand up so he _____
He tried walking one ____
Fell down flat in the _____
And he nearly squashed the _____ .

C Read the limerick in B with a partner and make a list of the words that rhyme. Think of three more words that rhyme with cat and day.

133

④ Learning objectives

Infer the meaning of unknown words from the context.

Practise reciting poems.

Read aloud with expression to engage the listener.

Students guess the meanings of new words from the context. They read a limerick aloud with expresssion, identify the rhyming pattern and understand that it is a funny poem.

Remember to display the child-friendly learning objectives to the class along with the child-friendly checklist that students can use to assess how well they achieve them.

We know that we have achieved these because:

▶ We can guess the meanings of words from the context.

▶ We can read a limerick with expression.

⑤ Word Cloud definitions

Focus students' attention on the Word Cloud and ask them to guess the meanings. After reading the list, ask students to think of other words they associate with the word 'laugh'. *Examples:* smile, grin, funny, humour, comedy.

amusing making you laugh or smile.
joke something that you say or do to make people laugh.
laugh to make a sound to show you are happy and that you think something is funny.
limerick a funny poem with five lines.

⑥ Student Book teaching notes and exercise answers

Ask students to think of the funniest thing that has ever happened to them. Ask them to turn and talk about this with their partner. Students share stories. Students do exercises A and B in pairs.

Students repeat the words in the Word Cloud and match the words to the meanings.

Answers:

1 laugh   **2** amusing   **3** limerick   **4** joke

Students copy the limerick and use the words to fill the gaps.

Answer:

There once was a pony so **fat**
He couldn't stand up so he **sat**
He tried walking one **day**
Fell down in the **hay**
And he nearly squashed the **cat.**

Students make a list of rhyming words and share these with the class. They think of three other words that rhyme with cat and day.

Answers:

fat, sat, cat (*Examples:* pat, bat, mat)
day, hay (*Examples:* way, bay, may)

Do a choral reading of the limerick. Encourage students to read with expression. Explain that a limerick is a song-like poem with a distinct pattern, one verse and five lines. Lines 1, 2 and 5 rhyme and lines 3 and 4 rhyme, forming a AABBA rhyming pattern. Ask students to practise reciting the limerick in pairs and ask for volunteers to perform.

Learning objectives

Read a range of story, poetry and information books and begin to make links between them.

Infer the meaning of unknown words from the context.

Practise to improve performance when reading aloud.

Read aloud with expression to engage the listener.

Students read a funny narrative poem and focus on what makes a poem a narrative. They compare and contrast this poem with other poems they have read so far and compare this story with others they have read. They continue to guess the meaning of unfamiliar words using the clues available to them. They practise reciting the poem aloud with feeling.

Remember to display the child-friendly learning objectives to the class along with the child-friendly checklist that students can use to assess how well they achieve them.

We know that we have achieved these because:

▶ We know what a narrative poem is.

▶ We can recognize similarities and differences between different poems and between stories and poems.

▶ We can correctly guess the meaning of unfamiliar words by using the different clues we have available to us.

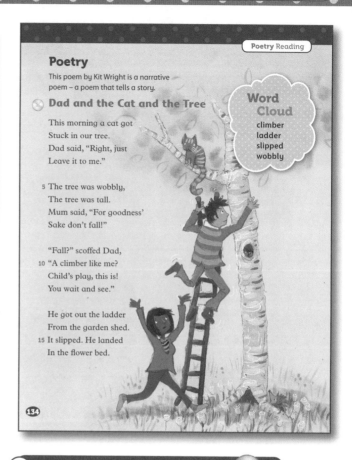

Poetry Reading

Poetry
This poem by Kit Wright is a narrative poem – a poem that tells a story.

Dad and the Cat and the Tree

This morning a cat got
Stuck in our tree.
Dad said, "Right, just
Leave it to me."

5 The tree was wobbly,
The tree was tall.
Mum said, "For goodness'
Sake don't fall!"

"Fall?" scoffed Dad,
10 "A climber like me?
Child's play, this is!
You wait and see."

He got out the ladder
From the garden shed.
15 It slipped. He landed
In the flower bed.

134

Word Cloud
climber
ladder
slipped
wobbly

② Poetry reading notes

Introduce the poem by telling students that this poem tells a story. **Ask:** *Have you read another poem that tells a story?* ('The Sound Collector' in Unit 3 told a story.) Ask students to quickly look over that poem. It told about a mysterious event when a thief took the sounds away. This poem tells a different kind of story – a funny story. Ask students to look at the illustration on page 134 of the Student Book and the title of the poem and make predictions about the story.

Begin reading the poem or refer to the CD-ROM. Read with feeling and exaggerated expressions. Stop at unfamiliar words and the words in the Word Cloud. Ask students to guess the meanings with the help of clues (*see* page 10).

③ Word Cloud definitions

Look at the Word Cloud and read out each definition or refer to the CD-ROM. Ask students to locate the terms in the text. Make sure that they understand the words in the Glossary, too.

climber someone who climbs hills and mountains for sport.

ladder something used to help you climb up or down something, with two long pieces of wood or metal with steps between them.

slipped lost his balance and fell.

wobbly not steady, moving from side to side.

Ask students to classify the words into nouns (climber, ladder), adjectives (wobbly) and verbs (slipped) and add the words to the charts created earlier. Focus their attention on the verb 'slipped'. Ask students whether the verb is in the present or past tense and how they know (past tense; the verb ends in 'ed'). Remind students of the rules they learned in Unit 2 about adding 'ed' to verbs that end with a short vowel followed by a consonant. Remind students to write all new words in their New Word List (*see* Workbook).

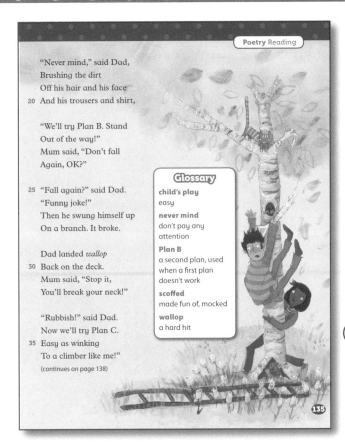

"Never mind," said Dad,
Brushing the dirt
Off his hair and his face
20 And his trousers and shirt,

"We'll try Plan B. Stand
Out of the way!"
Mum said, "Don't fall
Again, OK?"

25 "Fall again?" said Dad.
"Funny joke!"
Then he swung himself up
On a branch. It broke.

Dad landed *wallop*
30 Back on the deck.
Mum said, "Stop it,
You'll break your neck!"

"Rubbish!" said Dad.
Now we'll try Plan C.
35 Easy as winking
To a climber like me!"
(continues on page 138)

Glossary

child's play
easy

never mind
don't pay any attention

Plan B
a second plan, used when a first plan doesn't work

scoffed
made fun of, mocked

wallop
a hard hit

135

④ Poetry reading notes

Direct students' attention to the illustration on page 163 of the Student Book and ask them to make predictions about this part of the poem. Ask students whether they think Dad is going to give up. Or will he try another way to get to the cat? Ask them what they think he will try next.

Ask students whether they have ever had or seen a cat stuck in a tree. Direct students' attention to the fact that Mum and Dad in this poem are actually talking to each other. Ask students whether this makes the poem more or less interesting and whether it helps to make the poem funny. Both Mum and Dad use some interesting expressions such as 'Rubbish!' and 'easy as winking'. **Ask:** *What do these mean?* ('Rubbish' means 'things that are thrown away', but here it is used to mean 'nonsense'. 'Easy as winking' is used to mean 'very easy' because winking is something that you can do quickly and without any trouble; ask students to wink.) Ask students to collect ways of saying 'Nonsense!', 'Rubbish!' and 'Easy as…' or other sayings in their home languages,

preferably with the sayings written in the home languages and the English translation. Display these on a chart.

Ask students to find words and expressions in the poem that help to make it funny. This may be because of the words themselves or because the words create funny pictures in their minds.

When you come to the end of page 135 of the Student Book, ask students whether they understand why this is called a narrative poem (because it tells a story). Ask them to think about other ways of telling a story and how poems are different from other stories they have read, such as the story about Abdullah in Unit 1 (use of verses and rhyme, etc.).

⑤ Extension

In groups of three, students practise reciting this part of the poem aloud, taking turns in reading the different parts. One reads the words spoken by Dad, another reads the words spoken by Mum and the third student reads the other lines. Encourage students to recite the poem with feeling, using appropriate intonation in their voices to convey the feelings of Mum and Dad (Mum's worry and Dad's determination).

Learning objectives

(1)

Answer questions with some reference to single points in the text.

Begin to infer meanings beyond the literal, for example about motives and character.

Consider words that make an impact, for example adjectives and powerful verbs.

Listen and respond appropriately to others' views and opinions.

Students review the plot of the story in this poem and answer specific questions about the text. They answer questions by inferring things about the characters and events in the poem that are not explicitly stated in the text. They focus on words that give the poem special meaning and make the events funny. They take part in a whole-class discussion about what makes a poem funny.

 Remember to display the child-friendly learning objectives to the class along with the child-friendly checklist that students can use to assess how well they achieve them.

We know that we have achieved these because:

▶ We can answer questions about specific points in the poem.

▶ We are able to answer questions about things that are not explicitly stated in the poem.

▶ We can identify words that give special meaning to events and characters.

▶ We are able to listen to others and respond appropriately in a discussion.

(2) Student Book teaching notes and comprehension answers

Elicit from students the events in this part of the poem. **Ask:** *What happened first? Then what happened?* Repeat what the students say, changing the grammar just enough, minimally, to make the sentence more accurate. When you repeat the sentence, make sure to use the past tense of verbs.

As a group, write down the similarities and differences between a story written in text form and a story written as a poem. You can do this simply in two columns or draw a Venn diagram (*see* Guidelines) on the board.

Encourage students to use their own words to answer the questions rather than copying word for word from the text.

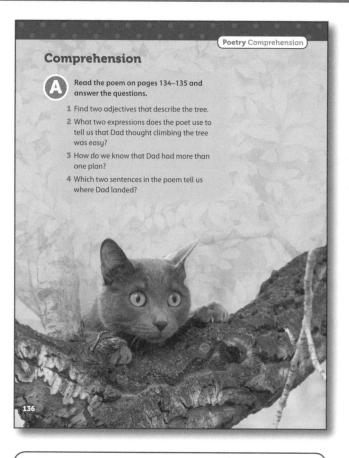

Poetry Comprehension

Comprehension

A Read the poem on pages 134–135 and answer the questions.

1 Find two adjectives that describe the tree.

2 What two expressions does the poet use to tell us that Dad thought climbing the tree was easy?

3 How do we know that Dad had more than one plan?

4 Which two sentences in the poem tell us where Dad landed?

136

A

Students re-read the poem on pages 134–135 of the Student Book and answer the questions.

Answers:

1 wobbly, tall

2 child's play and easy as winking. Ask students to think of other things that are very easy and invent new sayings. **Examples:** as easy as eating ice cream; as easy as playing with a dog.

3 We know Dad had more than one plan because he said that he would try Plan B, which means that he had thought about what he was going to do first, and had already come up with a second plan. He tried Plan A, but it didn't work, so he wanted to try Plan B. Ask students for examples of when they have had to 'try Plan B'.

4 The sentences in lines 15/16 and lines 29/30.

Poetry Comprehension

B **What do you think?**

Use phrases from the poem to help with your answers.

1 Why do you think the poet sometimes uses exclamation marks in the poem?

2 What do you think Mum thinks about Dad climbing the tree?

3 Which verbs and adjectives do you think are most effective in the poem so far? Explain why you like them.

4 Which words and phrases in the poem do you find most funny?

C **What about you?**

Think about something funny that has happened to you. Tell a friend your funny story.

Discussion time

Do you think this poem is funny? Why? With your class, make a list of the kinds of things that can make a poem funny.

137

C

Students think of something funny that has happened to them and tell their partner the story. Tell students to jot down notes that will help them tell their story.

4 Discussion time

Ask: *Is it funny when someone falls?* (Only when the person insists on doing something that makes them fall and when the person isn't hurt.) Students discuss whether it is just the events in a poem that make it funny or whether it is also the words the poet chooses. Make sure students wait for their turn and listen to each other's opinions.

5 Extension

1 Ask students to work in pairs or groups of three to write the story in text form rather than a poem. They will complete the story when they read the second part of the poem.

2 To apply what students learned in Unit 2 about giving instructions, ask them to develop a 'to do' list for telling funny stories, or a guide for a comedian (someone who tells jokes).

3 Student Book teaching notes and comprehension answers

B

Encourage students to use their own words rather than copy word for word from the poem.

Answers:

1 Remind students of what they learned about exclamation marks in Unit 2 (*see* Student Book page 33) – exclamation marks are often used at the end of commands and also to show surprise, excitement or force. Ask students which of these effects is achieved where exclamation marks are used in the poem.

2 Mum is worried because she doesn't want Dad to fall and hurt himself.

3 The adjective 'wobbly' is effective because it gives us a sense of how dangerous it might be to climb the tree; the verb 'scoffed' is effective because it tells us that Dad was not going to pay attention to being told not climb the tree; the verb 'swung' is effective because it gives us an image of Dad's movement.

4 Students can pick any words or phrases as long as they can say why they think they are funny. **Examples:** The phrases 'Child's play', 'Funny joke!', 'Rubbish!' and 'Easy as winking' are all funny because Dad does not find it as easy to climb the tree as he thinks he will.

⇨

Learning objectives

Read a range of story, poetry and information books and begin to make links between them.

Infer the meaning of unknown words from the context.

Students finish reading the funny poem and finish writing the text version of the story. They consider the different ways that stories can be told, comparing narrative poems with fiction they have encountered. They continue to guess the meanings of unfamiliar words using the clues available to them.

Remember to display the child-friendly learning objectives to the class along with the child-friendly checklist that students can use to assess how well they achieve them.

We know that we have achieved these because:

▶ **We can identify the different ways that stories can be told.**

▶ **We can correctly guess the meanings of unfamiliar words by using the different clues available to us.**

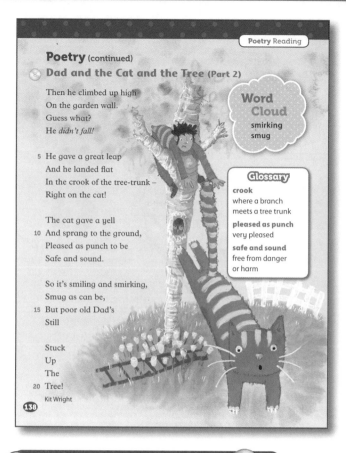

Poetry Reading

Poetry (continued)

Dad and the Cat and the Tree (Part 2)

Then he climbed up high
On the garden wall.
Guess what?
He *didn't fall!*

5　He gave a great leap
And he landed flat
In the crook of the tree-trunk –
Right on the cat!

The cat gave a yell
10　And sprang to the ground,
Pleased as punch to be
Safe and sound.

So it's smiling and smirking,
Smug as can be,
15　But poor old Dad's
Still

Stuck
Up
The
20　Tree!

Kit Wright

138

Word Cloud
smirking
smug

Glossary
crook
where a branch meets a tree trunk
pleased as punch
very pleased
safe and sound
free from danger or harm

② Poetry reading notes

Before reading the last part of the poem, review the story of the poem so far. Direct students' attention to the illustration on page 138 of the Student Book. Ask them to predict what Dad is going to do next. Write down some of the predictions and ask students to vote for the prediction they think is most likely to happen.

Begin to read the remaining part of the poem or refer to the CD-ROM. Stop at unfamiliar words and the words in the Word Cloud and ask students to guess their meanings.

Compare the predictions that students made to the actual ending of the poem. Ask students what they think of the ending. Which is funnier: that Dad falls one more time from the tree (very likely to be one of the students' predictions) or that he gets stuck in the tree instead of the cat (the actual ending of the poem)? Let students vote on which one they think is the funnier ending.

③ Word Cloud definitions

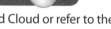

Read aloud the words in the Word Cloud or refer to the CD-ROM.

smirking smiling in an unpleasant way because you are pleased with yourself or you are glad about someone else's troubles.

smug feeling very pleased with yourself.

④ Extension

1　Ask students to finish writing the story they started earlier of the poem in text form. Students read their story in both forms and decide which one they like better.

2　Students rewrite the poem as a play script, following the models in Units 3 and 6. They will now have three forms of the same story. They can compare and contrast them, and vote on which form they like best.

Poetry Comprehension

Comprehension

A Which three sentences below are true?

1 Dad climbed onto the garden wall.
2 Dad rescued the cat.
3 The cat landed safely on the ground.
4 Dad got stuck in the tree.

Challenge
Find the words that rhyme in the poem. Do you notice a pattern? Read the poem aloud as a class. Use as much expression as you can.

B What do you think?

Use phrases from the poem to help with your answers.

1 Which verse in the poem do you find most funny? Give reasons for your answer.
2 What phrases tell us how the cat feels at the end of the poem?
3 Towards the end of the poem, the poet describes the cat as 'smiling', 'smirking' and 'smug'. Why do you think he chose those words?
4 What does the poet do to make the ending seem more dramatic?

C What about you?

What do you like best about this poem? What surprised you at the end of the poem?

139

---

(5) Learning objectives

Answer questions with some reference to single points in the text.

Begin to infer meanings beyond the literal, for example about motives and character.

Consider words that make an impact, for example adjectives and powerful verbs.

Read aloud with expression to engage the listener.

Students answer the questions about characters and events that are not directly stated in the poem. They identify words and phrases that convey special meaning and they learn to read the poem with feeling and expression.

Remember to display the child-friendly learning objectives to the class along with the child-friendly checklist that students can use to assess how well they achieve them.

We know that we have achieved these because:

▶ We can answer questions about characters and events that are not explicitly addressed in the poem.

▶ We are able to identify words that convey special meaning in the poem.

▶ We can read the poem aloud with feeling, adapting the tone of our voices.

---

(6) Student Book teaching notes and comprehension answers

A

Students read the poem on page 138 of the Student Book again and say which three sentences are true.

Answers:

1, 3 and 4

B

Encourage students to write the answers in their own words rather than copying word for word from the text.

Answers:

1 Let each student choose the verse that they think is the funniest. Walk around the classroom and ask them to tell you why they picked the one they chose. Get a show of hands as to how many students picked each verse as the funniest (there are 14 verses). You can connect this activity to mathematics and draw a bar chart with the numbers of the verses on the horizontal axis and the number of votes on the vertical axis.

2 'Pleased as punch', 'smiling and smirking' and 'smug as can be'.

3 These words convey a feeling that a simpler word, like 'happy' does not. These words make the reader realize that the cat was very happy with itself and it was laughing a little at Dad, who was now stuck in the tree himself. These words all start with the letters 'sm' so the sound they make when read aloud helps to create more impact.

4 The poet strings out the last few words with only one word on each line of the last verse. This makes you read the words slowly, one by one, and get the full effect of the funny ending.

C

Students can work in pairs or individually, to choose what they liked best about the poem and what surprised them most. They share their opinions with the whole class.

---

(7) Challenge

The last word in the second and fourth lines of each verse rhyme. Read the whole poem as dramatically as you can, exaggerating expressions and spoken words. Then, read it again with students joining in. Encourage them to read with as much expression and feeling as possible. To make it more interesting, you can have one student be the dad and another student be the mum, and whenever they say anything, those students read the lines on their own.

Learning objectives

Use a dictionary to find the spelling and meaning of words.

Collect examples of nouns, verbs and adjectives, and use the terms appropriately.

Generate synonyms for high frequency words.

Explore vocabulary for introducing and concluding dialogue, for example said, asked.

Students practise looking in a dictionary and a thesaurus to find the meanings of words and find other words with similar meanings. They continue to categorize words into nouns, verbs and adjectives.

Remember to display the child-friendly learning objectives to the class along with the child-friendly checklist that students can use to assess how well they achieve them.

We know that we have achieved these because:

▶ We can find definitions of words in a dictionary.

▶ We can identify words as nouns, adjectives and verbs.

▶ We can replace common words with more interesting words by using a thesaurus.

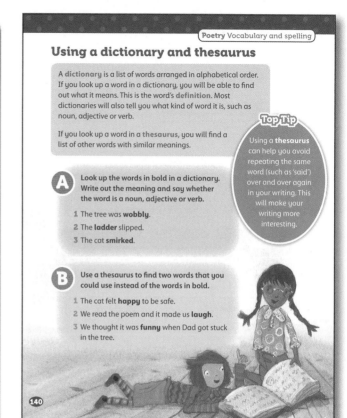

Poetry Vocabulary and spelling

Using a dictionary and thesaurus

A **dictionary** is a list of words arranged in alphabetical order. If you look up a word in a dictionary, you will be able to find out what it means. This is the word's **definition**. Most dictionaries will also tell you what kind of word it is, such as noun, adjective or verb.

If you look up a word in a **thesaurus**, you will find a list of other words with similar meanings.

Top Tip

Using a **thesaurus** can help you avoid repeating the same word (such as 'said') over and over again in your writing. This will make your writing more interesting.

A Look up the words in bold in a dictionary. Write out the meaning and say whether the word is a noun, adjective or verb.

1 The tree was **wobbly**.
2 The **ladder** slipped.
3 The cat **smirked**.

B Use a thesaurus to find two words that you could use instead of the words in bold.

1 The cat felt **happy** to be safe.
2 We read the poem and it made us **laugh**.
3 We thought it was **funny** when Dad got stuck in the tree.

140

Answers:

1 adjective
2 noun
3 verb

 B

Students can work in pairs to find the alternative words in a thesaurus. Read each sentence once with the more common word that appears in the book and once with the synonym or similar word found in the thesaurus. Ask students how the sentences seem different and whether they evoke different images with the two words.

② Student Book teaching notes and vocabulary and spelling exercise answers

Show students a dictionary and a thesaurus. Remind them that they list words in alphabetical order. **Ask:** *What is the difference between a dictionary and a thesaurus?* (A dictionary gives the meaning and classification of words; a thesaurus gives other words with similar meanings.)

Ask students what other types of dictionaries they have used. Remind them that some dictionaries are in one language and others have two languages. Ask students if any of them use a bilingual dictionary in their home language. Ask whether they prefer to use a bilingual dictionary or a dictionary in one language.

A

Students look up the meaning of each word in a dictionary. If students are using different dictionaries, compare definitions. Add the words to the NOUNS, ADJECTIVES and VERBS charts.

⇨

③ Top Tip

Ask students, in pairs, to look at stories that they have seen in other units and find examples of words that authors have used instead of 'said'. Ask them to think about what effect this has on the reader. If you have samples of students' work on the walls, or in students' notebooks, ask them if they would like to revise their writing, replacing common words such as 'said', 'like', 'good', 'bad', etc. with more interesting words that they can find in the Vocasurus.

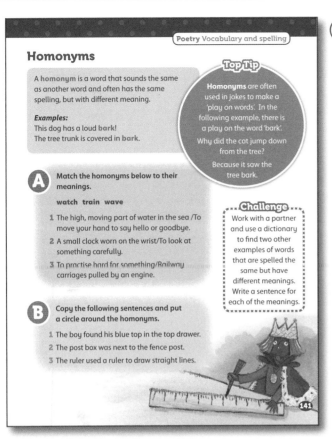

Homonyms

A **homonym** is a word that sounds the same as another word and often has the same spelling, but with different meaning.

Examples:
This dog has a loud **bark**!
The tree trunk is covered in **bark**.

Top Tip

Homonyms are often used in jokes to make a 'play on words'. In the following example, there is a play on the word 'bark'.

Why did the cat jump down from the tree?

Because it saw the tree bark.

A Match the homonyms below to their meanings.

watch train wave

1 The high, moving part of water in the sea /To move your hand to say hello or goodbye.
2 A small clock worn on the wrist/To look at something carefully.
3 To practise hard for something/Railway carriages pulled by an engine.

Challenge
Work with a partner and use a dictionary to find two other examples of words that are spelled the same but have different meanings. Write a sentence for each of the meanings.

B Copy the following sentences and put a circle around the homonyms.

1 The boy found his blue top in the top drawer.
2 The post box was next to the fence post.
3 The ruler used a ruler to draw straight lines.

141

Learning objectives

④

Explore words that have the same spelling but different meanings (homonyms), for example form, wave.

Consider how choice of words can heighten meaning.

Students contrast what they just learned about synonyms with homonyms in text that they have read in the book as well as text that they have written themselves.

⊙ Remember to display the child-friendly learning objectives to the class along with the child-friendly checklist that students can use to assess how well they achieve them.

We know that we have achieved these because:

▶ We can identify homonyms correctly.

▶ We can recognize words that make sentences more interesting.

---

⑤ Student Book teaching notes and vocabulary and spelling exercise answers

Tell students that they have learned about and have been using different words that mean the same or similar things. Draw the following diagram on the board:

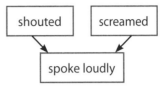

Tell students they are now going to learn about words that sound the same but have different meanings. Draw the following diagram next to the previous one:

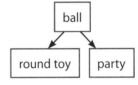

Explain that when two words sound the same but have different meanings, they are called homonyms. Ask students to look up the word 'top' or 'hide' in their dictionary and comment on the number of different meanings each has.

Students match the homonyms with their definitions.

Answers:

1 wave
2 watch
3 train

Students copy the sentences and put a circle around the homonyms.

Answers:

1 top
2 post
3 ruler

---

⑥ Top Tip

Explain that because many words in English sound the same but mean different things, we can pretend that we are meaning one thing and say another. This can be funny. Give the example in the book.

---

⑦ Challenge

Students share the words they found with the rest of the class and they take turns adding the words to the NOUNS, ADJECTIVES and VERBS charts.

① Learning objective

Identify different types of stories and typical story themes.

Students identify the distinct pattern in a limerick and how rhyming words help create this.

Remember to display the child-friendly learning objective to the class along with the child-friendly checklist that students can use to assess how well they achieve it.

We know that we have achieved this because:

▶ We know what a limerick looks like.

▶ We know that it has five lines and rhyming words.

▶ We can see how it is different from other forms of writing.

② Writing workshop teaching notes

Model writing

Give out some drawing paper and tell the students you are going to tell them a limerick and you would like them to draw whatever image comes into their head. Ask them to think back to the 'Fat Pony' limerick they read on page 133 of the Student Book. Elicit the features (song-like, five-line rhyming poem that is funny).

Read aloud the limerick on page 142 of the Student Book twice (Student Books closed). Exaggerate the rhyming pattern. Repeat if they need to hear the limerick again. Students draw the images that come into their heads. Line up all the pictures on the floor and let the students walk around and look at each other's work. Elicit what made them draw birds (the word 'nests').

Ask students to return to their seats and look at the drawing on page 142. **Ask:** *How many birds are there?* (Eight.) Tell students to read the Glossary and ask if they can see the larks and the wrens in the picture.

Read the limerick aloud together a couple of times. Tell the students that Edward Lear was a poet who is famous for writing a book of limericks. It was called *A Book of Nonsense*. **Ask:** *Why do you think it was called that?* (Because limericks are funny and often do not make sense.)

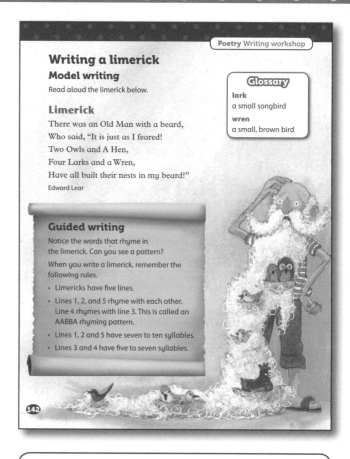

Poetry Writing workshop

Writing a limerick

Model writing

Read aloud the limerick below.

Glossary

lark
a small songbird

wren
a small, brown bird

Limerick

There was an Old Man with a beard,
Who said, "It is just as I feared!
Two Owls and A Hen,
Four Larks and a Wren,
Have all built their nests in my beard!"

Edward Lear

Guided writing

Notice the words that rhyme in the limerick. Can you see a pattern?

When you write a limerick, remember the following rules.

• Limericks have five lines.

• Lines 1, 2, and 5 rhyme with each other. Line 4 rhymes with line 3. This is called an AABBA rhyming pattern.

• Lines 1, 2 and 5 have seven to ten syllables.

• Lines 3 and 4 have five to seven syllables.

142

Guided writing

Read through the features listed in the Guided writing section. Count out the syllables in each line of the limerick and clap them a line at a time. In pairs, students practise reciting the poem and clapping to the syllables. Read the limerick chorally with expression.

Your writing

Use the ideas below to help you write your own limerick.

Top Tip

When writing a limerick, it helps to say the words out loud and tap out the rhythm.

	Example
1 Choose the name of a boy or girl and use it at the end of the first line.	*There was a young boy named Guy*
2 Make a list of words that rhyme with the name.	*shy, pie, why, try, fly, sky, cry, spy*
3 Write line 2, using one of the rhyming words from the list.	*Who ate such a very big pie*
4 Write lines 3 and 4 to continue the story.	*It made him explode All over the road*
5 Write the last line to complete the story – end with another rhyming word from your list.	*And even into the sky!*

When you have finished your limerick, ask a friend to check it:

- Does the poem have five lines?
- Does it have an AABBA rhyming pattern?
- How many syllables does each line have?
- Is it funny?

Does your friend have any tips for how you could make the limerick better?

143

---

3 Learning objectives

Write and perform poems, attending to the sound of words.

Choose and compare words to strengthen the impact of writing.

Adapt tone of voice, use of vocabulary and non-verbal features for different audiences.

Students write and perform limericks, making use of actions and their voices to get their story across to an audience.

Remember to display the child-friendly learning objectives to the class along with the child-friendly checklist that students can use to assess how well they achieve them.

We know that we have achieved these because:

- We can write a limerick, choosing words that will create the right rhyme and rhythm.

- We can perform our limerick in an entertaining way using the syllabic rhyming pattern to tell our stories.

- We know that limericks are supposed to make people laugh.

---

4 Writing workshop teaching notes

Your writing

If possible, bring samples of limericks to class. Students read and choose their favourite one to perform for the class. Tell the class they are going to write their own limericks, and when they have finished and practised reading them you will invite another class or parents to come and hear them.

Read through the five points in the table on page 143 of the Student Book together. Ask students to begin writing their limerick. Circulate, and help them in extending their lists of words that rhyme. Beginner second language learners can illustrate simple limericks and write a couple of sentences in their home languages to say what the limerick is about.

When students have finished writing their limericks read the Top Tip together and ask them to check their limerick with a friend using the checklist on page 143.

Ask students to write what their limerick is about in their home languages. Remind them that limericks are silly and for fun. They do not need to do a literal translation; give them the idea by reminding them that the first limerick they read was about a fat pony that nearly sat on the cat. So they should write something in their home language such as 'My short five-line poem is about…'

When the students have created their limericks and are happy that they meet the criteria for writing a limerick, they could jumble up the lines and ask a partner to rearrange the limerick back to the correct order (developing their sequencing skills). Give students ample time to practise reciting their limericks. Encourage them to create/bring in props that will help them tell their story. Write invitations to the limerick event to parents/other classes. Display the 'laugh' chart created during the unit warm up, as well as the illustrated limericks and the synopsis of them in home languages. And encourage laughter – it is good for the health!

End of Unit Test

Question Paper

Reading: poetry

Read the extract and answer the questions.

The Snow, Peebles and Me

Last evening the snow
Came quietly down
Covering everything around
I went out in my nightgown

5 Calling for our Peebles, the dog
I looked in the shed
Mum saw me and
Shouted "You should be in bed!"

Dad came out to see
10 What was going on
"Good gracious me
The day's nearly gone."

"But Dad, I'm looking for Peebles"
Said me
15 "Get in the warmth; sit down by the fire,
It's freezing," said he.

The snow was blowing this way and that
I made my way to the kitchen door
But we can't leave Peebles outside in that!"
20 "Zzzzzzz," I was interrupted by a snore.

I looked by the fireside and there
Was Peebles as comfy as can be
Cuddled up on his cushion
He stirred, barked and made room for me.

25   The silence of the falling snow
    And the blazing fire lullabied us to the land of dreams
    Tomorrow is a snow day
    A fun, no-school day, or so it seems.

Glossary

comfy comfortable.

cuddled up sitting or lying in a comfortable position.

good gracious me what people say when they are surprised.

interrupted stopped from speaking.

lullabied quieted by a low song-like noise (from lullaby, a song that is sung to send a baby to sleep).

snore a rough breathing noise made while sleeping.

stirred to move slightly or start to move after sleeping or being still.

Comprehension

A **Give evidence from the poem to support your answers.**

1 Why did the child in the poem go outside?

_____ [1]

2 What is the first thing that Dad says in the poem?

_____ [1]

3 What did Mum want her child to do?

_____ [1]

B **Give evidence from the poem to support your answers.**

1 What time of year is it in the poem (winter, spring, summer, autumn)?

_____ [1]

2 How do we know the child was ready for bed?

_____ [1]

3 What happened when the child lay down next to Peebles?

_____ [1]

C **Give evidence from the poem to support your answers.**

1 What did the child in the poem think had happened to Peebles?

_____ [1]

2 Do you think the poem has a happy or sad ending? Why?

_____

_____ [2]

3 Was the child looking forward to the next day? Give reasons for your answer.

_____ [2]

Writing: poetry

Read the limericks below, the first one is describing someone and the second one is telling a silly story. Notice the following features:

- Both limericks have five lines and an AABBA rhyming pattern.
- Lines 1, 2 and 5 have eight syllables.
- Lines 3 and 4 have five syllables.

Read the limericks a couple of times to yourself and use the glossary to help you understand new words.

Limerick 1

There was a young lady whose eyes
Were blue like the seas and the skies
The sparkle from each one
Was like the rising sun
The dear blue-eyed queen of sunrise.

Limerick 2

There was a young man with a dog
That he lost one night in the fog
He searched night and day
From April to May
Then found him on top of a log.

Glossary
fog thick mist.
rising going upwards.
sparkle bright, shining light.

Write your own limerick. Remember to follow the AABBA pattern and use:

- Seven to ten syllables in lines 1, 2 and 5.
- Five to seven syllables in lines 3 and 4.

Please use a separate sheet of paper.

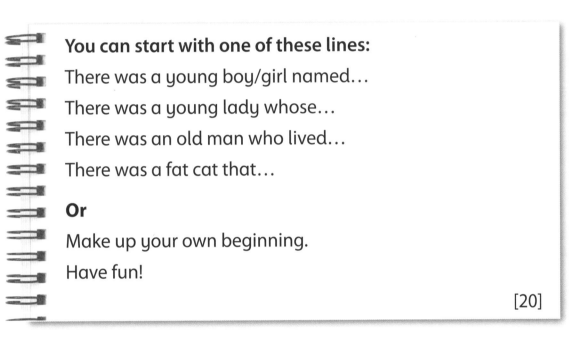

You can start with one of these lines:

There was a young boy/girl named…

There was a young lady whose…

There was an old man who lived…

There was a fat cat that…

Or

Make up your own beginning.

Have fun!

[20]

Revise and Check ❶

Questions

Vocabulary

1 Choose the correct word to complete the sentences.

a A tiny kitten was _____ softly on the sofa. (purring, swishing)

b The driver noticed the _____ and stopped the car just in time. (butterfly, pedestrian)

c There was a _____ sign by the side of the road. (warning, scraping)

2 Match the prefixes to the root words and write a sentence for each of the new words.

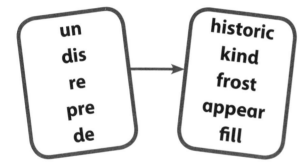

un
dis
re
pre
de

historic
kind
frost
appear
fill

Punctuation

1 Rewrite the text below with the correct punctuation (capital letters, full stops, question marks and exclamation marks).

dolores crept up to the old house she heard a whistling noise near the door it was the strangest sound she had ever heard what was it what should she do

Grammar

1 Copy the following sentences. Underline the nouns, circle the verbs and tick the adjectives.

a The artist created a beautiful sculpture.

b The noisy schoolchildren shrieked all afternoon.

c Robbie is washing the sticky pots.

Spelling

1 Copy the table below and put the following words in the right columns.

cyclist delicious flavour butterfly porridge marmalade

Three syllable words	Two syllable words
dangerous	journey

2 Copy the sentences below and complete the words with two vowels that make a single sound.

ea   ai   ou

a A sn__l crept onto the plant.

b It didn't make a s__nd.

c The spider started to w__ve a web.

Revise and Check ❷

Questions

Vocabulary

1 Copy the sentences below. Replace the words in bold with a word with a similar meaning from the following list.

noise   giggle   large   honest   teacher   little

a The **instructor** told the children not to **laugh**.

b The **big** drum made a very loud **sound**.

c My **small** brother was always **truthful**.

Punctuation

1 Rewrite the following sentences, adding the missing punctuation (capital letters, speech marks, commas, full-stops, exclamation marks and question marks).

a you need to put a stamp on that letter the man told her

b are you sure you have the right address she enquired

c the boy chased the van shouting stop I have an important letter

d oh no we've missed the post yelled the boy

2 Copy these sentences, writing the words in bold in full.

a **They're** going to the aquarium on Sunday.

b They **couldn't** wait to see their friends.

c **We'll** pick you up at 4 o'clock.

Grammar

1 Rewrite the sentences with the correct verbs.

    a I ____ getting ready to meet my friends. (is, am)

    b Ravi ____ my favourite cousin. (are, is)

    c There ____ a basket of clothes by the river. (was, were)

Spelling

1 Copy the table below and complete with singular or plural nouns.

Singular	Plural
beach	
	glasses
	fields
watch	
box	
	dishes

2 Write these words in alphabetical order.

care   warm   pain   slow   price   colour   power

3 Add the suffix –*ly* to the following words, using the correct spelling.

happy   quiet   easy   loud

Revise and Check ❸

Questions

1 Copy the sentences below, filling the gaps with the correct word.

  a The Arctic is a _____ place. (remote, amusing)

  b The ladder was _____. (smug, wobbly)

  c Precious wanted to solve the _____. (adventure, mystery)

2 Write two sentences for each of the following homonyms. Use a different meaning of the word in each sentence.

  bark   wave   ruler

3 Choose one word from the top row and one word from the bottom row to make four compound words. (Remember, compound words are made when two words are joined together to make a new word.)

  tooth   lady   rain   sun
  flower   bow   bird   brush

1 Copy the following sentences, adding commas in the correct places.

  a Lions eat zebras giraffes hippos and deer.

  b After he had found the muddy footprints the detective solved the crime.

  c Once it had landed safely on the ground the cat felt smug.

  d Because he lives a long way from school Michael does his schoolwork at home.

Grammar

1 Copy these sentences, filling the gaps with the correct pronouns.

 a Karl's dad said he would take _____ to play basketball. (him, he)

 b Karl asked _____ and Rahim if we wanted to go, too. (me, I)

 c Karl said _____ would pick us up at 3 o'clock. (they, them)

 d After the game, Karl's dad took _____ home. (we, us)

2 Rewrite the following sentences, underlining the subordinate clause.

 a Although female lions are the hunters, the males eat first.

 b Dad decided to climb the tree because the cat was stuck.

 c When they heard a loud noise, the children were scared.

 d Tapiwa talked to her teacher after the cake went missing.

Spelling

1 Match the prefixes to the correct word and write a sentence for each word.

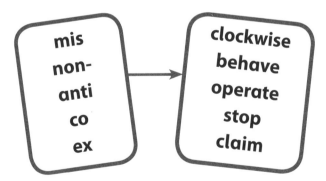

mis
non-
anti
co
ex

clockwise
behave
operate
stop
claim

Yasmin's Parcels

Synopsis

This enchanted story shows that when we do good deeds and help others who are in greater need than us, we are rewarded. Yasmin is a young girl who lives in a tiny house with her mum and dad and six little brothers and sisters. Yasmin goes out to find some food, but instead she encounters people who are suffering more than her. She helps them and, in return, they give her mysterious parcels.

Background information

Many children's stories from around the world have the main character go out of their way to help others who are in trouble. For their kindness, they receive a reward. The moral of the story is this: when you show genuine kindness to others in need, you get an unexpected reward. In this story, Yasmin is that kind of character.

Group or guided reading

Introducing the story

▸ Ask the students to look at the pictures and try to predict what the story is about. Write down the predictions without repeating any and keep them on a chart so you can refer back to them. Use the future tense to write these predictions.

▸ Find out which 'help-someone-and-get-rewarded' stories the students might know from their own culture. Ask some students to tell the stories briefly.

Strategy check

Remind students of the four types of clues that help them understand the meaning of unfamiliar words, pointing to the wall chart you have been using throughout the year: 1) illustrations, 2) the context of the story, 3) what they know about the structure of English and 4) what they know about their own mother tongue. **Learning objective:** Infer the meaning of unknown words from the context.

Many words in this story might be unfamiliar to students. Pay particular attention to: parcels, squashed, croaky, fluttery, pottery, jugs, ajar, kiln, reward, reeds, jogged, loom, thread, spinning wheel, dyed. Guide students through the four types of clues to help them guess the meaning of these words when they appear in the story. Whenever possible, show pictures or objects that represent these words if students cannot guess their meaning.

Group or partner reading

Chapter 1

▸ Ask students to read the first chapter then pair up with a partner to talk about it. Point out the words that may be difficult for them (parcels, squashed, croaky, fluttery, pottery, jugs, ajar).

▸ When they are done, write down the following contrasting words on the board: poor/rich; cruel/kind; happy/sad; dull/smart. Ask students to make a guess as to which words fit the characters or the story. **Learning objective:** Identify the main points or gist of a text.

▸ **Ask:** Why do you think the mother says "If only papa's back would get better." (His back hurts, and he cannot work or care for the children, which is why they are poor and don't have enough to eat.) **Learning objective:** Begin to infer meanings beyond the literal, for example about motives and character.

Chapter 2

- Return to the students' original predictions and see if they would like to eliminate any of them based on what they read in Chapter 1.

- Ask students to predict what may happen in the second chapter.

- Students continue reading with their partner and see if their predictions were accurate.

- Summarize the events that have happened so far with the whole class and focus their attention on the mysterious quality of the milk jug. **Learning objective:** Answer questions with some reference to single points in text.

- Ask students whether they have read another story about something turning into something different. Remind them of Bawang's story, the Balinese folk tale, in Unit 4. In that story, Bawang begs the golden bird, Tjilalongan, to peck her because she thinks she has done something bad. The bird does peck her but it turns her sarong into gold because Bawang had been so good. Ask students to talk about the similarities in Bawang's and Yasmin's stories regarding this phenomenon. **Learning objective:** Identify different types of stories and typical story themes.

Summarize the plot so far

- When students have finished reading the first two chapters, review the plot of the story so far, asking questions about specific events. **Learning objective:** Answer questions with some reference to single points in a text.

- Elicit ideas from the class as a whole and, on the board or chart paper, write down brief summary sentences to recap the story. **Learning objective:** Identify the main points of gist of a text.

- When you have finished recapping the story of Chapter 1, review the summary sentences:

  1 Yasmin's family is very poor and everyone is very hungry.

  2 Yasmin decides to go to town to find some food.

  3 Instead, she finds a door through which a croaky voice invites her to come in.

  Ask: *Do we know whose voice it was?* (No). *Why do you think that the author stops just before you know who's behind the door?* (To build up suspense and make you want to turn the page.)

- Continue on to recap the story of Chapter 2 and review the summary sentences:

  1 Inside was an old man who made jugs.

  2 To help him, Yasmin got some wood for his kiln.

  3 The old man thanked her by giving her a parcel.

  4 At home, she opened it and discovered that it was a mysterious jug that kept filling up with milk.

  5 In the middle of the night, a cat broke the jug.

- Again, point out that the author leaves us hanging at the end of the chapter. So, now we have to go on to the next chapter. **Learning objective:** Sustain the reading of books, noting how a text is organized into sections or chapter.

Independent reading

Chapters 3 to 5

- Students continue to read the story, either on their own or in pairs. If the reading is done in class, circulate among students and make sure that they understand the story. If students read the story at home, allow them time to ask questions and to clarify any doubts they might have.

- Continue writing the summary sentences on the board or chart paper for Chapters 3, 4 and 5 just as you did for the first two chapters. **Learning objective:** Sustain the reading of books, noting how a text is organized into sections or chapters.

Returning and responding to the text

▸ When everyone has finished the story, return to the predictions and rewrite the most accurate one, changing it if necessary to fit the story and changing the future tense that was originally used to the past tense. **Learning objective:** Continue to improve consistency in the use of tenses. Compare this summary to the list of sentences that were elicited above, and correct any inconsistencies or errors as necessary. **Learning objective:** Identify the main points or gist of a text.

▸ Go through the list of summary sentences and begin to identify the main sections of a story: the beginning and introduction of the main character(s); the middle where a problem emerges and mystery builds up; and the resolution of the problem and mystery solved.

▸ Ask students, in pairs, to identify:

  ▸ How characters are introduced

  ▸ How the excitement is built up in the story

  ▸ How the setting is described

  ▸ How the mystery is resolved.

  Learning objective: Consider words that make an impact.

▸ Ask students to practise telling the story to each other so that they can tell it to their parents. **Learning objective:** Speak clearly and confidently in a range of contexts, including longer speaking turns. Students can ask their parents if they know a similar kind of story where children do something good and are rewarded for their kindness. These stories can be shared in the classroom, parents can be invited to tell their stories or, if books or written versions of the home culture stories are sent from home, they can be exhibited in the classroom.

Book review and critique

▸ Students compose a group book review and critique. Introduce the activity by telling students about critiques. If possible, bring copies of book reviews written by children for children (see http://www.guardian.co.uk/childrens-books-site). Share with students a time when you consulted a review of a film before going to see it, or of a book before you bought or borrowed it.

▸ Elicit opinions from the whole class about things they liked or did not like in Yasmin's story. Write down one or two words on the board for each idea suggested by the students, under columns titled 'We liked' and 'We didn't like'.

▸ Divide the class into five groups, putting the students at the beginning level of proficiency together in one of the groups. This group will write the summary of Yasmin's story, using the sentences that have been generated from each chapter. Two of the remaining groups will each write about one thing they liked about the story, and the remaining two groups will each write about one thing that they did not like about Yasmin's story.

▸ Circulate, and help the groups finish their task in a satisfactory way. When all groups have finished their task, each group passes what they wrote to another group for editing.

- Read the whole review through, starting with the summary, then the 'like', and finally the 'didn't like' comments.

- Now it is time to put the review/critique together. You can do this by entering the text into a computer and printing it, or writing it on chart paper. Make sure you cite the 'author' (Classroom X or Ms Y's class).

- The review/critique can go on a wall in the school library or could even be submitted to an appropriate book review site on the web. **Learning objectives:** Write book reviews summarizing what a book is about. Use ICT to write, edit and present work.

Extending reading

- Students turn the story in to a play. **Learning objective:** Write simple play scripts based on reading. It can be acted out and presented to others. **Learning objectives:** Speak clearly and confidently in a range of contexts, including longer speaking turns. Practise to improve performance when reading aloud. Begin to adapt movement to create a character in drama.

- If possible, the teacher brings in a 'special' tablecloth, and students bring a dish from their home culture and put it on the tablecloth. They share a meal and write a story about their experience. Students can choose to write the story as a folk tale, in which case they would invent animals or objects that talk, or they write a story about how children from different places created a world of food on a special tablecloth. **Learning objective:** Write first-person accounts and descriptions based on observation.

- Students write a set of instructions for Yasmin to follow as she goes out to find food. **Learning objective:** Establish purpose for writing, using features and style based on model texts.

- Students write a letter to Yasmin to congratulate her for the good deeds that she did. **Learning objective:** Write letters, notes and messages.

- Ask students in pairs to complete any of the following activities for this book and others they have read:
  - List common themes.
  - Describe similarities and differences between the main characters: Do they face similar issues? Do they resolve them in the same way?
  - Decide whether the outcomes in the various stories are different or similar.

- Ask students to find out some facts about the author. If it is possible to obtain other books by the same author, ask students to decide whether the author's cultural background or childhood is reflected in the stories. Ask them to think about whether the author is like Yasmin or characters in other books by the same author. Ask students whether the setting in Yasmin's story is similar to or different from the settings in other books by the same author. **Learning objective:** Read and comment on different books by the same author.

- Students discuss whether Yasmin is a typical lead character. Why or why not?

E-books

The e-books have various tools that you can use in your lessons. Some of the functions are explained below but please go to the 'User Guide' tab on the CD-ROM for further information.

The e-books can be displayed on an interactive whiteboard and are a fun way of reading through the fiction, non-fiction texts and poetry or play scripts. The following tools can be used effectively in your lessons:

1 The **Spotlight** tool can be used to focus on one image or character on the page. Everything else is hidden so the students remain focused on what they can see. You can use this tool to introduce the students to the story. Using the example pictures below, we could ask: *Who do you think the girl is?* (One of the main characters.) *What do you think this story is about?* (A young girl and her family.)

2 You can use the **Highlighting Pen** tool to highlight words in different colours. You might want to highlight in green any difficult words that you would like to explain, verbs in red, nouns in blue, etc.

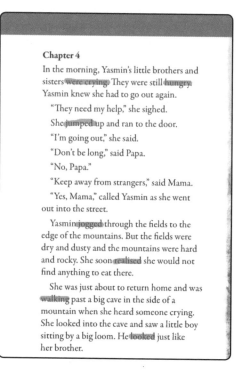

3 The **Sticky Note** tool can be used to add any teacher notes or reminders to any e-book page. These can be hidden if necessary.

4 If you make a mistake then simply select the **Eraser tool** and then click on the text that you would like to delete.

5 Finally, click on the 'Play' button to hear the audio. This will help students with their pronunciation.

Guidelines for working with second language students

Second language students are faced with the challenge of learning a new language and, at the same time, of having to learn through that language. It requires more linguistic skills to use language for academic purposes than it does for everyday conversation. Second language students need to use the new language for both purposes at the same time. It takes at least one to two years for these students to develop the skills needed to converse in social situations such as everyday, straightforward conversations. The speakers in such situations may use gestures, and communication is aided by contextual support. It takes much longer to acquire the skills to use language for academic purposes. This is because the language used in the classroom is academically demanding, and is often abstract and lacking in contextual support such as real objects and face-to-face interaction. Academic language consists of specialized vocabulary and language functions that students need in order to understand and process concepts in the various academic subject areas such as history, mathematics and biology. These functions include comparing, describing, explaining, giving reasons and persuading. Discrete language elements such as vocabulary, grammatical structures, spelling and pronunciation should be integrated into the teaching of these language functions. Our goal should be to enable second language students to develop an extensive range of skills necessary to communicate in social situations as well as learn academic content as they learn English through the activities outlined in *International English*.

Cognitive psychologists say that we learn by integrating new input with our existing cognitive structures or schemata. In other words, we need to activate prior knowledge and provide background knowledge where necessary. Anna Uhl Chamot sums this up well (see Gallagher, 2008):

'Nowhere is the role of prior knowledge more important than in second language educational contexts. Students who can access their prior knowledge through the language and culture most familiar to them can call on a rich array of schemata whereas students who can only use the language explicitly learnt in the second language are limited in their access.'

By activating prior knowledge and background knowledge, we increase students' cognitive engagement and enable them to function at a linguistically and intellectually higher level. We also show that we value the cultural and linguistic knowledge they bring to the classroom.

Reducing anxiety

Because second language students do not always understand everything that is said in the classroom, it is important to have set routines, patterns and signals to help them relax. If they know what to expect, they will be less anxious. When you have new arrivals, ask a child who speaks the same home language to explain classroom rules and routines to the new child. Establish set places where certain activities occur so that students know what to expect when they move to a certain area. Consistently model what has to be done and always contextualize directions.

Realia

Realia is a term for real things – concrete objects – that are used in the classroom to build background knowledge and vocabulary. The use of realia allows students to see, feel, hear and even smell the objects being explored. This sensory information is a powerful aid to comprehension. When real things are not available, use photos or illustrations. Visual scaffolding is an approach in which the language used in instructions and learning is made more understandable by the display of drawings or pictures, allowing students to hear the English words and connect them to the images. Students can do this while they engage in fun activities such as Total Physical Response (see below) where they actively manipulate objects or pictures (Asher, 1982). Be aware of opportunities to use realia as you plan lessons. Begin to collect and store things that can be used to aid instruction.

Promoting other languages

If a teacher does not speak Japanese or Urdu, then they cannot teach Japanese or Urdu but they can do a lot to promote the learning of these and other home languages. As Gallagher (2008) says:

'Openness to all languages of the classroom is critical. Teachers need to abandon their fear of the unknown and work collaboratively with parents and students to learn more about the home languages of the children in their classes.'

Two important concepts relating to the promotion of other languages are:

1 Interlingual teaching and learning

The term 'interlingual' was coined by Gallagher (2008). The 'inter' prefix brings the notion of everyone being open and responsive to learning about other languages. It stands for international-mindedness and for all languages of the classroom. In the interlingual classroom, students not only learn their own mother tongue but they learn about the other classroom languages as well. Interlingual classrooms are places where children are allowed to use their home languages as cognitive tools. They can transfer skills, concepts and learning strategies across languages. To read more on this see: http://www.eithnegallagher.net/

2 Translanguaging

The term *trawsiethu* or 'translanguaging' was first coined by Cen Williams (see Baker *et al*, 2012) to describe a method he used in bilingual classes in Wales. Translanguaging gives children the freedom to move in and out of languages while they are working. The teacher introduces the topic in the classroom language but the task is carried out in the students' home languages. Ofelia Garcia (2010) also uses this term and has carried out a lot of research in dual language English/Spanish schools in the United States. She reports that it is a highly successful strategy for working with young children. Garcia says that the opportunity to use home languages in the classroom gives second language students a voice and allows them to formulate their personal identities. To read more on this see: http://ofeliagarcia.org/

Learner profiles

Developing learner profiles is a useful way of learning about individual learners. This can be done through informal interviews with parents, questionnaires and setting up classroom activities that allow the learners to write or speak about their experiences (for newcomers to the school and the country you may require the services of an interpreter).

Connecting home and school

Connecting home and school is of paramount importance especially for second language students. We need to draw on the 'funds of knowledge' that our diverse students have and connect what happens inside the classroom to what happens outside. Students from diverse backgrounds have a wealth of cultural capital – attitudes, beliefs, experience, knowledge and skills. Activities that incorporate a student's home language and culture validate the home language and culture. This, however, requires effort from the teacher, who must strive to know and understand the socio-cultural contexts of their students' lives so that they become partners with parents in the students' schooling.

Parents can help with their children's education by understanding the important role they play in developing and maintaining the home language. Parents should be encouraged to:

- share stories with their children in the home language
- listen to their children reading aloud in the home language and English

- speak to their children about the concepts and main ideas being taught in school in the home language
- collaborate with their children on writing projects, in English and the home language
- tell their children stories that transmit family beliefs and cultural values
- share stories, read books or give presentations in the classroom
- translate children's work
- buy resource books, such as bilingual dictionaries, etc.
- volunteer to help in the school, translating signs, making multilingual displays, etc.

Too often in schools intercultural practices are entertaining events that celebrate differences, such as days that focus on food, costumes or flags. This approach often amounts to tokenism, as it relegates cultural issues and languages to special days. It focuses on the surface aspects of culture. However, the more important aspects of culture are hidden. Our understanding of friendship, how we deal with authority, the importance we give to time, a preference for competition or cooperation, and approaches to problem solving lie well below the visible surface (Hamayan, 2012). However, they permeate every aspect of the lives of second language students at school. To be effective and inclusive we need to weave the home languages and cultures into the learning that takes place every day in our classrooms.

Families are key participants in the academic success of children learning English. When our classroom doors are wide open to them, our learning environment becomes more multilingual and multicultural. We must also be aware that to focus solely on the classroom language by negating the home language can have a negative impact on a child's overall development, resulting in the loss of the home language and possible alienation of children from parents.

Supporting home languages and biliteracy awareness

It is important to have books in the home languages of the classroom and bilingual books available. Discuss the books and talk about the similarities and differences in the customs and situations that are depicted in the books. Make time in your lesson to stop and ask students how they say things in their home languages. Explore key vocabulary in home languages and encourage students to make a note of new words in their New Word List (see Workbook). The primary reason for integrating the two languages is that moving between languages helps learning. When the teacher plans and guides this movement by creating bridges between languages, it becomes possible for learners to access the full range of resources they have available to them in their two languages (Hamayan, 2010).

Talk

Talk is fundamental in a class of second language students. Second language students need to hear a lot of talk in order to learn how to talk themselves and they need lots of opportunities to interact in various contexts. However, beginner second language students should not be forced to talk; rather they should be encouraged to participate by listening and observing until they feel ready to talk. We learn to talk by talking and we talk when we have an authentic reason to do so. Some authentic reasons for talking are:

- asking and receiving information
- expressing feelings and ideas
- getting to know someone in both formal and informal situations
- clarifying thoughts
- communicating knowledge
- questioning understanding.

Teachers need to provide occasions for children to talk about tasks, subjects and topics in various circumstances – as a whole class, in small groups and in pairs. They need to ask questions that require stretches of language rather than one-word answers. We also need to give second language students plenty of time to answer questions. It is important to bear in mind that second language students are trying to come to terms with a new language and are not only learning how to speak: they are also learning what is appropriate to say. For more on the importance of talk for language acquisition see Gallagher (2008).

We should also encourage children to talk through their learning in home language groups whenever possible.

Reading

Research has shown that being able to read in one's own language is one of the most important factors in learning to read in a second language. Teachers need to be aware that children who are already literate in their home language can transfer their existing skills to English. However, it is important that teachers familiarize themselves with the home literacy practices of the students in their classes so that they can identify areas of misunderstanding. If, for example, the student is used to reading from right to left at home, the teacher needs to aware of this. Reading skills just like writing skills need to be developed across the whole curriculum. Texts from different subject areas have different features both in the language they use and in the way the text is constructed. We need to build activities into our reading instruction that focus on three levels.

1 **Before reading:** we need to set up the context, establish prior knowledge and teach vocabulary to prepare children for the work ahead.

2 **During reading:** this is the time to encourage children to think through their learning and talk about it.

3 **After reading:** teachers should use the reading text as a springboard for writing or responding creatively to what they have read as well as extending into everyday application of what they read.

We need to encourage students to read in their home languages. They need to know that our classroom is a place where it is acceptable to read in many languages. The promotion of home languages and literacies in the classroom helps students to develop bilingual and biliteral skills.

Writing

The development of written skills depends to some extent on oral language skills. Teachers can help second language students to become more effective writers by giving them opportunities to explore and practise oral language as it is used in a variety of situations and for a variety of purposes. However, talk as preparation for writing is not enough on its own: students also need the explicit teaching of the various written genres. They must also understand the differences between the oral and written modes of writing. Many second language students write as they speak and their writing may appear rambling and immature. They need help to understand that oral language and written language are not the same. Through writing workshops, teachers can demonstrate to their students what writers 'do' by modelling the construction of texts with their students. Teachers need to give students time to work through the stages of the writing process. They need time to discuss the topic, and time to think, plan, research and draft. Second language students should also have opportunities to write in their home languages in class. Whether they are writing in their home languages or in English, they are still working through the same processes. Allowing students to write in their home languages affirms their linguistic and cultural identities and it also gives value to texts written in languages other than English. It motivates the students and it is inclusive practice.

Conferencing with writers

Teachers should conference individually with students, focusing at this stage on meaning over form. As the students' confidence develops, teachers can ask them to identify spelling errors in their writing and give them strategies to help them learn words they find difficult.

NB: Second language learners may use their home languages when they cannot find the English words. Spelling and syntax may reflect patterns used in their home languages, too. When this occurs, the teacher should not consider it an error but rather a teaching point.

Genre

The genres of spoken and written English are specific to English culture. Second language students may well know the different features of genres in their own languages (because genre is culture specific), but they need to be taught English genres. Some of the most common genres used in school are:

▸ personal genre: recount, narrative, memoir and reader response

▸ factual genre: procedural writing, directions, retelling of events, summaries and research reports

▸ analytic genre: personal accounts, persuasive essays, expositions, discussions, explanations, and comparisons.

Each of these genres uses language differently and each genre has certain patterns (Knapp and Watkins, 2005; Schleppegrell, 2012). These patterns need to be taught explicitly to second language students so that they can be successful in school.

Techniques and strategies for working with second language learners

Second language proficiency develops when students actively use the language both orally and in writing. Instructional strategies that encourage oral language include: cooperative learning activities in which students interact with their peers, drama, role-play, and activity-centred instruction where students share an experience making something or completing a task, such as preparing an exhibit or producing a map of the school. These oral strategies, in turn, can promote creative writing as students write about the experience or the activity they just completed. Texts that are polished and well edited can be produced as books and placed in the classroom or school library. These texts can be in English, the home language or both. One type of dual language text is what Jim Cummins calls 'identity texts' (Cummins and Early, 2011).

Dual language texts/identity texts

The creation of dual language texts or 'identity texts' promotes students' identities and the knowledge and experiences they bring with them to the classroom. Students use both their languages to create personal or collaborative books. These books can be related to classroom themes or based on personal experiences. They can be prepared in the classroom or with the help of parents at home. They should be a regular activity in your classroom. Displaying this work will reflect the multilingual, multi-literate character of your classroom.

Bilingual dictionaries

Bilingual dictionaries should be available in your classroom for second language students. You may need to spend some time showing the children how to use them.

New Word Lists

The Workbook has a place reserved for the learning of new words. Encourage the students to record the new vocabulary they learn in the units in English and their home languages. Ask parents to check the spelling of words written in the home scripts.

Charts

A home language chart should be permanently on display. Enlist the help of parents to write their languages in the original script.

Every time you start a new unit, put the main concept/theme on a chart and invite students to write in the concept in their home scripts.

Graphic organizers

Graphic organizers such as the T chart and Venn diagram below can be used to help second language students participate even when their knowledge of English is quite limited. Graphic organizers such as this help students to compare concepts and ideas, and show what they know without having to write in complete sentences.

T chart

Venn diagram

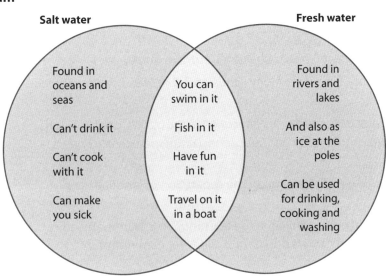

Total Physical Response (TPR)

Total Physical Response is an approach to second language instruction based on first language acquisition research. When children learn their first language they listen and acquire receptive language before they speak. They develop understanding through moving their bodies and they speak when they are ready to do so. In TPR, the teacher gradually introduces directions by performing actions to demonstrate them. Gradually the teacher's demonstrations are removed and the students respond to verbal directions.

The Language Experience Approach (LEA)

The Language Experience Approach is an activity-based writing lesson that helps students to see the connections between oral and written language. The students participate in an experience (making or doing something). The teacher engages the students in a discussion of their experience and as they talk about what they did, the teacher models writing their words on chart paper. Students can read along with the teacher or repeat the sentences. The teacher can ask leading questions such as 'And what did we do next?' When the students have dictated the entire text, they can read it with the teacher. LEA lessons support the development of English vocabulary and syntax.

Free Voluntary Reading (FVR)

Free Voluntary Reading (Krashen, 2004) is a powerful tool for involving students in reading. Students self-select books at their independent reading level and read for a given period of time. The students are encouraged to read what they would like to read, putting down a book if they don't like it and choosing another one. Free Voluntary Reading is not intended to replace the literacy or language programmes: it is meant to compliment them. Krashen tells us that when children read for pleasure they acquire a large vocabulary and they develop the ability to understand more complex structures.

Conclusion

Second language learners strive and succeed when we weave their home languages into instruction. In every lesson we need to establish prior knowledge and build background knowledge to aid their comprehension. We need to support their learning with realia, visuals and contextualized language. They need a learning environment that encourages risk-taking and welcomes their home languages. Multilingual, multi-literate and multicultural 'interlingual' classrooms are exciting and fun places to be for students and teachers. Enjoy the experience and the journey!

Bibliography

Asher, J. (1982) *Learning Another Language Through Actions: The Complete Teachers' Guidebook*. Los Gatos, CA: Sky Oaks

Baker, C., Jones, B. and Lewis, G. (2012) 'Translanguaging: origins and development from school to street and beyond'. In *Educational Research and Evaluation*, Vol. 8, issue 7. New York: Routledge

Cummins, J. and Early, M. (eds) (2011) *Identity Texts*. Chester: Trentham Books

Gallagher, E. (2008) *Equal Rights to the Curriculum: Many Languages One Message*. Clevedon: Multilingual Matters

García, O. (2010) *Latino language practices and literary education in the U.S.* In Farr, M., Seloni, and Song, J. (eds) (2010) *Ethnolinguistic Diversity and Education: Language, Literacy and Culture*. New York: Routledge

Hamayan, E. (2010) 'Separado o together? Reflecting on the separation of languages of instruction'. *Soleado*, Winter 2010, pp. 1–9

Hamayan, E. (2012) 'What is the role of culture in language learning?' In E. Hamayan and R. Freeman Field (eds) *English Language Learners at School: A Guide for Administrators*. Philadelphia, PA: Caslonters

Knapp, P. and Watkins, M. (2005) *Genre, Text, Grammar: Technologies for Teaching and Assessing Writing*. Sydney: University of New South Wales Press, Ltd

Krashen, S. (2004) *The Power of Reading* (2nd edn). Englewood, CO: Libraries Unlimited Inc.

Schleppegrell, M. J. (2012) 'Systemic functional linguistics: exploring meaning in language'. In Gee, J. P. and Handford M. (eds) *The Routledge Handbook of Discourse Analysis*. New York: Routledge

Glossary

adjective An *adjective* is a word that describes somebody or something.

1 *Adjectives* are usually found in front of a noun. ***Examples:*** **Green** emeralds and **glittering** diamonds.

2 *Adjectives* can also come after a verb. ***Examples:*** It was **big**. They looked **hungry**.

3 Sometimes you can use two *adjectives* together. ***Example:*** tall and handsome. This is called an adjectival phrase.

4 *Adjectives* can be used to describe degrees of intensity. To make a comparative adjective you usually add *–er* (or use more). ***Examples:*** quicker; more beautiful.

5 To make a *superlative* you add *–est* (or use most). ***Examples:*** quickest; most beautiful.

adverb An *adverb* is a word that describes a verb, or how something was done. Many are formed by adding *–ly* to an *adjective*. ***Example:*** slow/slowly.

Adverbs often come next to the verb in a sentence. They can tell the reader:

How something was done: quickly, stupidly, amazingly. ***Example:*** She ate her lunch quickly.

Where something happened: there, here, everywhere. ***Example:*** After the rainstorm, there was water everywhere.

When something happened: yesterday, today, now. ***Example:*** I went to the circus yesterday.

How often something was done: occasionally, often. ***Example:*** I visit my grandmother often.

agreement An *agreement* is when the verb has the correct form for the subject of the sentence. ***Examples:*** I am/I was; you are/you were. The **storm was** becoming worse. The **storms were** becoming worse.

alliteration *Alliteration* occurs when two or more nearby words start with the same sound. ***Example:*** A slow, sad, sorrowful song.

antonym An *antonym* is a word or phrase that means the opposite of another word or phrase in the same language. ***Example:*** *closed* is an antonym of *open*.

apostrophe An *apostrophe* (') is a punctuation mark that is used in two ways:

1 To show where letters are missing. ***Examples:*** don't (for 'do not'), can't (for 'cannot'), I'm (for 'I am').

2 To show possession. ***Example:*** My dog's collar. (This explains that the collar belongs to my dog.)

In the plural the apostrophe follows the *s*. ***Example:*** The boys' cards. (This explains that the cards belong to the boys.)

bold Letters or words can be written in *bold* print, which is darker than normal. It can help to highlight words for the reader. ***Example:*** Promise me, you will **never** do that again.

brackets These can be used to add an extra comment, fact or aside into a sentence. ***Example:*** I am as thirsty (who wouldn't be?) as a camel.

capital letter A *capital letter* starts the first word of a new sentence. It is a letter written in the upper case. ***Example:*** **J**oin now.

The names of persons and places, the days of the week, and the months of the year also begin with a capital letter. ***Examples:*** **N**ovember, **M**ary.

caption A *caption* is a short sentence or phrase used to say what a picture is about.

cinquain A poem of five lines with the syllable pattern 2, 4, 6, 8, 2.

clause A *clause* is a group of words that contains a subject and a verb. Every full sentence contains at least one main clause. ***Example:*** I ran. (In this clause, 'I' is the subject and 'ran' is the verb.)

Complex sentences contain one or more subordinate clauses. A subordinate clause does not make sense on its own and relies on the main clause. ***Example:*** When I had finished reading it, I returned the book to the library. (In this sentence, the clause 'When I had finished reading it' is a subordinate clause, which depends on the main clause, 'I returned the book to the library' to make sense.)

colon/semicolon A *colon* is a punctuation mark (:) often used either:

1 To introduce a list in instructions. ***Example:*** You will need: a notebook, a pencil, etc.

2 To add further information to a sentence. ***Example:*** I am quick at running: I can run as fast as a cheetah.

A *semi-colon* is a punctuation mark (;) that separates two main clauses. ***Example:*** I like cheese; it is delicious.

Glossary

comma A *comma* is a punctuation mark (,) used to separate parts in a sentence. When you read you must pause briefly when there is a comma. Commas can be used:

1 To separate items in a list.
   Example: a sunny day, a stretch of sand, several rock pools and an ice-cream van.

2 To place a section of a sentence in parenthesis (as brackets do).
   Example: The dog, happy to be outside, was sniffing everything in sight.

3 When addressing someone by name.
   Example: I understand you, Patricia.

4 After a subordinate clause that starts a sentence.
   Example: Although it is cold, I am warm.

5 After many connecting conjunctions that we use to start a sentence.
   Example: However, penguins can get cold…

command A *command* is a type of sentence that gives an order or instruction. Commands start with imperative verbs. *Example:* Catch the ball!

comparative See *adjective*.

complex sentence See *sentence*.

compound sentence See *sentence*.

conjunction A *conjunction* is a word used to link clauses within a sentence.
Examples: and, but, so, until, when, as.
Example: He had a book when he stood up.

connective A *connective* is a word or a phrase that links clauses or sentences. *Connectives* can be conjunctions.
Examples: but, when, because.
Example: I wanted to catch the bus but I got to the bus stop too late.

Connectives can also be connecting adverbs.
Examples: then, therefore, finally.
Example: I waited for the next bus and finally it arrived.

context The *context* is the part of a spoken or written text that gives details about a word or passage and clarifies its meaning.

definition A *definition* is an explanation of the meaning of a word.
Example: **purse** a small bag for holding money.

dialogue A *dialogue* is an oral or written conversation.

discussion This type of text sets out both sides of an argument and draws a conclusion, supported by reasoning and evidence. Discussion texts set out to provide a balanced argument. Discussions can also be oral, where people talk about their opinions about a topic.

exclamation mark An *exclamation mark* is a punctuation mark (!) used to end an exclamation of joy, anger, surprise. *Example:* Oh dear!

explanation This type of text explains a process: how or why things happen. *Example:* How a kite flies.

fiction This type of text describes imaginary events and people.

full stop A *full stop* (.) is a punctuation mark used at the end of a sentence.

haiku A poem of three lines with the syllable pattern 5, 7, 5.

heading A *heading* is a title that shows the reader what a paragraph or section of text is about.

homonym A homonym is one of two or more words that sound the same and share the same spelling, but differ in meaning.
Examples: bark, wave, train, top.

homophone A *homophone* is one of two or more words that sound the same but have different meanings. They may have the same or different spellings.
Examples: right, write, rite, wright.

hyphen A *hyphen* is a short dash (-) used to join words together. *Example:* snake-pit.

idiom An *idiom* is a colourful expression that cannot be understood from the meaning of its separate words.
Example: It's raining cats and dogs. (This means that it is raining very hard.)

imperative The *imperative* is the form of the verb used to make commands. *Example:* Go away!

inflection An *inflection* is a change in the form of a word (often the ending) according to how it is used in a sentence.

Nouns inflect to show plurals.
Example: one cat, two cat*s*.

Verbs inflect to show number, person and tense.
Examples: I jump, he jump*s*, they are jump*ing*, he jump*ed*.

Some adjectives inflect to show comparative and superlative forms.
Examples: brave, brav*er*, brav*est*.

instruction This type of text helps readers to make something or to carry out a step-by-step operation.

irregular verb An *irregular verb* is a verb that does not form its past tense in a regular way. In the case of regular verbs, if the verb ends in a consonant or vowel other than the letter *e* you add –*ed* to form the past tense. If the verb ends in the letter *e*, you add the letter *d*. Irregular verbs do not follow this pattern.
Examples: take/took; swim/swam; go/went.

limerick A *limerick* is a funny poem of five lines; lines 1, 2 and 5 rhyme and are long, lines 3 and 4 rhyme and are short.

main clause See *clause*; *sentence*.

metaphor A *metaphor* is a way of speaking or writing in which one thing is actually said to be something else. This way of speaking or writing is called a figure of speech.
Example: This man is a lion in battle. (This means that he is very brave.)

non-fiction This type of text is informative and factual rather than fictional.

noun A *noun* is a word that names something or somebody.
Examples: fox, chicken, brother, rock.

Nouns can be singular (dog) or plural (dogs). A collective noun refers to a group.
Example: a flock of birds.

A proper noun begins with a capital letter and names a person, a place or something specifically.
Examples: Mrs Brown, London.

onomatopoeia The use of words that sound like the thing they describe.
Examples: bang, crash, gurgle, hiss, sizzle.

person (1st, 2nd or 3rd person) The *1st person* is used to talk about oneself – I/we. The *2nd person* is used to address the person who is listening or reading – you. The 3rd person is used to refer to someone else – he, she, it, they.

personification The technique of giving human qualities to things that are not human, such as an animal, concept or inanimate object.
Example: The sun beamed happily while the kittens played hide-and-seek, and life danced by.

persuasive writing This type of text intends to persuade the reader to a certain opinion or point of view. Powerful language may be used with supporting arguments and evidence. For example, a piece of writing that shows the benefits of eating snacks that are nutritious instead of sweets or fatty foods that are not healthful.

phrase A phrase is a small group of words that forms part of a clause. Phrases do not make sense on their own.

phoneme A *phoneme* is a speech sound. The phonemes of a word do not correspond to the letters used to spell it.
Example: The phoneme *ee* appears in *feel*, *seal* and *metre*.

play script A *play script* is the written down version of a play and is used by actors. It tells actors what to say and also how to say it and what they should be doing while they are saying their lines.

plural See *singular*.

poem A *poem* is a text that creates or recreates experience in a compressed and intense way, using rhythm, or rhyme and language effects to create images and sound effects. Most poems have short lines, and many have line endings that rhyme.

point of view In fiction, the narrator's or a character's view of the story from their place in it.

prefix A *prefix* is an element placed at the beginning of a word to modify its meaning.
Examples: In the word 'misunderstand', the prefix *mis*– makes the word 'understand' mean 'not understand correctly'. In the word 'unhappy', the prefix *un*– makes the word 'happy' mean 'not happy'.

preposition A *preposition* is a word that indicates place (on, in), direction (over, beyond) or time (during, on) among others.
Examples: I put the book **in** the drawer. I read my book **during** lunch.

pronoun A *pronoun* is a word that can replace a noun.
Examples: I, me, mine, myself.

punctuation *Punctuation* is the term given to special marks used to help a reader get the meaning of text.
Examples: full stop (.), question mark (?), comma (,), exclamation mark (!), speech mark ("), colon (:), semicolon (;).

question mark A *question mark* (?) is a punctuation mark that is used to end a question sentence.
Example: What did you eat for lunch?

recount This type of text tells the reader about what has happened. *Examples:* news, a diary.

report This type of text provides information about a given subject.

root A *root* is what remains when all prefixes and suffixes are removed from a word. Sometimes a root word is a root in its own right.
Example: un**happy**. (In this word. *un*– is a prefix and the root word is 'happy'.)

sentence A *sentence* is a group of words that expresses a complete thought. All sentences begin with a capital letter and end with a full stop, question mark or exclamation mark. There are four types of sentences:

1   Statements – that declare something and end in a full stop (.).
    Example: The class yelled in triumph.

2   Questions – that ask something and end in a question mark (?).
    Example: Where is the dog?

3   Exclamations – that exclaim and end in an exclamation mark (!).
    Example: I'm so tired!

4   Imperatives – that command or instruct and can end either in a full stop or an exclamation mark.
    Example: Put on your coat right away!

Simple *sentences* are made up of one clause.
Example: I am hungry.

Compound *sentences* are made up of two or more main clauses, usually joined by a conjunction.
Example: I am hungry and I am thirsty.

Complex *sentences* are made up of one main clause and one, or more, subordinate clauses. A subordinate clause cannot stand on its own and relies on the main clause.
Example: When I joined the drama club, I did not know that it was going to be so much fun.

simile A *simile* is a figure of speech in which two things are compared using the linking words 'like' or 'as'.
Example: In battle, he was as brave as a lion.

simple sentence See *sentence*.

singular/plural *Singular* refers to one thing. *Plural* refers to more than one thing.
Examples:

dog (singular)   dogs (plural)

sky (singular)   skies (plural)

wolf (singular)   wolves (plural)

speech marks *Speech marks* (" and ") are punctuation marks that enclose speech, including the relevant sentence punctuation.
Example: "What is it?" she gasped.

In direct speech you write down what is said.
Example: "Hello children," said Tom.

In indirect speech you report on what was said and you do not need to use speech marks.
Example: Tom said hello to the children.

speech verbs *Speech verbs* are the verbs used before or after direct speech to show how the words have been spoken. The most common is the word said. Others include – asked, roared, whispered, etc.

standard English *Standard English* is the form of English used in most writing and by educated speakers. It can be spoken with any accent. There are many slight differences between standard English and local ways of speaking.
Example: 'We were robbed' is standard English but in speech some people say, 'We was robbed.'

story A *story* is a text type that recounts an invented tale. It is usually used to entertain. Stories normally have a setting, characters and are structured by a plot. A story could also be true.

subheading A *subheading* comes below a heading and indicates to the reader the contents of smaller units of text.

subordinate clause See *clause; sentence*.

suffix A *suffix* is an element placed at the end of a word to modify its meaning.
Example: The suffix –*less* makes the word 'tasteless' mean 'with no taste'.

superlative See *adjective*.

syllable A *syllable* is a unit of pronunciation that forms part of or the whole of a word. Each syllable in a word contains one vowel sound.

synonym A *synonym* is a word or phrase that means exactly or nearly the same as another word or phrase in the same language.
Example: *shut* is a synonym of *close*.

tanka A poem of five lines with the syllable pattern 5, 7, 5, 7, 7.

tense A *tense* is a verb form that shows whether events happen in the past, present or the future.
Examples:

The Pyramids are on the west bank of the River Nile. (present tense)
They were built as enormous tombs. (past tense)
They will stand for centuries to come. (future tense)

Most verbs change their spelling by adding –*ed* to form the **past tense**.
Example: walk/walked.

Some have irregular spellings.
Example: catch/caught.

Most verbs use 'will' to form the **future tense**.
Example: I will go to school tomorrow.

thought map A *thought map* helps present information by dividing the key points of an oral or written presentation into main topics and subtopics branching off the main topics. Colour is used to highlight the different 'branches' in a thought map.

title A *title* is the overall heading given to a text.

verb A *verb* shows the action in a sentence and can express a process or state.

1 Verbs are often known as 'doing', 'being' or 'happening' words.
Example: The boys **run** down the hill. (In this sentence the word 'run' is the *verb*.)

2 Sometimes several words make up the verb.
Example: The boys are running. (In this case *running* is the main verb and *are* is an extra verb that adds to the meaning. It is called an *auxiliary verb*.)

vowel A *vowel* in writing is one of the five letters, a, e, i, o or u. In speech, a *vowel* is a sound made with the mouth open and the airway unobstructed. Each syllable in a word has one *vowel* sound.

Useful websites

The links below are intended for teacher use only. It is recommended that students are not given access to these links.

Units 1 and 2

Information on journeys to school, with downloadable booklets in various languages on road safety issues, including a teaching pack that includes an exercise to create a collage of road safety signs.

http://www.journeytoschool.com/

Unit 4

A video link to a traditional Balinese tale and an opportunity for students to hear a snippet of Balinese.

http://vimeo.com/11074221

Unit 6

An example of a flow chart graphic organizer.

http://www.eduplace.com/graphicorganizer/pdf/flow.pdf

A video link for teachers to hear the chant 'As I was walking down the street'.

http://www.youtube.com/watch?v=4_1BJGocYrw

A link to the Maori Source website providing ideas for making book marks and masks.

http://maorisource.com/Maori-Carving-Designs.html

Unit 8

The National Geographic website, providing information reports on animals.

http://kids.nationalgeographic.co.uk/kids/animals/creaturefeature/

The World Atlas website, giving information on population density.

http://www.worldatlas.com/aatlas/populations/ctydensityl.htm

Unit 9

'The Limerick Song' – a video about how to write limericks.

http://www.youtube.com/watch?v=k-rN3DGMCsE

Notes